This Book Comes With a Website

Nolo's award-winning website has a page dedicated just to this book, where you can:

DOWNLOAD FORMS – All the forms and worksheets in the book are accessible online

KEEP UP TO DATE – When there are important changes to the information in this book, we'll post updates

READ BLOGS – Get the latest info from Nolo authors' blogs

LISTEN TO PODCASTS – Listen to authors discuss timely issues on topics that interest you

WATCH VIDEOS – Get a quick introduction to a legal topic with our short videos

You'll find the link in the appendix.

And that's not all. Nolo.com contains thousands of articles on everyday legal and business issues, plus a plain-English law dictionary, all written by Nolo experts and available for free. You'll also find more useful **books, software, online services,** and **downloadable forms.**

5th Edition

Special Needs Trusts

Protect Your Child's Financial Future

Stephen Elias & Kevin Urbatsch

FIFTH EDITION	APRIL 2013
Editor	BETSY SIMMONS HANNIBAL
Cover Design	SUSAN PUTNEY
Production	SUSAN PUTNEY
Proofreading	SUSAN CARLSON GREENE
Index	MEDEA MINNICH
Printing	BANG PRINTING

ISSN 2167-5716 (print)
ISSN 2325-4920 (online)

978-1-4133-1815-9 (pbk)
978-1-4133-1816-6 (epub ebook)

Please note

We believe accurate, plain-English legal information should help you solve many of your own legal problems. But this text is not a substitute for personalized advice from a knowledgeable lawyer. If you want the help of a trained professional—and we'll always point out situations in which we think that's a good idea—consult an attorney licensed to practice in your state.

Dedication

I dedicate this work to my brother Bob and my sister-in-law Lois and their wonderful family.   —Stephen Elias

I would like to acknowledge my lovely wife, Elizabeth, who enhances my quality of life each and every day.   —Kevin Urbatsch

About the Authors

Stephen Elias spent ten years doing legal aid work in California and New York and as a public defender in Vermont's Northeast Kingdom. Steve wrote and edited more than 30 Nolo books and was one of the original authors of Nolo's bestselling *WillMaker* software. Steve was featured in such major media as *The New York Times*, *The Wall Street Journal*, *Newsweek*, *Good Morning America*, *20/20*, *Money Magazine*, and more.

Kevin Urbatsch is a principal of the boutique estate planning firm, Myers Urbatsch P.C. in San Francisco, California. He is a nationally recognized expert in the unique planning needs of individuals with disabilities and their families. Mr. Urbatsch is a charter member of the national organization, the Academy of Special Needs Planners. He writes and is a frequent lecturer both locally and nationally on planning for persons with disabilities, primarily concerning special needs trust drafting and administration.

Table of Contents

Appendixes

Your Legal Companion for Special Needs Trusts

If you have been providing care for a child or another loved one with special needs, you've no doubt thought about what will happen when you're no longer able to give that care. Of course, you can leave property to your loved one, but—as you are probably aware—doing so without some careful planning will almost certainly jeopardize his or her ability to receive benefits under the Supplemental Security Income (SSI) and Medicaid programs. Unless you make the right legal arrangements, benefits simply won't be available until the inheritance is used up.

A special needs trust allows you to protect your loved one's government benefits while continuing to supplement his or her special needs. This book explains how special needs trusts work and how you can set one up yourself. We give you the documents you need with plenty of explanation, examples, and easy-to-understand instructions. It will take a little time and concentration, but you can do it, and probably without the help of a lawyer. When it's done, you will be at ease knowing that your loved one's benefits will be protected when you're gone.

Step by step, this book:

- explains how special needs trusts protect your loved one's government benefits

- describes the role of the trustee and helps you figure out who should serve as trustee and successor trustees during and after your lifetime

- shows you how to draft a special needs trust and make it legally valid

- tells you how to set up a trust bank account and how to modify your estate plan to leave money to the trust at your death

- shows you how to leave a detailed letter or diary about your loved one's needs

- explains how to keep up on SSI and Medicaid rules, file taxes, keep track of successor trustees, and make sure that the trust continues to meet your loved one's needs

- details the duties of the trustees who will serve when you're gone, and
- suggests investigating a "pooled trust," if you don't want to set up your own special needs trust.

This book also shows you how to work with experts to make the most of your special needs trust. For example, at times you may want to consult a lawyer, an accountant, or a financial planner. This book suggests when that might be a good idea, and helps you find the support you need. And because you'll have a solid understanding of the important issues, you'll be able to work confidently with professionals.

This Is a Third-Party Trust

The trust in this book is specifically designed to be used for funds that come from a "third party"—that is, someone other than your loved one. It is a stand-alone trust that can receive property from your will, living trust, life insurance policy, or other beneficiary designation at your death.

This book does not help you create a special needs trust within a larger estate planning document such as a will or living trust. For that you will need an attorney—typically the same attorney you are using for your entire estate plan.

Also, the trust in this book cannot be used for money your loved one receives directly, whether by court award, gift, or inheritance. However, as the material in Chapter 7 explains, you can use a pooled or community trust for these types of funds as well as funds that pass directly from a third party to the trust itself.

Whether or not you make the trust provided, this book offers you a wealth of information that will prepare you for having an informed discussion with a lawyer about special needs trusts.

We hope that this book will give you not only the legal documents you need, but also peace of mind from knowing that you've taken steps to protect your loved one after you're gone. ●

Planning for a Loved One With Special Needs

Millions of us love and care for someone who lives with a disability—a son with Down syndrome, a daughter with cystic fibrosis, a niece with severe autism, a grandchild with schizophrenia, a spouse with multiple sclerosis. Such a disability usually means your loved one will require long-term support and medical assistance under the Supplemental Security Income (SSI) and Medicaid programs.

This chapter introduces the special needs trust—a way to leave property to a loved one with special needs without jeopardizing those crucial SSI and (especially) Medicaid benefits.

Why You May Want to Make a Special Needs Trust

Special needs trusts are powerful tools that can be used to:

- protect the assets of a loved one with a disability, while retaining eligibility for needed government benefits for health care and financial assistance

- protect your loved one with special needs from predators who target young or vulnerable individuals

- provide guidelines for how your loved one with special needs should be supported to enhance his or her quality of life

- name the right people to manage money and advocate for your loved one

- protect your loved one from claims of divorced spouses or creditor claims (such as car accident plaintiffs), and

- protect your loved one from making poor financial decisions due to lack of capacity, immaturity, or good nature—such as giving money away to strangers.

Preserving Health Care for People With Disabilities

One of the primary reasons to protect the inheritance of a person with a disability is to maintain eligibility for his or her health care coverage. Health care and caregiving costs can be the two most expensive needs

A Special Needs Trust Will Not Protect the Assets of a Person With a Disability

This book will not help to protect assets that belong to a person with a disability. Rather, this book helps you protect that person's eligibility for benefits when you give that person assets as a gift or an inheritance.

When a person with a disability already has assets—perhaps from a personal injury award, retirement plan, life insurance policy, or an inheritance—there are ways to protect those assets, but not through the type of trust described in this book. Trusts that can help protect the assets that already belong to a person with a disability are "first-party" trusts that go by a variety of names such as "first-party special needs trust," "payback special needs trust," "litigation special needs trust," "Miller Trust," "pooled SNT," "(d)(4)(A) SNT," and "(d)(4)(C) SNT." All of these first-party trusts are subject to specific federal and state rules designed to keep applicants from sheltering their property in order to meet program eligibility requirements. They are also generally subject to "payback" rules that require that the state be reimbursed for medical expenses after the trust beneficiary dies. Because each state has very specific rules that constantly change, you'll need the help of a lawyer in your state who has experience with first-party special needs planning. See Chapter 10 for information about finding and working with such a lawyer.

This book is designed to help families leave money to a loved one with a disability in a "third-party" special needs trust. The rules are a lot easier to follow in third-party planning than in first-party planning, simply because the government wants to encourage people to leave money for the benefit of their loved ones with disabilities. By contrast, it does not want people to give away their own money in order to stay eligible for public benefits. To discourage this, the rules for first-party trust planning are more restrictive than those for third-party planning.

for a person with a disability. And these needs must be planned for when leaving an inheritance.

There are really three health care systems in America: the private system, Medicare, and Medicaid. These three systems share doctors, hospitals, and other medical resources, but each provides access to these resources in radically different ways. Here is a brief description of each:

- **Private health care.** The private health care system is most frequently available as an employment-related benefit. Great, perhaps, for working people, but usually not available for those with disabilities after they are no longer able to stay on their parents' health care plans. And paying for private health care individually has rarely been an option because health insurance companies consider nearly all people with disabilities ineligible for coverage due to their "preexisting" conditions. The new Affordable Health Care Act (sometimes called Obamacare) does away with this limitation. Thus, when this law goes into effect (January 1, 2014), it may be possible for persons with disabilities to obtain insurance for private health care.

- **Medicare.** Medicare is a government-run health care system that pays for most medical services (but only very limited long-term and in-home care) required by people with disabilities who are eligible for Social Security or Social Security Disability Insurance (SSDI) benefits. A person need not be poor to get Medicare benefits, but because eligibility for Medicare is based on work history, many people with disabilities fail to qualify for coverage.

- **Medicaid.** Medicaid is a state-managed program that pays for virtually all health care delivered to people who don't have private insurance and who don't qualify for Medicare. To get Medicaid you must be classified as either "disabled" or older than age 64. In most states, you also must be poor enough to qualify for SSI—an income-support program designed exclusively for people with limited income and few resources.

For the many people with disabilities who don't qualify for Medicaid, health care costs cause serious financial complications. For example, if parents leave money directly to an adult child with a disability, the gift— if over $2,000—will disqualify the child from SSI and so from Medicaid until the money is used up. This is where the special needs trust comes in. It allows a person with special needs to enhance his or her quality of life with money and assets received from others without losing SSI and Medicaid.

Special needs trusts also provide the trust maker an opportunity to:

• leave instructions about how to use the inheritance (which helps to protect the beneficiary from financial predators), and

• decide when a trustee should hire an advocate or caregiver for the beneficiary.

In other words, the special needs trust can be viewed as a parent (or loved one) replacement when that person is no longer there to provide necessary support and guidance.

Medicaid Eligibility Rules

Within limits set by federal law, each state can determine who is eligible for its Medicaid program. In most states, someone who is eligible for SSI is also automatically eligible for Medicaid. (Some states give Medicaid a different name—for example, Medi-Cal in California and MassHealth in Massachusetts.)

In 11 states, however, eligibility for Medicaid is determined separately from eligibility for SSI. In these states, the income and resource limits for Medicaid are either roughly the same as for SSI or somewhat lower. So someone could be eligible for SSI but not for Medicaid. These states are listed below. They're called "209 states" after a section of the Social Security Act that allows states to determine Medicaid eligibility separately.

This book assumes that someone who is ineligible for SSI because of excess income or resources is also ineligible for Medicaid. However, in most states, a person with excess income or resources can become eligible for Medicaid by spending down the resources or excess income. And a person with disabilities who does not qualify for SSI could still qualify for Medicaid by being determined to be "medically needy."

Medicaid and SSI Eligibility: State Differences		
Eligibility for SSI and Medicaid determined separately ("209 states")	Medicaid for all SSI recipients, but must separately apply to Medicaid agency ("SSI Criteria States")	Eligibility for SSI same as eligibility for Medicaid ("1634 states")
Connecticut New Hampshire Hawaii Illinois North Dakota Indiana Ohio Minnesota Oklahoma Missouri Virginia	Alaska Utah Idaho The Common- Kansas wealth of the Nebraska Northern Nevada Mariana Oregon Islands	All other states and the District of Columbia

For more information about Medicaid eligibility requirements in a 209 state, contact that state's Medicaid agency.

How Inherited Money Can Make SSI and Medicaid Unavailable

Inheriting money seems like a good thing. But for someone who relies on SSI and Medicaid, receiving an inheritance can have a disastrous side effect: losing support and, perhaps more important, health care. That's because the SSI and Medicaid programs are available only to people who have low incomes and few resources.

To qualify for these programs, a person's monthly income usually must be no more than about $650 to $1,000 (it varies from state to state), and the person must own less than $2,000 worth of liquid assets (bank accounts, securities, and the like) and many other types of property. Someone whose property is worth more than the limit is not eligible for benefits. However, importantly, the value of the person's home, car, personal effects, and household furnishings are not usually counted and are considered exempt.

EXAMPLE: John's daughter Yolanda was born with cerebral palsy and will likely need lifetime medical benefits under the Medicaid program. John wants to provide for Yolanda after his death but has been cautioned that leaving her property might disqualify her from Medicaid and support under SSI.

John is right to be concerned. An inheritance that would cause Yolanda to exceed the SSI resource limit would probably also make her ineligible for Medicaid. (Most states operate under this rule, as discussed above.) Yolanda would likely see the property she inherits quickly evaporate in a blizzard of medical bills and living expenses until she once again became eligible for those programs and then had to live a bare-bones existence with no assets to enhance her quality of life.

A person with a disability who comes into money must either put the money in a trust (a first-party special needs trust or pooled trust) or spend it—or at least enough of it so that what's left doesn't exceed the resource limit of $2,000—before reapplying for SSI and Medicaid benefits. The money doesn't have to be spent on support or medical care. However, the money should not be given away. If a person were to give away the money, he or she would be disqualified from SSI for up to three years and from Medicaid for up to five years.

How a Special Needs Trust Can Help

How, then, can you make sure that your loved one receives the full benefit of your inheritance without losing eligibility for Medicaid and SSI? The answer is a third-party special needs trust.

The beneficiary of a properly drafted special needs trust doesn't have a legal claim to property in the trust. This means that the money isn't counted as the beneficiary's resource and so it doesn't interfere with eligibility for benefits. The funds from the trust can be used for your loved one's benefit for any good or service. However, if the trust pays for food or shelter it may reduce how much he or she receives from SSI. Generally, this is a good trade-off because the small loss of SSI is more than offset by having a better place to live or enough food to survive. However, these rules vary from state to state, so be sure to understand your state's rules about using funds from third-party special needs trusts. To learn the rules in your state, you can contact your local Social Security agency or an attorney experienced in special needs planning. See Chapter 10 on how to find such an attorney.

> **EXAMPLE:** Janine, 45, an only child, has had schizophrenia since child-hood. She is able to function under heavy medication, but she cannot work and depends on SSI for her income and Medicaid for health care costs. Janine's sole surviving parent, Helen, wants to leave Janine her property, which consists of a house and assets worth $75,000.
>
> Helen creates a special needs trust for the benefit of Janine, naming herself as trustee to manage the trust while she is alive. Helen writes her will to state that her property should pass directly to the special needs trust rather than to Janine herself. When Helen dies, the house and liquid assets are passed to Jim, the person Helen has named to succeed her as trustee (the successor trustee) in the trust for Janine.
>
> In his new role as trustee, Jim allows Janine to live in the house, liquidates the other assets into cash, and adds the cash to the trust bank account Helen opened when she created the trust. Jim uses the trust funds to pay for items that are not counted by SSI and Medicaid. Because Janine has no control over how the trust money is spent, the money is not counted as a resource by SSI or Medicaid. She gets to keep all of her SSI and Medicaid and gets to use the money in the trust to pay for things and services to enhance her quality of life.

Do you need a lot of money to set up a trust? No, though you may decide that a trust isn't worth the trouble if you don't expect that you (or anyone else) will leave money or other assets to the beneficiary. Typically, you would draft the trust and name yourself as trustee of the special needs trust and either not place any money in trust or make an initial deposit of about $500 in a trust bank account. Be careful: Some states do not allow a trust to be established without any money being added to it. So it is usually best to open a small bank account in the name of the trust. Then after you die, you leave additional property to the trust through your will, revocable living trust, insurance policy, or beneficiary designations. You would also encourage the beneficiary's other relatives to leave money or property to the trust.

Even if the trust ends up with only $5,000 or $10,000, it may be well worth creating because even that little amount of money can be stretched over a long period of time. If the successor trustee (the person you named to serve as trustee after your death) has even $100 a month over five years to spend, it could make your loved one's life easier.

Who Can Benefit From a Special Needs Trust

Third-party special needs trusts can benefit those of any age who have disabilities that qualify them (or may qualify them) for SSI and Medicaid benefits. They may also be useful for people with disabilities who do not have the capacity or capability to manage their own assets. If you think a loved one may at some time need SSI or Medicaid, or may need help in managing assets, consider creating a third-party special needs trust like the one described and provided by this book.

To determine whether someone may be eligible for government public benefits, you need to know at least the basic rules of the programs. The federal programs that provide assistance to adults with disabilities who are younger than 65 focus almost exclusively on whether someone has the ability to be gainfully employed. In other words, employability defines whether or not someone is "disabled"—at least for the purpose of qualifying for federal benefits. A person doesn't have to actually be working. It is their ability to work and not their actual work that determines eligibility.

For SSI purposes, disability is determined under a complex set of criteria fashioned by the Social Security Administration. Generally, the disability must be severe and be expected to last longer than 12 months. Some conditions are considered to be automatically disabling—Down syndrome, for example. Others (like an amputation) require that a number of factors be taken into account, including age, work experience, and the type of function affected by the medical condition.

Chapter 2 discusses disability in more detail, and also discusses some other situations in which you may want to set up a special needs trust for a loved one.

Who Can Set Up a Special Needs Trust

Most articles on special needs trusts speak to a parent or grandparent leaving property to a disabled child or grandchild. However, third-party special needs trusts can work for individuals of any age and relationship. You don't have to be the beneficiary's parent or any other relative to set up a third-party trust.

Older couples sometimes set up special needs trusts for the survivor, to take effect when one spouse or partner dies. However, if the couple is married, these types of special needs trusts must be established through a will and cannot be established during life or through a revocable living trust.

EXAMPLE 1: Gavin and Denise, both 70, have been married for the past 20 years. Denise has been diagnosed with Alzheimer's disease and will need Medicaid in the near future. Gavin creates a special needs trust in his will for Denise, naming a friend as trustee. In his will, Gavin leaves $75,000 to the trust, to be used for Denise's benefit. When Gavin dies, the trust will be set up to supplement Denise's SSI and Medicaid benefits with money from the trust by paying for items not covered by those programs.

EXAMPLE 2: Rolf and Juanita are both in their 60s and live together but are not married. Rolf suffers from severe rheumatoid arthritis and has been receiving SSI and Medicaid for ten years. Juanita has a stock portfolio worth $50,000 in her name alone. She wants to leave the stock to Rolf but doesn't want him to lose his SSI or Medicaid. Juanita creates a third-party special needs trust naming herself as trustee and uses a transfer-on-death beneficiary designation to leave the stock to the trust. When Juanita dies, title to the stock passes to the trust and the person Juanita has named to succeed her as trustee can manage the stock to enhance Rolf's quality of life. Note, however, that if Rolf and Juanita get married, she must create a new special needs trust by will.

You can also set up a special needs trust for someone to whom you're not related at all.

EXAMPLE: Agnes, age 75, leads a simple life in the house she grew up in. She puts in volunteer time at the local Boys and Girls Club and The Arc (an organization dedicated to the developmentally disabled). Unbeknown to the community, Agnes is worth several million dollars because of property she inherited from her father and mother. She gives handsome annual donations to the groups she works with, but has never given much thought to how to leave her property.

When Agnes learns about special needs trusts, she decides to create special needs trusts for 12 disabled children she has grown close to in her volunteer work. In her will, she directs that at her death, each trust will receive an equal share of her property. If during her life she meets other children who she wants to include, she can make arrangements to include them as well.

Alternatives to a Special Needs Trust

Special needs trusts aren't the right solution for every family. Trusts can cost time and money to administer, and the person serving as trustee may be called on to make difficult decisions about investing and spending trust assets.

Leaving Money to a Friend or Relative

Rather than rely on a special needs trust, you may be inclined to leave some money to a friend or relative who agrees to watch out for your loved one's needs after your death.

Unfortunately, this informal approach has several serious downsides. The main problem is that because the person to whom you leave the property will own it outright; there is no way to ensure that the money will end up benefiting your loved one, no matter how honorable the intent at the outset. For example, the money would be subject to that person's creditors in a lawsuit or bankruptcy. Or the property could pass to that person's heirs if he or she suffers an untimely death. Or it could go to a spouse in the event of a divorce. Also, because the laws that govern trustees (described in Chapter 5) won't apply, if the person spends the money on a new car instead of on your loved one's needs, there is nothing that anyone will be able to do about it.

If you don't expect to leave much property to your loved one, this approach may be preferable to setting up a trust that will last only a year or two before the money has been spent. You could attach a letter to your will or living trust explaining what you are doing and request that the money be spent in a way that doesn't interfere with your loved one's SSI and Medicaid benefits. However, this is not preferred if you want the most protection for your loved one with special needs.

Leaving Money Directly to Your Loved One

Leaving money directly to a person with a disability will almost certainly eliminate his or her eligibility for SSI and Medicaid. It also may have a devastating result if that person lacks the capacity to manage money. The only time it may be better to leave property directly to your loved one with a disability is if that person is unlikely to ever qualify for SSI and Medicaid and can be trusted to manage the funds.

Using a Pooled Trust

If you don't want to set up your own special needs trust, you may be able to join an existing "pooled trust." Almost every state has at least one nonprofit organization that operates this type of trust, in which gifts to many disabled beneficiaries are combined so that they can be efficiently and professionally managed. The trustee invests and spends funds for the beneficiaries without affecting their eligibility for SSI and Medicaid. If you sign up for one of these pooled trusts, you can leave the trust details to them. Chapter 7 discusses pooled trusts in detail.

 RELATED TOPIC

Look to the glossary for help with legal terms. In classic plain-English Nolo style, this book explains a complicated legal topic with a minimum of legalese. However, talking about legal things requires at least some use of legal terms, and when that's necessary, we want to make those terms as clear as possible. So, in addition to having legal terms defined in the text, this book also provides a glossary of legal terms for your reference. You'll find the Glossary between Chapter 10 and Appendix A.

How a Special Needs Trust Works—Nuts and Bolts

A special needs trust is an arrangement under which a person (called the "grantor" or "settlor") places property in the hands of a manager (the "trustee"). Typically, the grantor of a special needs trust names himself or herself as trustee and another trusted person successor trustee. The grantor serves as trustee until he or she dies, becomes incapacitated, or resigns; at that time the successor trustee takes over. Each person who serves as trustee is legally obligated to follow the terms of the trust document to use the property for the benefit of the person with a disability identified in the trust document (the "beneficiary").

> **EXAMPLE:** Albion (the grantor) creates a special needs trust for the benefit of his daughter Chloe (the beneficiary). Albion names himself as trustee and his sister Rosie as successor trustee. Rosie will take over when Albion dies, becomes incapacitated, or resigns.

All special needs trusts are defined by two basic characteristics:

• The trust document states that the beneficiary with a disability cannot direct the use of the funds in the trust for his or her support or maintenance.

• The trust document expressly states that the beneficiary with a disability cannot revoke or terminate the trust.

By including these two provisions in the trust document, you ensure that the Social Security Administration (SSA) won't consider the property in the trust as a resource available to the beneficiary.

Of course, the typical special needs trust contains many more words to deal with various events that may arise. For instance, what happens if the beneficiary recovers and is no longer concerned about SSI and Medicaid eligibility? Or if the beneficiary dies, leaving a lot of property in the trust? These and other issues can be resolved by including basic statements of intent in your trust document. (Chapter 8 takes you step by step through all the major issues and offers plain-English provisions to address each of them.)

When the Trust Takes Effect

This trust will take effect when you sign it and have it notarized. Not long after that (when you get the trust's tax identification number from the IRS), you can add a little cash to the trust by opening a bank account with a minimal deposit. Then you can leave additional property to the trust at your death through a will, living trust, or beneficiary designation or another estate planning document. It is possible to put additional property into the trust while you are alive. However, see an experienced estate planning attorney or tax professional for help, as putting large amounts of personal property or real estate into the trust during your lifetime could have serious estate and gift tax implications.

> **EXAMPLE:** Barbara's daughter Kristin suffers from schizophrenia. Barbara, at age 55, creates a special needs trust for Kristen, opens a bank account with $500, and drafts a will that leaves $100,000 to the special needs trust. Twenty years later, both Barbara and Kristin are still alive. Barbara no longer has $100,000 to leave to the trust, but she does own a house. She creates a revocable living trust, places her house in the trust, and includes language in the trust instructing the trustee who will take over at her death (the successor trustee) to deed the house to Kristin's special needs trust. A year later Barbara wins $25,000 at a local casino. She deposits that money in the special needs trust bank account. Barbara is certain that she will never need the $25,000 for her own care. A year later Barbara dies. The special needs trust will now have her house and the casino winnings (plus interest) to provide for Kristin's needs.

CAUTION
Keep an eye on the federal gift tax. The federal government limits the amount of tax-free gifts you can make in your lifetime. This includes gifts you make to a special needs trust. However, the limit is high—over $5 million—

so most people don't need to worry about avoiding gift tax. This exemption amount can change however, and it is tied to the estate tax. So, if you expect to leave millions of dollars as gifts either during your lifetime or at your death, it makes sense to keep tabs on this tax. To learn more, go to the Estate & Gift Tax section of Nolo.com. And if you are concerned that this tax might apply to your situation, see an attorney or a tax professional for advice.

Revocable Living Trusts: The Basics

Revocable living trusts have become a common estate planning tool. They are a private way to legally pass property without the delay and expense of a probate court proceeding that wills often require. In the trust document you name yourself as trustee to manage the trust during your life and appoint a successor trustee to take over at your death. In the trust you also state who should inherit trust property. Because the trust is revocable, you—the grantor—can amend the trust or revoke it completely during your life.

By comparison, the third-party special needs trust in this book is an irrevocable trust. This means that you can't revoke it and you can amend or terminate it only under specific circumstances provided for in the trust itself. If you wish to completely change a third-party special needs trust, you simply create another special needs trust and amend your living trust to leave assets to the new special needs trust.

To learn more about living trusts and other types of trusts, go to the Estate Planning section of Nolo.com.

Who Can Give Property to a Special Needs Trust

Anyone (except the person with a disability) can contribute property to a third-party special needs trust. Although these trusts are most often created by parents for their children, you don't need any family relationship to create or give money to a trust for someone. And there is no limit to the number of trusts that may be created for a particular beneficiary.

EXAMPLE: Jennifer's cousin Harvey wants to leave her some money. Instead of leaving the property directly to Jennifer, he creates a special needs trust for her and names Jennifer's mother, Helen, as trustee (after getting her agreement to serve). In his will, Harvey leaves $20,000 to the trust.

Jennifer's close friend Ruth also wants to give Jennifer some money—both as a gesture of friendship and because she is making gifts as part of a plan to get her estate under the estate tax threshold. Ruth creates a separate special needs trust, names Jennifer's mother, Helen, as trustee, and transfers a $13,000 CD into the trust.

Jennifer's aunt Frieda wants to leave Jennifer $15,000. Rather than create yet another special needs trust, Frieda uses her will to name the trust created by Ruth for Jennifer as the recipient of the $15,000.

What Types of Property Can Be Held in the Trust

Virtually any type of property can be held in a special needs trust, including real estate, stocks, collections, a business, patents, or jewelry. But because the primary purpose of a special needs trust is to use cash money to pay for items that aren't provided by SSI or Medicaid, special needs trust documents typically give the person serving as trustee authority to sell tangible items (cars or jewelry, for example) to raise cash. Whether or not the trustee sells property will depend on:

- the significance of the items to the beneficiary, and
- the likelihood that the assets will appreciate in value (if they won't, it's better to convert them to cash that can be invested elsewhere).

For instance, a home or an heirloom ring might be important to the beneficiary, and the trustee probably wouldn't sell them. A valuable coin collection might be likely to appreciate in value, warranting keeping it in the trust as long as possible. On the other hand, jewelry that is of little interest to a beneficiary might as well be sold, with the proceeds invested in an asset that will produce income. Clearly, in order to make this type of decision, the person serving as trustee will need a good understanding of the beneficiary's personal needs and basic sound investment rules. (Chapter 5 helps you create a written statement communicating these needs to the person you name as your successor trustee.)

How Assets Get to the Trust

The person who creates a special needs trust often makes the initial transfer of assets into the trust—usually, just a small amount of money. Then, commonly, a parent, a grandparent, or another relative leaves property to the trust by:

- leaving it through a will or revocable living trust directly to the trustee of the special needs trust, or
- naming the trustee of the special needs trust as a beneficiary on a designation form that controls what happens to a deposit or brokerage account, retirement plan, or stocks and bonds.

More about this in Chapter 4.

How Trust Assets Can Be Used

Trust assets can be used for almost anything that is not illegal or contrary to the terms in the trust. Because the primary purpose of a special needs trust is to enhance the quality of life of the beneficiary with a disability, the list of things that can be paid for is quite broad. Generally, trust funds can be used to pay for:

- caregiving (such as a personal attendant or therapies not paid for by Medicaid)
- experiences (such as travel or concerts)
- services (such as cell phone, Internet, or cleaning service)
- pet care (such as pet food or veterinarian care), or
- things (such as a computer, clothing, or new furniture).

However, the trustee of a third-party special needs trust must perform a balancing act between making distributions that do not violate the rules of SSI and Medicaid and providing sufficient goods and services to person with special needs.

This balancing act is particularly tricky when the trustee wishes to make payments for the beneficiary's food or shelter, because such payments often trigger a reduction in SSI benefits. However, even though it's tricky, it often still makes sense for a trustee to use trust funds for food and shelter because there are exemptions and rules that make the trade-off worthwhile.

EXAMPLE: Eva, a 34-year-old woman with cystic fibrosis, lives in a studio apartment in a "low-rent" part of San Francisco, where she still must pay $800 a month. Eva's SSI grant—her sole source of income—is $700 a month. Obviously, Eva needs some help with her rent. Under SSI rules explained in Chapter 3, the trust can pay the entire $800 rent, and Eva will lose only about $256 from her grant.

Whether or not to use trust property for food and shelter is entirely up to the person serving as trustee. In the example above, Eva couldn't force the trustee of her special needs trust to pay the rent money. If the beneficiary did have that kind of power over the trustee, all the funds in the trust would be considered available resources for SSI and Medicaid eligibility purposes. So, although a special needs trust may give the trustee authority to make rent payments, the trust or state law may prohibit such payments if they would interrupt the beneficiary's eligibility for SSI and Medicaid.

Chapter 3 explains the ins and outs of paying for shelter and associated services, such as utilities. It also provides a long list of items that are typically considered supplementary to the SSI and Medicaid programs and, therefore, appropriate for special needs trust expenditures without any reduction of benefits.

The Trustee's Role

It's almost a cliché that the operative word in the phrase special needs trust is "trust." The person you choose to succeed you as trustee will manage and spend, without court supervision, the property you leave for the beneficiary. You will need to pick one or more successor trustees to step in should you die or become incapacitated. Even if you pick someone else as the initial trustee, you should name successor trustees so that there is someone in line to take over management of the trust if the initial trustee can no longer serve.

When picking trustees and successor trustees, you want to pick people you have complete faith in. In addition to being responsive and sensitive to the beneficiary's personal needs, the person serving as trustee has the absolutely crucial job of investing and spending trust assets.

You also need someone who will keep up on the law. Generally, trustees are supposed to use trust funds only for goods and services that supplement—but don't disqualify the beneficiary for—benefits provided by SSI and Medicaid. For this, the trustee needs a good working knowledge of how to spend trust money without affecting eligibility. This can be easy when the goods and services are obviously supplemental but more problematic where food or housing costs are involved. The person serving as trustee will learn about the rules from the SSI program administrators and their regulations, or from a qualified professional resource. (Chapter 10 has more on resources.)

In addition to dealing with the SSI and Medicaid programs, the person serving as trustee has a legal duty to invest the trust assets prudently. Trustees must obey state laws about trust management and must also obey the terms of the trust document itself.

Trustees may be required to spend judiciously to make the trust's funds last as long as possible. This can be one of the hardest aspects of a trustee role, especially when the beneficiary's desires conflict with a trustee's duty to conserve trust funds.

EXAMPLE: Adrian, a 28-year-old with quadriplegia, rents a cheap apartment in a downscale Cleveland neighborhood. He receives SSI and Medicaid and is the beneficiary of a special needs trust containing roughly $200,000 left by his father. Adrian wants to live in a better neighborhood and asks the person serving as trustee of the special needs trust to buy him a house that's for sale. If the trustee buys the house, almost all of the trust property will be used up. Should the trustee comply with Adrian's wishes, or refuse so the trust funds will last longer? Because Adrian has no authority to direct the trustee's disbursements, he'll have to abide by the trustee's choice.

So how should Adrian's trustee go about making this decision? He or she will have to consider the purposes of the trust. One purpose is to supplement the SSI and Medicaid benefits Adrian receives—food, shelter, and basic medical services. Another purpose of the trust is to enhance the quality of life for Adrian. The trustee should also consider the costs of maintaining the home after purchase. Ultimately, the trustee will have to weigh these factors and make a decision. This situation highlights the importance of naming a trustee that you can count on to make difficult decisions.

Unlike Adrian, some beneficiaries cannot coherently express their wishes because of their particular disability—for example, severe autism can have this effect. In such cases, trustees must rely on their own knowledge of the beneficiary's needs and desires, or on information provided in the trust document or by the beneficiary's family in a written needs statement (explained in Chapter 5).

Trustees are also responsible for accounting for the trust income and disbursements and filing annual tax returns for the trust. Unless the trustees have tax and accounting expertise, this might be something that should be handled by an outside expert and paid for with trust funds. Of course, if the trustee only writes a few checks a month out of the same checkbook, the accounting will mostly done on the check stubs.

The special needs trust in this book provides that the trustee can be paid a reasonable amount from trust assets for doing trust-related work. Also, because a trustee's role can be demanding, you may want to name cotrustees to share the load. If the property in the trust has or will have a sufficient value—roughly $250,000 or more—you might also consider turning over the financial management of the assets to a private professional fiduciary or corporate trustee.

The trust will be managed under fiduciary law, which requires the person serving as trustee to do what a prudent person would do under similar circumstances. If necessary, however, the trust document authorizes the person serving as trustee to get expert help—and to pay a reasonable amount for it with trust funds.

Chapter 5 helps you get a grasp on these and other trustee issues so you'll know what's in store for trustees and successor trustees you name to manage the trust. A sample letter to trustees, which outlines the information your trustees will need to competently manage the trust, is available in Appendix B and as a downloadable eForm.

Pooled Trusts

In almost all states, you can join an existing special needs trust that is managed for people with special needs by a nonprofit organization. This option, called a pooled trust, may be just the ticket if either of the following applies:

- You need a place to park your loved one's current assets without jeopardizing their eligibility for SSI and Medicaid.
- You can't come up with a good candidate to serve as trustee or successor trustee.

Chapter 7 discusses pooled trusts in detail.

Terminating the Special Needs Trust

The special needs trust ends when it's no longer needed. There are four reasons to end a special needs trust:

- Trust funds are depleted.
- The beneficiary no longer needs government benefits.
- The beneficiary is no longer eligible for government benefits.
- The beneficiary dies.

The first reason to terminate a trust is simply because the funds run out. This may happen if the trust wasn't funded with many assets to begin with, or if the beneficiary lives much longer than originally antici-pated. The person serving as trustee doesn't have to spend the last dime; when funds dwindle to a low level, it may no longer make sense to keep the trust going, given the cost of expenses such as record keeping and expert advice.

EXAMPLE: Eden, age 60, is the beneficiary of a special needs trust that went into effect when she was 20. Eden has outlived her original life expectancy by 20 years. The trust was originally funded with the proceeds of a $200,000 life insurance policy, but over the next 40 years the funds were slowly depleted. Now, only $3,000 is left in the trust, and the trustee can no longer justify keeping the trust in effect, given the expenses of administration.

The second reason to terminate a trust is if it appears that the beneficiary either doesn't need or doesn't qualify for SSI or Medicaid. This may happen because eligibility rules change or because the beneficiary's condition improves.

EXAMPLE: Robert, who suffers from chronic schizophrenia, is the beneficiary of a special needs trust established when he was 28. Now Robert is 55 and, thanks to a new class of antipsychotic drugs, no longer has symptoms of his illness as long as he takes his pills. Because Robert is now able and willing to work, he no longer needs to rely on SSI and his medical care will be picked up by a work-related medical insurance program.

The third reason to terminate the trust would be because a change in program rules made the beneficiary ineligible for SSI, Medicaid, or similar programs if the trust continues in effect.

EXAMPLE: Clara is the beneficiary of a special needs trust created when she was 21. At that time, the laws allowed a person who was addicted to drugs to be considered disabled. Fifteen years later, the SSI rules have changed so that drug addicts are no longer considered to be disabled. In this case, the trustee may have rights to terminate the trust because it can no longer be used for its primary purpose.

In any of these three situations, after all taxes and debts legally owed by the trust have been paid, the trust document provided by this book directs the person serving as trustee to distribute as much of the property to the beneficiary as possible without interfering with his or her eligibility for benefits. If the beneficiary has a legal guardian or conservator, or a person who has been designated to receive benefits on his or her behalf (representative payee), the trustee distributes the property to that person.

EXAMPLE: The person serving as trustee of Emma's special needs trust decides to terminate the trust because federal law changes will make Emma ineligible for Medicaid benefits if the trust stays in existence, and Emma really needs the benefits. There's about $10,000 in the trust.

The trustee distributes $1,999 to Emma, which keeps her under the $2,000 resource limit (she doesn't have any other nonexempt assets) so she can continue to receive SSI and Medicaid. The trustee gives the rest of the money to Emma's sister, who is named as the remainder beneficiary in the trust document.

If the beneficiary won't lose any needed benefits as a result, the trustee gives all of the trust funds to the beneficiary or may buy an exempt asset like new furniture or a car.

EXAMPLE: Eli no longer needs government benefits, so the trustee of his special needs trusts ends the trust and gives all of the funds directly to Eli.

The last reason to terminate the trust is when the beneficiary dies. In this case, the person serving as trustee is directed to distribute any remaining trust funds to the person you named in the special needs trust to inherit them. This person is called the "remainder beneficiary" of the trust. (Chapter 5 discusses remainder beneficiaries.)

Checklist: Making a Special Needs Trust

☐ Decide whether or not you really want to create a special needs trust.

- Will you be leaving enough money to make administering a trust worthwhile after you die?
- Are you willing to serve as trustee during your lifetime, or do you know someone who is?
- Is someone willing and able to serve as successor trustee?
- Will your loved one need SSI and Medicaid after your death?
- Would a pooled trust serve your needs better? (See Chapter 7.)

☐ Choose an initial trustee (typically yourself) and one or more successor trustees.

☐ Educate the people you want to name as successor trustees.

- Prepare and give the successor trustees the Trustee's Duties Letter (Appendix B) and the Beneficiary Information Letter (Appendix C).

☐ Draft the special needs trust document.

☐ Decide how much cash to deposit in the trust bank account you'll set up after you create the trust.

☐ Decide how much property you wish to add to the trust during your life.

☐ Decide how much property you wish to leave to the trust when you die.

Who Can Benefit From a Special Needs Trust

Special needs trusts are designed to enhance the quality of life of a person with a disability by maximizing the resources available to him or her. It preserves eligibility for Supplementary Security Income (SSI) and Medicaid (which pay for food, shelter, and medical care but little else). The special needs trust can then pay for all other additional things that make life better.

Someone With a Permanent or Severe Disability Who Is Unable to Earn a Living

Special needs trusts are most commonly used for people who likely will need government assistance from the SSI and Medicaid programs their entire lives because of a permanent or severe disabling condition.

Not all persons with a disability qualify for SSI or Medicaid. Someone who is commonly understood to be disabled may not qualify for these public benefits if, despite the disabling condition, the person is able to earn a living. SSI's definition for disability for an adult is:

> The inability to engage in any "substantial gainful activity" (SGA) due to any medically determinable physical or mental impairment, or combination of impairments, that has lasted or can be expected to last for a continuous period of at least 12 months, or result in death.

So, the two qualifications are: The person has a disability that will last at least a year or is expected to result in death, and the person must be unable to engage in SGA. SGA is the maximum amount that a person with a disability may earn each month while maintaining eligibility for benefits. In 2013, the SGA figure is $1,040/month. The Social Security Administration reasons that an individual who is able to earn at least this amount per month is able to engage in competitive employment in the national economy. (Of course, this is contrary to what many people would view as a reasonable figure.)

Only United States citizens automatically qualify for SSI benefits if they meet these qualifications. Noncitizens can qualify for SSI if they are legally in the country and meet some additional qualifications.

Low-income people 65 or older are also eligible for SSI. When someone under the age of 65 applies for SSI or Medicaid benefits, the Social Security Administration makes a determination as to whether or not the person is "disabled." (Chapter 10 lists references to the rules and other sources of law regarding SSI and Medicaid rules that affect special needs trusts.)

People with blindness, developmental disabilities, Down syndrome, organic brain damage, chronic mental illness, physical paralysis (paraplegia), or congenital disabling afflictions, such as cerebral palsy or cystic fibrosis, have been the most common automatic beneficiaries of government benefits for persons with disabilities. But there are many other physical and mental conditions that meet the Social Security Administration's definition of disability and that are likely to last a lifetime. Some of them are listed below.

Conditions That Can Cause Permanent Disability: A Partial List

agoraphobia	hemophilia	organic brain syndrome (OBS)
Alzheimer's disease	HIV	
amputations	Huntington's chorea	Parkinson's disease
bipolar disorder	kidney malfunction	phenylketonuria (PKU)
cancer (many types)	leukemia	severe autistic disorder
congenital heart disease	lupus	sickle cell anemia
diabetes mellitus (type 2)	multiple chemical sensitivity	spina bifida
		Tay-Sachs disease
emphysema	multiple sclerosis	thalassemia
fetal alcohol syndrome	muscular dystrophy	traumatic spine damage
	obsessive-compulsive disorder	Turner's syndrome
fragile X syndrome		

Someone Who May Get Better

Many disabling conditions are not permanent. For example, many combat veterans suffer from posttraumatic stress disorder, which produces a combination of mental, emotional, and physical symptoms, making it impossible to work for years, but not necessarily for a lifetime. Even then, however, it may make a lot of sense to create a special needs trust in such a case because it's impossible to tell just how long the disability will last.

How the Definition of "Disabled" Is Changing

Many factors make it hard to predict whether someone who currently has a disability will always need to rely on SSI and Medicaid.

Changes in the workplace. For SSI eligibility purposes, someone who can't work is disabled. So as the workplace changes, so does the definition of disabled. For instance, when most people worked on farms, someone with a developmental disorder might not have been considered disabled for the purposes of an SSI-type program, because formal learning wasn't necessary to heft a pitchfork, milk cows, plant corn, or do housework. In 21st-century high-tech America, however, a pronounced difficulty in learning makes it difficult to find a job. On the other hand, technological advances in the medical field have made it possible for people with paraplegia or severe visual impairment to perform a large range of productive work.

New treatments for old disabilities. Modern medical techniques and discoveries in areas such as gene therapy, stem cells, and neuro-transmitters (molecules that facilitate nerve impulse transmissions) offer the possibility of cures for a broad range of conditions that currently are incurable. Parkinson's and Alzheimer's disease are two devastating conditions that may be amenable to treatment in ten or 20 years. Similarly, techniques to regenerate damaged or severed nerve cells may someday offer relief to people who cannot move their limbs because of a spinal injury. Mentally disabling conditions also are reaping the benefits of modern medical technology. The pharmaceutical industry has given us drugs that let people with a large range of formerly incapacitating mental conditions engage in productive activity.

Technological advances. There have been profound changes in technologies available to ameliorate physically disabling conditions. For example, hearing aids or surgery largely eliminate the disability of deafness for many Americans. More change is on the way in such fields as robotics and nanotechnology. For example, research is underway to help people whose arms or legs have been amputated to regain near-full functionality with the help of "intelligent" prostheses and to develop a computerized interface that helps blind people experience visual feedback from the environment.

Planning With Recovery in Mind

The SSI and Medicaid programs have not, by and large, taken medical and technological advances into account when determining disability. A condition that prevented employment in 1950 is often assumed to do so today. However, this could change at any time. Your loved one may not always be eligible for SSI and Medicaid, either because disabilities are defined differently or because he or she enjoys a dramatic recovery.

There's no way to know whether your loved one's disability will improve with time, either naturally or through medical and technological intervention. But even so, you can create a special needs trust without worrying that you will needlessly tie up your loved one's inheritance. The trust document takes into account the possibility that the trust, for whatever reason, may not always be necessary, and gives the trustee (you or the trustees who succeed you) power to terminate the trust under certain conditions. For example, the trust allows the trustee to end the trust if at some point the beneficiary no longer needs or qualifies for SSI and Medicaid.

EXAMPLE: Jeanne leaves $100,000 in her will to a special needs trust she created for the benefit of her daughter Cassie, who is ten and has been diagnosed with schizophrenia. Jeanne named Joanne, Cassie's aunt, to take over as trustee when Jeanne dies. The trust gives the trustee complete discretion as to how the funds may be spent for Cassie's benefit, provided that disbursements do not disqualify Cassie for SSI and Medicaid.

The trust document also states that if someday Cassie does not need or does not qualify for SSI or Medicaid, the person serving as trustee may terminate the trust and distribute the remaining trust money to Cassie outright.

Twenty years later, when Jeanne dies, the $100,000 passes to the trust. By that time, Cassie, now 30 is no longer considered disabled for purposes of SSI and Medicaid. Joanne, the person serving as trustee, terminates the trust and distributes the property to Cassie outright.

If you think that a disability is likely to get better, another option is to leave the funds to your loved one outright, with the expectation that a first-party special needs trust will be created if needed. (A first-party special needs trust is one funded with the beneficiary's own money—unlike the trust you make with this book, which is funded with your money or someone else's.) Remember though, a first-party special needs trust is more expensive to set up than the special needs trust covered in this book, can only be set up for someone under the age of 65, and requires payback to the state's Medicaid agency on the termination of the trust (which results from the death of the beneficiary). You will need an attorney's help to make sure that the trust complies with the Medicaid eligibility rules of your state.

Someone Who May Need a Special Needs Trust Later

Some people who aren't disabled now may need assistance from SSI or Medicaid at some point because of a condition that is likely to get worse, making it impossible for the person to be self-sufficient.

In this situation, creating a special needs trust involves some guess-work. But if you think it's more likely than not that a loved one will need government assistance for a significant length of time, it makes sense to set up a special needs trust. There's really no risk. The trust in this book includes a clause that allows the person serving as trustee to terminate the trust if changes in the beneficiary's disability make a special needs trust unnecessary. If it turns out that the trust is needed, however, the trustee can use trust funds to pay for all kinds of useful things, such as tuition, travel, tools, cultural events, and companion services. (See Chapter 3 for a complete list.) And because the trustee has complete control over how funds are used, you don't need to worry about the beneficiary spending it in ways you wouldn't approve of.

Someone Who Is Eligible for Medicare or SSDI

A loved one who receives Medicare or Social Security Disability Insurance (SSDI) may not need a special needs trust because these programs do not base eligibility on the amount of money or assets an applicant has. There's no need to keep an inheritance in trust; your loved one can own it outright without losing SSDI or Medicare benefits.

If, however, the SSDI payment is low, SSI may be a valuable way to supplement your loved one's income. And Medicaid may be necessary to provide benefits not included in the Medicare program—for instance, long-term nursing home care.

In other words, if your loved one suffers from a degenerative mental illness that almost certainly will require long-term care in a nursing facility, then establishing a special needs trust might make sense even if he or she is eligible for Medicare. However, if you don't expect your loved one to need long-term nursing care, you may prefer to not tie up his or her inheritance in a special needs trust (assuming that you don't have concerns about you loved one's ability to spend the inheritance wisely and you're not worried about the possibility of your loved one becoming the victim of predators). Instead, you can leave the property directly to your loved one, who can continue to receive Medicare and SSDI.

EXAMPLE: Julia was born with cystic fibrosis. Her parents have worked for many years in jobs covered by Social Security, so they qualify for Social Security benefits should they become disabled or reach retirement age.

Because of her parents' work history, Julia also qualifies for Social Security benefits and Medicare.

TIP

Medicaid goes by different names in different states. Medicaid is a combined federal and state program, and is known by a different name in some states. For example, in California it's called Medi-Cal, and in Massachusetts, MassHealth.

Sources of Support and Medical Care for People With Disabilities		
	Who Qualifies	Benefits
SSI	People with limited income and few resources. If a noncitizen, must meet certain criteria.	Monthly cash payments (amount depends on living arrangement, marital status, and disability).
Medicaid	People who qualify for SSI. People who have too much income for SSI but might still independently qualify. People who qualify by Medicaid waiver.	Most medical services, including long-term nursing home care and pharmaceuticals.
SSDI & Social Security	People who have paid enough Social Security taxes, without regard to resources or income. People who become disabled before age 22, if their parents qualify for either SSDI or Social Security retirement benefits.	Monthly cash payments.
Medicare	People who are eligible for Social Security disability benefits because of their work history or that of an eligible parent.	Most medical services, but not long-term care.

For more information, see www.ssa.gov.

Someone Who Needs Assistance Managing an Inheritance

Even if a person is never eligible for SSI or Medicaid, it may still make sense to place that person's inheritance into a special needs trust. This is particularly true for those loved ones who are unfamiliar with or incapable of managing money in a prudent fashion. Even in the absence of an established disability, a special needs trust could be helpful for a person with mild developmental disabilities, mild autism, attention deficit disorder, or bipolar syndrome, or for someone who is easily influenced by financial predators.

In any of these circumstances, the special needs trust by its very nature would help, because the trust names a qualified person to help the beneficiary manage and spend trust assets. This is the trustee. The trust puts a host of laws and rules in place to make sure that that the trustee manages the money in the best interests of the beneficiary. Such trusts are often called "spendthrift" trusts when used to keep assets out of the hands of a beneficiary (and of his or her creditors) and in the firm control of a wise trustee. So, even for those persons who never need or use public benefits, a special needs trust can optimally manage an inheritance.

Ultimately, only you can decide whether it makes sense to provide the long-term management of a loved one's inheritance that a special needs trust provides or to leave the inheritance directly to your loved one. If you do decide to use a special needs trust, the beneficiary is sure to receive much the same benefit from the inheritance as would be the case with an outright gift, even though a small portion of the trust assets may be spent on administrative fees over the years.

How Trust Funds Can (and Cannot) Be Used

Τhis chapter explains how a special needs trust can provide your loved one with a disability with a large variety of goods and services while at the same time preserving his or her SSI and Medicaid benefits.

SSI Income and Resource Limits: An Overview

You're using a special needs trust so you can enhance the quality of life of a person with a disability without jeopardizing SSI and Medicaid benefits. That means people you choose to serve as trustee and successor trustee will need to know the rules about how trust money can be used. Otherwise, your loved one's benefits could be cut or even lost altogether. Much of the information in this chapter is summarized in a letter you can give to the people you name as trustee and successor trustee (see Chapter 5 and Appendix B).

 RESOURCE
Learn more about administering a special needs trust. For a detailed explanation about how to properly administer a special needs trust, read *Administering the California Special Needs Trust*, by Kevin Urbatsch (iUniverse).

Here's a quick summary:

- Monthly SSI payments can be reduced or eliminated if the person serving as trustee gives the beneficiary cash or pays for the beneficiary's food or shelter.

- SSI benefits can be lost for any month in which the beneficiary receives too much cash or owns too many "countable" assets. In most states, a beneficiary who no longer qualifies for SSI won't qualify for Medicaid either.

CAUTION

SSI and Medicaid rules can change at any time. The people you name to serve as successor trustees will be responsible for keeping up to date on SSI and Medicaid rules. See Chapter 10 for information about how to keep up to date.

Resource Limits

Anyone who owns more than $2,000 worth of countable resources is not eligible for SSI. (The limit for a couple eligible for SSI is $3,000.) Countable resources are cash, any asset that could readily be converted to cash, or real estate that isn't the person's primary residence.

Countable Resources: Examples
• Cash
• Checking and savings accounts
• Stocks and bonds
• Vacation home, rental property, or other real estate that is not the beneficiary's primary residence
• IRA, 401(k), and other retirement assets
• Investment accounts
• Uniform Transfer to Minor Accounts

There are some assets that are not counted toward the $2,000 limit. Some examples are listed below.

Noncountable Resources: Examples

- Beneficiary's primary residence (house and land, condo). This home may be of any value, if the beneficiary is on SSI. If the beneficiary receives only Medicaid—and not SSI—the home's value may be limited to $500,000 or $750,000.
- Car or van of any value
- Furnishings and personal effects
- Burial and life insurance with a face value of up to $1,500

How does the SSI program know what and how much a recipient owns? Generally, the bureaucracy relies on the recipient's own required reports and on information from the IRS, state motor vehicles department, and banks. If for some reason an investigation is begun, the recipient's financial affairs will be examined more closely.

Income Limits

An SSI recipient can receive only a certain amount of income in a given month. Federal regulations divide income into three categories: earned, unearned, and in-kind. Each is treated differently.

Earned income comes from a job (including wages earned in a sheltered workshop) or a business. If the beneficiary earns more than $65 a month, his or her SSI payment is reduced one dollar for every two dollars earned. If earnings are too high, the SSI grant (and as a result, Medicaid benefits) can be lost altogether.

Unearned income is cash (or assets that can be easily converted into cash) from gifts, donations, prizes, rental income, interest from bank accounts, dividends, and similar sources. If a trustee gives a beneficiary money from the special needs trust, that's counted as unearned income. If you leave money directly to your loved one, that will be unearned income in the month it is received; whatever is left the next month will be treated as a resource and subject to the $2,000 resource limit.

The first $20 of unearned income each month has no effect on a beneficiary's SSI grant. After that, the grant is reduced, dollar-for-dollar, up to the amount of the unearned income.

EXAMPLE: Sadie, who receives SSI, receives a $200 check as a birthday gift. Her SSI grant is reduced by $180 that month.

However, here's why a special needs trust works: Gifts of items that aren't countable resources aren't considered unearned income.

EXAMPLE: The person serving as trustee of Maya's special needs trust buys her a big TV. Because the TV is a noncountable home furnishing, it doesn't count as income. Maya's SSI grant is not reduced at all by the gift.

In-kind income consists of food or shelter, including payments for such shelter costs as rent, a mortgage, or utilities. Gifts of other items are not in-kind income (though they may count as unearned income (see above) and as a resource after the month in which they are received).

In-kind income reduces an SSI grant up to the lesser of:

• the value of the gift, or

• one-third of the maximum federal portion of the SSI grant plus $20. For 2013, the maximum reduction is $256.67.

How these rules will affect management of the trust funds by you and the people you name as successor trustee is discussed in more detail in the rest of the chapter.

RESOURCE
More information on SSI and related issues. For an in-depth discussion of the SSI system, see *Social Security, Medicare & Government Pensions*, by Joseph Matthews with Dorothy Matthews Berman (Nolo).

Assets in the Special Needs Trust

Assets contributed by you or another third party to a properly drafted special needs trust are not considered resources of the beneficiary because the beneficiary has never had control over them. So they are not subject to the $2,000 resource limit. Theoretically, a special needs trust could hold millions of dollars in cash, houses, cars, jewelry, stocks, and commercial properties of enormous value, and yet the trust beneficiary would still financially qualify for SSI.

> **EXAMPLE:** A vacation cabin that Estelle's family has owned for years has been left to a special needs trust naming Estelle as the beneficiary. Although the cabin is worth far more than $2,000, it isn't considered a resource owned or controlled by Estelle, and so it doesn't affect her eligibility for SSI.

What Special Needs Trust Funds Can Be Used For

The person serving as trustee of the special needs trust can pay for anything for your loved one, as long as the purchase is not against public policy or illegal and does not violate the terms of the trust. Certain types of disbursements, most notably those for food or shelter, may reduce the amount of SSI but are generally still allowed.

It's common for the trustee to pay for a broad variety of services provided to the beneficiary—for example, travel, education, caregiving, or medical services not provided by Medicaid.

The person serving as trustee can also buy the beneficiary noncountable assets without worrying about how much they're worth. That means the beneficiary can own a substantial amount of property without losing eligibility for SSI and Medicaid.

> **EXAMPLE:** Pauline, the trustee of Meg's special needs trust, buys Meg a special van that Meg, who can't drive an ordinary car, can use. Because the van is a noncountable asset under SSI rules, Meg still qualifies for SSI even though the van is worth much more than $2,000.

Here are details about some of the main noncountable resources:

One Home of Any Value

Owning one home as a primary residence won't disqualify your loved one from receiving SSI. However, it might be better to leave the home in the special needs trust so the person serving as trustee (you or a successor trustee) can make important decisions about the home—such as selling it someday if your loved one doesn't need it anymore. Also, if your loved one owns the house outright, trust expenditures on maintenance will be counted as in-kind income. But if the trust owns the home, the trust can spend whatever is necessary to maintain the home without affecting the beneficiary's SSI grant.

On the other hand, in the month that the trust buys the home, the beneficiary will lose the $256.67 in-kind income from his or her SSI check. However, going forward, even if the beneficiary doesn't pay market rent, there is no reduction in SSI because the trust is considered to have an "equitable" ownership interest in the house.

> **EXAMPLE:** If the trustee purchases a home where the beneficiary will live for $800,000, the beneficiary would lose only $256.67 of SSI in the month of purchase. Going forward, the beneficiary may live in the home rent-free without any further reduction of SSI. The beneficiary may also move from the home at any time without affecting SSI.

CAUTION

Additional restrictions apply to homes owned by some Medicaid recipients. Many Medicaid programs limit the value of a home owned by a person who receives Medicaid benefits to $500,000 or $750,000. However, this limit does not apply if a trust owns the home. So if a person with a disability does not qualify for SSI, but does receive Medicaid, it is important that either the value of the home is lower than these amounts or the home is owned by the special needs trust.

One Motor Vehicle

The beneficiary can own one motor vehicle, regardless of value, without affecting SSI eligibility.

> **EXAMPLE:** Conor, the beneficiary of a special needs trust, urges the person serving as trustee to buy him a second car. If the trustee spent $10,000 on a second car, Conor's resources would go over the $2,000 resource limit and make him ineligible for SSI. Such a purchase is forbidden by the terms of the trust in this book, because the trustee is required to avoid disbursements that would make Conor ineligible for SSI and Medicaid. However, the trustee could purchase a second car and have the special needs trust own it and it would not affect his SSI eligibility.

Home Furnishings and Personal Effects

These categories are extremely broad and have no limiting definition. Pretty much anything that can fit in your loved one's home is covered.

> **EXAMPLE:** Bob, a trustee of a special needs trust for his niece Sandra, buys her a $1,200 computer. The computer is not counted as a resource because it's considered a household furnishing. Owning it doesn't affect Sandra's SSI eligibility.

Property Essential to Self-Support

This category encompasses property that is used for work, either as an employee or running a trade or business. There are limits on the value of these items depending on the rate of return they provide and other variables.

More information about this category is available in the guidelines relied on by workers at the Social Security and local district offices. For more about these guidelines, called the *Program Operations Manual System* or POMS, go to http://policy.ssa.gov. If you still are uncertain about whether a particular type of property will be treated as a resource, consider asking for a written opinion from the applicable SSA agency.

Things Special Needs Trusts Can Pay for Without Worry

Here is a list of items that a special needs trust can pay for without jeopardizing eligibility for public benefits. This list is not meant to be exhaustive, but it shows how many useful things and services can be paid for without worry.

Automobile (car, van)

Accounting services

Acupuncture/acupressure

Appliances (TV, VCR, DVD player, stereo, microwave, stove, refrigerator, washer/dryer)

Bottled water or water service

Bus pass/public transportation costs

Camera, film, recorder and tapes, development of film

Clothing

Clubs and club dues (record clubs, book clubs, health clubs, service clubs, zoo, advocacy groups, museums)

Computer hardware, software, programs, and Internet service

Conferences

Cosmetics

Courses or classes (academic or recreational), including books and supplies

Curtains, blinds, and drapes

Dental work not covered by Medicaid, including anesthesia

Down payment on home or security deposit on apartment

Dry cleaning and laundry services

Education expenses including tuition and related costs

Elective surgery

Eyeglasses

Fitness equipment

Funeral expenses

Furniture, home furnishings

Gasoline and maintenance for automobile

Haircuts and salon services

Hobby supplies

Holiday decorations, parties, dinner dances, holiday cards

Home alarm, monitoring, and response systems

Home improvements, repairs, and maintenance (not covered by Medicaid), including tools to perform home improvements, repairs, and maintenance by homeowner

Home purchase (to the extent not covered by benefits)

House cleaning and maid services

Insurance (for automobile, home, or possessions)

Legal fees

Linens and towels

Magazine and newspaper subscriptions

Massage

Musical instruments (including lessons and music)

Nonfood grocery items (laundry soap, bleach, fabric softener, deodorant, dish soap, hand and body soap, personal hygiene products, paper towels, napkins, Kleenex, toilet paper, and household cleaning products)

Over-the-counter medications (including vitamins and herbs)

Personal assistance services not covered by Medicaid

Pets, pet supplies, and veterinary services

Things Special Needs Trusts Can Pay for Without Worry (cont'd)	
Physician specialists if not covered by Medicaid	Therapy (physical, occupational, or speech) not covered by Medicaid
Pornography (as long as legal)	Tickets to concerts or sporting events (for beneficiary and an accompanying companion, if necessary)
Private counseling if not covered by Medicaid	
Repair services (for appliances, automobile, bicycle, household, or fitness equipment)	Transportation (automobile, motorcycle, bicycle, moped, gas, bus passes, insurance, vehicle license fees, or car repairs)
Snow removal, landscaping, and gardening (lawn) services	
Sporting goods, equipment, uniforms, and team pictures	Tuition and other educational expenses
Stationery, stamps, and cards	Utility bills (satellite TV, cable TV, telephone—but not gas, water, or electricity)
Storage units	
Taxicabs	Vacation (including paying for a personal assistant to accompany the beneficiary if necessary)
Telephone service and equipment, including cell phone, pager	

Occupational Goals

Under SSI's Plan for Achieving Self-Support (PASS) program, the government allows SSI recipients to use specific assets toward an occupational goal, such as college, vocational training, or starting a business. The assets used might be earned income, unearned income, or even countable assets of over $2,000. Normally, using these assets would result in ineligibility for benefits or lowering the SSI monthly payment amount. However, under PASS, a person with a disability could use assets toward an approved occupational goal without penalty. To have a PASS plan approved, an SSI recipient submits form SSA-545-BK to an SSI field office for review. In the form, the recipient describes how using the funds will help that person obtain employment. If the office's PASS expert approves the plan, the assets used to fulfill the PASS will not be counted as resources. To learn more about PASS, go to www.ssa.gov.

Burial and Life Insurance Policies

Life insurance policies with cash surrender values less than $1,500 aren't counted toward the $2,000 SSI resource limit. Burial insurance policies of any value are not counted. However, funds set aside for burial expenses in an account or a trust are limited to $1,500 or less.

Gifts of Cash

There is no point in giving an SSI beneficiary cash from a special needs trust. That's because if a beneficiary receives cash or its equivalent (countable resources that can be readily converted to cash, such as a bank CD or shares of stock), the SSI grant will be reduced, dollar for dollar, in the month the income is received. (A small exception to this rule is that the first $20 of a gift received in a given month is not counted.) SSI recipients must make regular reports to the Social Security Administration about income they receive.

> **EXAMPLE:** Peter is the trustee of Erica's special needs trust. For Erica's birthday every year, Peter writes her a check from the trust for $100. Erica then goes shopping with the money. Erica must report the receipt of this cash and, as a result, $80 is deducted from her SSI grant.

The trustee can, however, give the beneficiary noncash items that aren't countable resources because such items are not income.

> **EXAMPLE:** Peter stops writing Erica checks and instead starts taking her shopping for her birthday. He lets her pick out $100 worth of birthday gifts and pays for them with trust funds. The gifts—things for her apartment and personal items such as clothing and jewelry—qualify as "personal effects and household furnishings" (discussed above), and Erica's SSI grant stays intact.

If a gift of cash is large enough to reduce the SSI grant to zero, in many states the recipient will also lose Medicaid eligibility for that month.

EXAMPLE: When Erica turns 21, Peter writes her a trust check for $1,000. Because Erica's monthly SSI grant is only $680, Erica will lose her SSI eligibility for that month as well as her Medicaid benefits. She will regain her SSI and Medicaid benefits the month after that, provided that the balance of the $1,000 doesn't send her over the $2,000 resource limit.

The trust in this book prohibits the person serving as trustee from making disbursements like this one, which would make the beneficiary ineligible for SSI and Medicaid. The trustee is also directed to conserve trust assets so they'll be available to the beneficiary for as long as possible. So, the trustee should avoid making disbursements that reduce the size of the SSI grant unless there is a very good reason to do so.

 TIP

Avoid making distributions directly to the beneficiary. To avoid wasting trust funds or interfering with SSI eligibility, trustees almost always make disbursements to a third party on the beneficiary's behalf, not directly to the beneficiary.

EXAMPLE: Jonas, age 35, receives SSI and Medicaid because the brain injury he suffered in a car accident as a teenager left him unable to work. Ten years ago, his mother left $50,000 in her will to a special needs trust set up for Jonas's benefit. The trust's value is now down to $30,000.

The person serving as trustee, Jonas's sister Peggy, would like to give Jonas $300 a month in spending money. But she knows that this would result in a dollar-for-dollar reduction of Jonas's SSI grant and so would be a waste of trust money. In addition, it would deplete the trust assets in about eight years. So Peggy doesn't give cash to Jonas, but instead uses trust funds to pay for goods and services he wants. That way, the trust disbursements don't affect his SSI grant.

Payments for Food or Shelter

If the person serving as trustee pays for a recipient's food or shelter, the amount paid is considered income to the beneficiary. Specifically, it's called in-kind income or in-kind support and maintenance (ISM). The SSI program treats ISM differently from other types of income.

If the ISM can be assigned a specific value, that amount is deducted from the SSI grant—up to a limit. The amount of the deduction is currently capped at $256.67 (for 2013). That's one-third of the maximum federal portion of the SSI grant ($710 in 2013) plus $20.

> EXAMPLE: Leo, who receives an SSI grant because of his Down syndrome, loves to eat out. Each month Leo's restaurant tab averages $120. If the cost of the meals is picked up by a special needs trust or another outside source, Leo's SSI grant will be reduced dollar for dollar by $120.
>
> If Leo had fancier tastes and, courtesy of his special needs trust, spent $500 a month eating out, his grant would also be reduced, but only by a maximum of $256.67 (in 2013).

These rules mean that if necessary, a special needs trust can provide your loved one with food or shelter—and still leave him or her with the lion's share of the SSI grant as well as continued eligibility for Medicaid benefits.

The question of ISM comes up most often with shelter, because the SSI grant is so inadequate when it comes to paying rent in the private housing market. Trust payments for rent or mortgage payments on a house owned by the beneficiary are considered ISM, so they trigger a reduction of the SSI grant. Still, if a beneficiary's shelter needs can be met only through rental assistance from the special needs trust, a $256.67 reduction in the monthly SSI grant is usually a great deal.

EXAMPLE: Sonya, the beneficiary of a special needs trust, receives SSI and Medicaid. When Sonya's group home closes, she is forced to seek shelter at private market rents. She finds a suitable apartment for $2,000 per month—considerably more than her total $680 SSI grant. The trustee of Sonya's special needs trust decides to pay for all of Sonya's rent and utilities, a total of $2,300 a month.

Trust payments for rent and utilities are ISM, so Sonya's SSI grant will be reduced. The federal portion of the grant in 2013 is $710, so Sonya will lose $256.67 of her SSI check. She will also continue to receive Medicaid. In other words, Sonya's trust pays $2,300 for a nice, safe and clean apartment for Sonya and she continues to receive $423.33 in SSI without any further reduction in SSI.

> ⓘ **CAUTION**
>
> **Know how much SSI a beneficiary is receiving.** If Sonya was receiving less than $256.67 in SSI because she was receiving income from another source, the payment of the rent in the example above would eliminate her eligibility for SSI. Thus, it is important to know how much SSI the person with a disability is receiving to make sure that there is not a total loss of SSI and an accompanying loss of Medicaid.

Once the ISM maximum reduction of $256.67 (in 2013) is reached, the trustee may pay for all the beneficiary's food, rent, and utilities without any further reduction in SSI.

EXAMPLE: Tonya is the beneficiary of a special needs trust. The trustee has been paying $3,500 for all Tonya's rent and utilities. Tonya's SSI check was reduced by $256.67 as a result of these ISM payments. Tonya then asks the trustee to pay her monthly grocery bill of $500. The trustee may pay the additional amount without any further reduction of SSI.

As mentioned earlier, if a special needs trust owns a house or has enough assets to buy one outright, the beneficiary may be able to live in the house rent free without affecting his or her SSI grant. (See "Resource Limits," above.)

However, if the trust pays other expenses associated with shelter—such as electricity, heat, or water—the amounts are considered ISM, and the grant is reduced dollar for dollar up to the $256.67 per month (in 2013) maximum deduction. If the trust were to make mortgage payments on the house, those payments would also be considered ISM and would result in an SSI reduction, up to $256.67 per month.

> **EXAMPLE:** Kathy, who uses a wheelchair because of a childhood accident, receives a $750 monthly SSI grant ($674 federal, $76 state) and Medicaid. Kathy is also the beneficiary of a special needs trust created by her mother. Kathy lives in the family home, which is now held in the special needs trust, rent free. Kathy's SSI grant is not affected by the market value of the shelter because her local SSA office does not count the value of the shelter as in-kind income.
>
> The trust pays for the utilities, which average about $180 a month. Because this amount is considered ISM, Kathy would lose $180/month from her SSI grant.

Computing the Maximum Deduction for ISM

The maximum federal SSI grant increases every year, as the cost of living increases. In 2013, it is $710. One-third of this amount is $236.67; add $20 to get the maximum deduction of $256.67 per month.

For more information on federal and state SSI benefits, visit the Social Security Administration's website at www.ssa.gov.

When to Use Trust Funds—And When Not To

If payment for food or shelter is:	Then use money from:
less than $256.67 (maximum reduction in 2013)	the SSI grant
more than $256.67 (maximum reduction in 2013)	the special needs trust

Government Benefits

Food stamps, low-income housing assistance, state-funded cash benefits, and noncash government benefits don't count as income in-kind for purposes of computing an SSI grant.

Gifts of Food or Shelter From Other Sources

When someone gives food or shelter directly to an SSI recipient, often it is unduly burdensome to place a precise dollar value on the gift. In that case, its value is presumed to be one-third of the maximum federal SSI grant, even though its actual value might be much lower or much higher. This is called the "presumed maximum value," or PMV.

EXAMPLE: Mohammed, an SSI recipient, lives with his family and receives his food and shelter for free. Because calculating the fair market value of what has been given can be unduly burdensome, SSI simply presumes the value is one-third of the federal SSI grant plus $20 ($256.67). So each month Mohammed receives $458.33 ($256.67 less than his $715 grant).

Generally, this isn't the trustee's concern. The person serving as trustee is responsible only for reporting trust activity; the beneficiary (or his or her representative payee) should report other income or income in kind separately in the month it is received. But there are two things the trustee will need to know:

- The maximum reduction to the grant is $256.67 (in 2013) regardless of the combined value of income in-kind received through the trust and from outside resources.

- If the person serving as trustee is responsible for making the reports to SSI (for example, the trust document may make the trustee responsible for reporting), then these outside gifts should be reported along with any income in-kind provided by the trust.

What the Trustee Should Not Pay For: Countable Assets

If the person serving as trustee (you or a successor trustee) buys the beneficiary things that are counted as the beneficiary's resources, there is a danger that the $2,000 resource limit will be exceeded, making the beneficiary ineligible for SSI as well as Medicaid. So the trustee must be careful.

The value of property is measured by how much it could be sold for, not what it originally cost.

EXAMPLE 1: Pete receives SSI and Medicaid and is the beneficiary of a special needs trust. He already owns a car that he uses for everyday transportation (not a countable resource). If the trustee spends $5,000 on a motorcycle, Pete will lose his SSI and Medicaid eligibility. That's because the motorcycle is a countable resource, so its value puts Pete over the $2,000 resource limit. The solution to this situation is to have Pete's special needs trust own the motorcycle.

EXAMPLE 2: Sam also owns a car and a motorcycle. But his cycle would bring only $1,500 if he sold it, so, by itself, it wouldn't make him ineligible for benefits. But if he owned $500 or more of other nonexempt assets—a savings account, for example—he would lose his SSI and Medicaid eligibility, at least temporarily, because the value of his assets would be more than $2,000. ●

Getting Money Into a Special Needs Trust

T his chapter takes a closer look at actually getting money into the special needs trust you create for your loved one. In legal language, this is called "funding." You also need to decide just what kinds of assets to leave in trust for your loved one; this chapter discusses that issue, too.

What Assets to Put Into a Special Needs Trust

You can hold virtually any type of property in a special needs trust. This includes real estate, collectibles, deposit accounts, stocks, bonds, heirlooms, furniture, jewelry, intellectual property (patents, copyrights, trademarks), businesses, cars, tools, hobby collections, wheelchairs, and just about anything else you can think of.

But a trustee usually has little use for assets that gather dust in an attic or a safe deposit box. The person serving as trustee needs cash to invest and spend on the beneficiary's special needs. The primary function of a special needs trust, after all, is to enhance the quality of life of the person with a disability. And trustees do that largely by paying for goods and services for the trust beneficiary.

To raise cash, most trustees sell tangible trust assets and keep the proceeds in liquid assets, such as deposit accounts, certificates of deposit, stocks, or other types of property that can easily be converted to cash.

EXAMPLE: Fred was born with Fragile X syndrome. Among other symptoms, Fred has profound mental deficiencies, qualifying him for SSI and Medicaid. In her will, Fred's mother, Jolene, leaves all of her property to a special needs trust she previously established for Fred's benefit. Jolene had named her brother Carl as successor trustee. When she dies, Jolene leaves a broad array of items to the special needs trust (actually to Carl as trustee of the trust), including clothing, furniture, appliances, a boat, a vacation cabin, and the house where Fred grew up and still lives. She leaves almost no liquid assets.

Although Fred can use some of what Jolene left, most of it is not essential to his well-being and has no particular sentimental value to him. What Fred does need is supplemental services from various health and disability professionals, which he won't get unless the trust can pay for them. To fulfill his duties as trustee, Carl keeps the house and furniture that Fred can use, but sells everything else to raise cash for Fred's special needs.

Sometimes a beneficiary wants to use tangible property owned by the trust. In that case, there is no point in selling it. However, if the trust owns items that have no direct practical benefit to the beneficiary— jewelry, for example—it will probably make sense to sell it and invest the proceeds in a way that will produce income.

EXAMPLE: Violet is the person named as successor trustee of a special needs trust created for her nephew Sam by Sam's mother, Peg. Peg funded the trust with jewelry valued at $14,000, a coin collection worth $5,000, family heirlooms valued at $25,000, and a house in which Sam lives rent free. The trust document gives Violet the power to sell any property in the trust to further the purpose of the trust.

Violet sells the jewelry, coin collection, and heirlooms and invests the $44,000 in a mutual fund. Sam continues living in the house.

How Much Money Will Your Loved One Need?

If your loved one is the only person you want to provide for after your death, then you'll probably want to put your entire estate into your special needs trust and hope it lasts as long as your loved one needs help. Many people, however, want to leave money not just to a loved one with a disability, but also to other family members or charities. Or you may have more money than you think your loved one will need. In either case, you'll need to decide how much to leave to the special needs trust and how much to others.

The answer depends on:

- **Your family.** Do you want to divvy your property up evenly or leave a larger share to the special needs trust, on the theory that your other loved ones can take care of themselves? There are no easy answers, but talking with family members may help you reach a conclusion you feel good about.

- **Your life insurance.** Many parents of children with disabilities obtain life insurance. This approach lets you leave a sizable sum to the special needs trust under the life insurance policy and still provide for your other family members out of your other property. Types of life insurance are discussed later in this chapter.

- **Your loved one's life expectancy.** Grim as it is, you'll have to take your loved one's life expectancy into account when deciding how much property to leave to the special needs trust. To state the obvious, if your loved one's life expectancy is short, then the trust will need less money than if it were long.

- **Your loved one's needs.** Although it involves some guesswork, you need to think about what you want the trust funds to supply for your loved one, and how much money that will take.

So, how should you juggle all of these factors so that you come out with the right funding for your special needs trust? The short answer is, you shouldn't—unless you are a professional in the area of financial management. It's almost impossible to come up with meaningful numbers without the right calculators and expertise at your fingertips.

Get help from a professional. At least three companies have created departments specially designed to assist in financial planning for persons with disabilities:

- MassMutual Financial Group has a program called SpecialCare, dedicated to special needs financial planning. In order to be a part of the program, MassMutual agents are required to take a week-long course on special needs planning. Call 800-272-2216 or visit the company's website, www.massmutual.com/specialcare.

- Merrill Lynch & Co. has set up a program that focuses on financial planning for special needs families and has a training program for its brokers. Call 877-456-7526 or visit the company's website, www.wealthmanagement.ml.com.

- MetLife Inc. has created a special needs unit to help families design financial plans and to refer people to groups that can help direct families to government benefits and services. Call 877-MetDESK (638-3375) or visit the company's website, www.metlife.com.

You can also get help from certified financial planners. (See Chapter 10.)

How to Leave Money to a Special Needs Trust

Nearly always, you'll leave money to a special needs trust after your death. You may want to use more than one method to do that.

CAUTION

See an expert if you want to fund a special needs trust during your lifetime. Unless there is a very specific reason to leave assets to a special needs trust while you are living, you shouldn't because doing so may have gift tax consequences. During your lifetime, you can use funds held in your name to take care of your loved one with special needs. So it is almost always unnecessary to fund a special needs trust before you die. If you believe that you need to add money to the trust while you are living, you should consult with a tax attorney or CPA to fully understand any gift tax consequences.

Wills

The best-known estate planning document is the will or "last will and testament." It's relatively simple to create and you can use it to specify which property you want held in the special needs trust.

EXAMPLE: In her will, Phyllis leaves her valuable art collection to her elder daughter, Katie, and her house to her other daughter, Ruth. She wants to leave her vacation cabin to her son, Mickey. However, Mickey qualifies for SSI because of a long-term disability and Phyllis knows that if he inherits property of more than $2,000 he will no longer be eligible for SSI and Medicaid. (See Chapter 3.)

So instead of leaving the cabin directly to Mickey, Phyllis creates a special needs trust and uses her will to direct that the cabin be held in the trust at her death.

Will Basics

You can leave almost any kind of property in your will—bank accounts, houses, businesses, personal property of any description, or intellectual property (patents, copyrights, trademarks), to name a few examples.

Contrary to popular belief, there is no need to use magic words or legal jargon in a will. In fact, the more simple and straightforward the language, the better. (Take the will of the French philosopher Rabelais: "I have nothing, I owe a great deal, the rest I leave to the poor.")

A will must, however, be signed in front of at least two witnesses who also sign it, stating that the person making the will appears to be of sound mind. Witnessing is intended to provide protection against forgery or duress.

You can prepare a will at any time during your life and change it whenever you wish, provided any changes are signed and witnessed. After you die, the person handling your estate—called an executor, a personal representative, or an administrator, depending on the circumstances—distributes your property to persons and entities you named in the will to inherit it (for example, the trustee of a special needs trust). These recipients are your will beneficiaries.

CAUTION

Property left through a will may get held up in probate after your death. One downside to passing property to a special needs trust through a will is that all property that passes through a will must go through probate. With a few exceptions (for example, many states have simplified probate rules for small estates), probate is likely to take many months and cost many thousands of dollars. This will cause a delay in funding the special needs trust and may reduce the sum available to your loved one. To avoid these problems, consider using a revocable living trust instead; see below.

What You Can't Leave Through Your Will

You cannot leave property through your will if you have already arranged for that property to pass under another estate planning document—such as a beneficiary designation form, a revocable living trust, or a joint tenancy deed. In these instances, your will won't have any effect on it. (The one exception is in the state of Washington, which has a "superwill" statute allowing a will to override a previous beneficiary designation.)

Jointly owned property. Certain forms of ownership give all co-owners the "right of survivorship." This means that when one owner dies, the surviving co-owners own the entire property. Forms of ownership that have the right of survivorship include joint tenancy, tenancy by the entirety, and community property with right of survivorship. If you're not sure how you own property with someone else, check the deed or other title document.

Property held in a trust. If you've transferred title to assets to yourself (or someone else) as trustee of a trust, your will has no effect on the asset. For example, if you've transferred property to yourself as the trustee of the special needs trust you created for your loved one, your will won't determine who gets that property.

Property for which you've named a beneficiary in a binding document.
If you've made an arrangement in writing with an institution that holds
an asset—for example, a bank that holds your money—to give your
money to a certain beneficiary at your death, then that agreement is
legally binding. Your will has no effect on what happens to the property
at your death.

EXAMPLE 1: On a beneficiary designation form provided by her bank,
Flora names her son Angelo as the pay-on-death beneficiary of her savings
account. Her will contradicts this and directs that the same account pass
to her daughter Rosa.

Who gets the money in the account? Angelo, because Flora's will has no
effect on property for which she has named a beneficiary. (See "Beneficiary
Designations," below, for more on these forms.)

EXAMPLE 2: Harvey makes a will leaving all his property in equal shares to
his nine children. In addition to household furnishings and personal effects
(worth a total of about $15,000), Harvey owns a house in joint tenancy
with his second wife, Clara. At Harvey's death, Clara will own the house.
Harvey's children will split the household furnishings and personal effects
in equal shares.

RESOURCE

**Let Nolo help you make your will or revocable living trust
online.** Nolo has put its best-selling and easy-to-make will and living trust
online. Nolo's Online Will and Online Living Trust help you make your will
or living trust on your computer anytime, with a minimum of cost and
effort. Nolo's will and living trust are updated regularly by Nolo's team of
lawyers, and if you have questions while making your document, Nolo
provides legal and practical help along the way. All you need to do is log in,
answer questions about yourself and your property, and then print out and
finalize your document. To start your document now, see samples, or get
more information about wills and trusts, go to www.nolo.com.

Revocable Living Trusts

Because most wills must go through the probate process—which can be both costly and time-consuming—other estate planning devices have become very popular. One of these is the revocable living trust.

Like a will, a living trust can be used to fund a special needs trust that will become effective at your death. The trust document lists the trust property that should pass to the trust rather than directly to the beneficiary.

> **EXAMPLE:** Adam creates a special needs trust for the benefit of his son, Porter, who has spina bifida. Adam also creates a revocable living trust and transfers title to his main asset, his house, into the trust. As part of the living trust document, Adam directs that, upon his death, his house be transferred to the special needs trust.

A simple revocable living trust works much like a will does to distribute property after your death. But a trust offers one big advantage over a will: Trust property does not need to go through probate court proceedings.

Here is how the most common kind of revocable living trust works. You, the "grantor," draft a trust instrument in which you name yourself as "trustee" of the trust and as its initial beneficiary. You transfer any property you want to pass after your death into the trust. Because you are both trustee and beneficiary while you are alive, you have absolute control over the property in the trust. And because the trust is revocable, you can change your mind and take some or all of the property out of the trust at any point.

In the trust document, you direct what is to happen to the trust property after your death. When you die, the person you named in the trust document as "successor trustee" takes over as trustee and distributes the trust property as you instructed.

No one will supervise your successor trustee. In contrast, with a will, the executor you name will probably be accountable to a probate court. But in both positions you want someone (perhaps the same someone) you trust completely.

A living trust controls only property that's legally held in the trust. As long as your property is formally held in trust, your will has no effect on it.

EXAMPLE 1: After creating a living trust and transferring title to his house to his name as trustee of the trust, Adam makes a will in which he leaves his house directly to Porter. The house will not pass to Porter under the will because it has already been disposed of in Adam's revocable living trust.

EXAMPLE 2: Joyce creates a living trust but forgets to transfer title to her house to her name as trustee of the trust. At her death, the house will pass under her will—not under her trust document, as she had intended.

Property that isn't held in your revocable living trust, or that hasn't been legally passed some other way, will pass under the terms of your will. It is precisely for this reason that most people with a living trust also make a will—to handle any property that hasn't been transferred to the living trust or left through some other means.

EXAMPLE: Julian creates a revocable living trust for his house, business, and investments. He then transfers title to these assets to the trust. He names two of his three children to each take one-third of the property. He leaves the remaining third to a special needs trust for his other child, who has cerebral palsy. Julian also creates a will that leaves any property subject to the will (that is, not held in his trust or left some other way) to the successor trustee of the trust, to be distributed under the terms of the trust document. This is sometimes called a pour-over will.

After he makes his will and living trust, Julian inherits $200,000 from his sister. He never gets around to adding the money to his revocable living trust. So after his death, the money passes, under Julian's will, to the successor trustee of his trust. The trustee distributes it under the terms of the trust just like the rest of the trust property.

Beneficiary Designations

These days, an increasing amount of property passes not by will or trust but under the terms of beneficiary designations that apply to specific accounts and items of property. For example, it's very common for people to name beneficiaries for bank and brokerage accounts, retirement plan money (IRAs, 401(k) plans), securities, and certificates of deposit. The owner of the funds simply uses a form provided by the fund or securities manager to designate who gets the property upon his or her death. Doing so ensures that the named beneficiary—a special needs trust, if you choose—will receive the property without probate. In a few states—Arizona, Arkansas, Colorado, Hawaii, Illinois, Indiana, Kansas, Minnesota, Missouri, Montana, Nevada, New Mexico, North Dakota, Ohio, Oklahoma, Oregon, and Wisconsin—you can use a "transfer on death deed," to transfer real property to a named beneficiary when you die, without probate.

> **EXAMPLE:** Justine wants to leave everything she owns to her only surviving relative, her younger brother Leonard. When she sets up her IRA, she names Leonard as the person to get the funds at her death. Similarly, Justine names Leonard as the pay-on-death beneficiary for her bank CD, using a form provided by the bank. And she can pass her stocks to Leonard by submitting a "transfer-on-death" beneficiary form to her broker.
>
> Once she's taken these steps, Leonard will inherit the funds in the IRA, the CD, and the stocks—all without the need for probate court proceedings.

> **TIP**
> **Name the trust as the designated beneficiary.** Keep in mind that leaving property directly to your loved one will jeopardize his or her eligibility for SSI and Medicaid. To avoid this, designate the special needs trust—not your loved one—as the beneficiary.

EXAMPLE: Suppose that Leonard has severe brain damage from a childhood accident. Justine creates a third-party special needs trust for him and opens a bank account in the name of the trust. Justine then asks her broker to arrange for her to change the beneficiary on her IRA from Leonard to the trustee of Leonard's special needs trust. When Justine dies, the money in the IRA will be delivered to the trustee of the special needs trust to be used for Leonard's special needs.

CAUTION

See an estate planning attorney or a tax professional if you want to make a special needs trust a "designated beneficiary" of your retirement plan. You can add a great benefit to your loved one with a special needs trust if you make the trust a "designated beneficiary" of an IRA. The trust must meet some rules but if it does, then the IRA will continue to earn tax-free income over the life expectancy of the trust beneficiary. This plan works best if the IRA has a significant value.

Life Insurance

For many people, life insurance is the only feasible way to raise enough money to help a special needs trust beneficiary over many years or decades. While it is impossible for most people to save $100,000 or more during their life out of their paychecks, many people can afford a small monthly payment for a $100,000 life insurance policy.

EXAMPLE: Frank and Jane, a married couple, buy a term life insurance policy that will pay out $100,000 when the surviving spouse dies, provided they keep the policy in force by paying the monthly premiums of roughly $25 a month. When it becomes clear to them that their daughter Emily will need SSI and Medicaid for life because of a childhood accident, Frank and Jane decide to route the insurance proceeds to a special needs trust by naming the trustee of the trust as beneficiary of the life insurance policy.

You can make sure that life insurance proceeds go to a special needs trust by creating the trust as detailed in Chapter 8 and naming the trust as the policy beneficiary.

> **EXAMPLE:** Frank and Jane create a special needs trust, naming themselves as cotrustees and Elmer, a close family friend, as successor trustee to take over after both Frank and Jane die. They also name the trustee of the special needs trust as the beneficiary of their life insurance policy.
>
> After the deaths of both Frank and Jane, the successor trustee receives the proceeds of the life insurance policy in his capacity as trustee and uses the money to provide for Emily's special needs under the terms of the trust.

There are many kinds of life insurance policies (or "products," as the companies call them) including term, universal life, whole life, and more. Term insurance is the simplest; if you die while the policy is in force, your beneficiary gets the proceeds. That's it. Other kinds of policies are part insurance and part investment; they build up equity you can borrow against or cash in. Annuities can give you a steady income throughout retirement.

 RESOURCE

More information on life insurance options. *Plan Your Estate*, by Denis Clifford (Nolo), discusses life insurance choices, including how to find the right kind of policy and a solid company. At least three financial companies have separate divisions specifically to deal with planning for loved ones with disabilities:

- MassMutual's special needs division. Call 800-272-2216 or visit the company's website, www.massmutual.com.
- Merrill Lynch & Co.'s special needs division. Call 877-456-7526 or visit the company's website, www.wealthmanagement.ml.com.
- MetLife's special needs division. Call 877-MetDESK (638-3375) or visit the company's website, www.metlife.com.

Don't Commingle the Beneficiary's Property With Trust Property

Once the special needs trust you create is up and running after your death, your loved one may come into some property of his or her own— perhaps a personal injury settlement or an inheritance from a relative. At first thought, it might seem like a good idea to put that money straight into the existing special needs trust, to keep it from being counted as the beneficiary's resource and disqualifying him or her from getting SSI. **Bad idea**. In fact, adding the beneficiary's own property to the special needs trust would make your loved one ineligible for SSI and Medicaid.

That's because if the beneficiary's own property is mixed with the property you left in the special needs trust, it could all be considered the beneficiary's resource. And the total amount would almost certainly exceed the resource limit (currently $2,000) that's imposed on SSI recipients. (Chapter 3 has more on resource and income limits.)

> **EXAMPLE:** Bonnie, who receives SSI and Medicaid, is the beneficiary of a special needs trust created by her father and funded by him in his will. This has worked out well for ten years. However, Bonnie unexpectedly wins $10,000 in the state lottery.
>
> She deposits the money in her existing special needs trust—and only later learns that as a result, all of the money in the trust is now considered her resource because her lottery winnings and the original funds from her father were mixed together.

A better alternative than adding property to a third-party trust is to create a separate first-party special needs trust. That way, assets in the original trust will remain off-limits as a resource, and eligibility for SSI and Medicaid will not be affected.

SEE AN EXPERT

See a lawyer to create a first-party special needs trust. First-party special needs trusts must meet several federal and state requirements that third-party special needs trusts (the kind you make with this book) are not subject to. For example, first-party special needs trusts must provide for reimbursement of Medicaid costs from trust assets to the state's Medicaid agency after the beneficiary's death. If you must decide what to do with funds owned by the beneficiary, see a lawyer. Chapter 10 can help you find and work with one. ●

The Trustee's Job

The trustee of your special needs trust will manage the trust for the benefit of your loved one. Whether the trustee is you, a relative, a friend, or a professional, the trustee has a critical job as the manager and guardian of the trust. Not only must the trustee spend trust funds in the best interest of the beneficiary (your loved one with a disability), the trustee must also keep up to date on SSI and Medicaid laws, invest trust funds, file taxes, maintain accurate records, and more.

This chapter describes the duties of the trustee. It will give you a sense of what your job will be as initial trustee, and it will also help you decide who should take your place when you (or the initial trustee you name, if not yourself) can no longer serve. Chapter 6 goes into more detail about how to choose the trustees.

Consider Signing Up for a Pooled Trust

If you don't know anyone you feel confident naming as trustee, you may want to consider joining a "pooled trust" instead of setting up your own special needs trust. If you use a pooled trust, you won't need to choose a trustee or successor trustee; the nonprofit organization that administers the trust will carry out that function. Chapter 7 discusses pooled trusts.

The Trustee's Basic Duties

A trustee's most fundamental legal duty is to always act honestly and put the interests of the trust beneficiary first. This is commonly called the trustee's fiduciary duty.

EXAMPLE: Peter is the trustee of a special needs trust created for his younger brother Paul. Peter's older brother Simon needs money to fund a high-risk start-up company. Wanting to help Simon, Peter invests part of the trust money in Simon's company. By unnecessarily risking trust assets, Peter has violated his fiduciary duty to act in Paul's best interests.

The trustee may, however, take actions that indirectly benefit other parties, as long as the sole purpose of the action itself is to help the beneficiary. For example, it's all right to use trust money to buy a home for a beneficiary even if a relative may also live in the home and so also benefit.

Trustees who act in good faith generally won't be personally liable for losses caused by their actions. Trustees could be held personally liable for acts that are judged (after the fact) to be unreasonably careless or, to use the legal term, negligent. Negligence is generally defined as the failure to take the proper care that a prudent person would take in similar circumstances.

For instance, if the beneficiary lost several months of SSI and Medicaid eligibility because the trustee forgot to prepare a report required by those programs, the trustee might be considered to have been negligent. The beneficiary, or the beneficiary's guardian, could sue the trustee.

Trustees must also:

- Avoid any activity that conflicts with the purpose of the trust—which is to enhance the quality of life of the beneficiary.

- Respond to the beneficiary's personal needs for goods and services that aren't covered by SSI or Medicaid.

- Keep up with SSI and Medicaid income and resource rules so that the trustee's spending doesn't affect your loved one's eligibility for SSI and Medicaid. (See Chapter 3.)

- Invest and manage trust property following the terms of the trust and state law, in the beneficiary's best interests.

- Keep your loved one with a disability and other interested persons up to date on trust activity.

- Keep accurate records, prepare reports that the SSI and Medicaid programs require, and file necessary federal and state tax returns.

- Go to court, if necessary and financially reasonable, to uphold the trust and require the SSI and Medicaid programs to comply with applicable law.

All of these responsibilities are discussed in this chapter. Remember, as you read, that trustees are entitled to reasonable compensation from the trust assets for the time they spend administering the trust.

> **TIP**
>
> **Share the burden.** As you can see, there is a lot on a trustee's plate. You don't have to choose one person to handle everything; these tasks can be shared by two or more cotrustees, handled by experts hired by an individual trustee as needed, or carried out by a trustee working for a pooled trust. The pros and cons of each approach are discussed in Chapter 6.

Working With a Guardian or Conservator

People with disabilities that interfere with some aspects of their cognitive functioning—such as Down syndrome or a traumatic brain injury—often need someone to help them make sound financial and personal decisions. The same is true of children under 18.

For many people, this assistance comes from an informal advocate—a friend or relative who is always there to help the disabled person cope with the world. But if the disability is severe, a court may need to appoint someone to make decisions on behalf of the beneficiary. This person is usually called a guardian or conservator.

If your loved one has a court-appointed guardian or conservator, the person serving as trustee of the special needs trust will have to work closely with that person. In essence, they must function as partners, each contributing to the business of meeting the needs of the person with a disability. Frequent communications—in person or by telephone or email—are necessary to make sure the guardian or conservator and the trustee are on the same page.

EXAMPLE: Nicolas was diagnosed with severe autism when he was three years old. His father died when he was ten. His mother, Theresa, cared for Nicolas until he turned 18. At that time, she asked the probate court to appoint her as conservator, in charge of Nicolas's person and property. She also created a special needs trust and used her will to leave everything to this trust for Nicholas's sole benefit. The trust document named her brother Zeke as successor trustee to take over after Theresa dies.

Shortly after Nicholas's 36th birthday, Theresa died. As part of the probate process, Theresa's executor (the person named in her will to wind up her affairs) asked the court to appoint Nicolas's aunt, Katie, as his conservator. As conservator, Katie made all necessary financial and personal decisions for Nicholas while Zeke, who became trustee when Theresa died, invested and spent trust assets for Nicholas's benefit. Katie couldn't require Zeke to make a disbursement, and Zeke couldn't second-guess any of Katie's decisions.

Katie and Zeke made it a point to talk at least once a month to discuss any issues that had arisen. Zeke relied on Katie to tell him about Nicholas's day-to-day needs because Katie was more attuned to them than Zeke was. Similarly, Zeke, who was more comfortable with financial decisions than Katie was, frequently had good suggestions for Katie in that area.

Sometimes the person serving as trustee of the special needs trust is also the court-appointed guardian or conservator. In that case, the roles must be kept strictly separate. For instance, income received by a guardian for the benefit of your loved one must be kept in a separate account—it can't be placed in the trust. Similarly, records of trust activity must be kept separate from records kept as part of the guardianship or conservatorship.

Investing Trust Property

Trustees must safeguard and invest the trust property, following the instructions in the trust document. The trust provided by this book directs the trustee to act in accordance with the Prudent Investor Act, a law that has been adopted by most states. It makes significant demands on trustees, but also gives them flexibility in making investments.

SEE AN EXPERT

The trustee can get help. Investment decisions can become complex. For that reason, many trustees hire financial advisers to help them come up with sensible investment strategies that comply with the Prudent Investor Act. Chapter 10 explains how to find such people.

The Prudent Investor Act sets out four major rules for trustees:

• Balance risk against return.

• Diversify investments.

• Act in ways that will further the trust purposes.

• Evaluate the investment portfolio as a whole.

When you examine each of these principles, they seem nothing more than common sense. Basically, they tell the trustee to invest conservatively if the circumstances indicate caution, as may be the case with assets in a special needs trust. But if the purpose of the trust, the amount of funds available to invest, and the knowledge of the trustee combine to make a more aggressive strategy reasonable under the act's guiding rules, then it's allowed.

The Old Rules for Investing

Many older state laws limited trustees to certain very low-risk, low-return investments. This gave trustees certainty, but didn't allow them to protect trust funds from being eroded by inflation or to diversify investments. Also, under the old rules, every investment decision could be scrutinized separately if challenged in court. Under the Prudent Investor Act, the trustee's performance as an investor is looked at in its entirety.

Trustees who act sensibly and follow the Prudent Investor Act rules will not be liable for losses to the trust caused by a particular investment that goes bad. Instead, a court (if there were ever a lawsuit) would look at the overall performance of the trust investments. Acting sensibly means having a reason for the investments you make that fairly balances the four rules set out above.

A fairly detailed explanation of the Prudent Investor Act is contained in the Trustee's Duties Letter provided by this book. Take a look at the investment portion of that letter so you'll have an understanding of what the trustee and successor trustee must do, and what will happen to trust assets after your death. Assuming that the special needs trust will primarily be funded at your death, you won't be investing trust funds as the initial trustee, and you don't need to absorb all the details of investment rules yourself.

Investing in a Recession
As this edition is being prepared (Winter 2012), the economy continues to be troubled. This latest downturn in the economy highlights the fact that special needs trusts are not immune to market fluctuations.
In fact, at this point, it's likely that some existing special needs trusts may have less value than they did when they were originally funded. How well an investment will recover depends on the type of investment in question. For example, mortgage-backed securities may not recover anything near their original value while investments in indexed mutual funds may recover in the not too distant future.
The question for you, a prospective creator of a special needs trust, is whether you can or should get more specific about how the funds in the trust should be managed. It may be wise to obtain a financial plan from an investment adviser who specializes in planning for persons with disabilities.
If you want to give very specific instructions about how the funds in the special needs trust you create should be invested, you'll need to consult an attorney to draft the appropriate provisions and a financial adviser to assist with creating a plan because the trust in this book would not allow your trustee to deviate from the Prudent Investor rule.

Spending Trust Money for the Beneficiary

When spending trust property, the person serving as trustee will have to keep an eye on two sometimes conflicting goals:

- meeting the trust beneficiary's current special needs (remember, basically that means things other than food and shelter), and

- keeping enough property in the trust to provide for the beneficiary's needs for as long as possible.

The second goal will usually come into play only after your death. Typically, only a small amount of money is placed in a special needs trust when it is initially created. The lion's share of the funding usually comes later, either over time in gifts or in one bulk amount in the form of a life insurance payout or bequest through a will or revocable living trust.

Calculating an Annual Budget

How much money can a trustee spend to meet the beneficiary's special needs? At the simplest level, to compute an annual budget, the trustee could divide the value of the trust property by the number of years the beneficiary is expected to live. For example, if the beneficiary's life expectancy is 30 more years, and there is $100,000 in the trust, the trustee could spend about $3,300 each year.

This calculation, of course, doesn't take into account any income that the trust assets might earn. If you assume an average return of 6% a year on the $100,000, then the annual budget would be increased to account for the trust income.

You or a successor trustee can get help in making these calculations simply by searching for the phrase "investment calculators" on the Internet. But most trustees consult a financial planner or another adviser who's had experience with trust investing and with estimating how much a disabled beneficiary's needs are likely to cost.

 TIP

Figuring life expectancy. Life expectancy tables are easily available on the Internet (search for "life expectancy tables"), but those figures may not apply to someone with a disability. If relevant figures aren't available, the trustee might ask the beneficiary's doctors for an estimated figure.

Knowing the Beneficiary's Needs

For a special needs trust to benefit your loved one in the way you want it to, the people who succeed you as trustee need to understand and respond to the beneficiary's needs. This won't be a problem if the beneficiary can communicate them clearly. But if the beneficiary's disability impairs his or her ability to think or communicate, then the more background information a trustee has about the beneficiary, the better. It is up to you to make sure that your successor trustees will be adequately informed.

A good way to start is to keep a diary of your loved one's needs or write a "beneficiary information letter." (A beneficiary information letter is different from the trustee's duties letter mentioned above. It sets out your loved one's needs, rather than focusing on the trustee's duties.) Keeping a diary or writing a beneficiary information letter is a good idea even if the person who serves as trustee is the beneficiary's parent, sibling, other close relative, or friend who already have a deep understanding of the beneficiary's likes, dislikes, proclivities, habits, needs, and desires. That's because your initial choices for trustee or successor trustee may die or become unable to serve because of circumstances you can't foresee. And if you use a corporate or professional trustee, or you opt for a pooled trust, the trustee will have only the information you provide. (Chapter 6 discusses professional trustees, and Chapter 7 explains pooled trusts.)

Sitting down to describe your loved one's intimate needs in a beneficiary letter can be emotionally taxing. After all, what you are really doing is preparing for a time when you won't be around to provide the primary care your loved one needs, and that thought alone can get the best of us down. Keeping a diary, on the other hand, spreads the task across many weeks, months, and years. This may make documenting the details of your loved one's life a little bit easier. On the other hand, many people aren't organized or habitual enough to keep an accurate diary, and for those folks, the beneficiary letter will be the best approach. You can give a copy of your diary or the beneficiary information letter to your choice for successor trustee, or attach it to the original special needs trust document so that it will be easily available to the successor trustee when the time comes.

The diary or letter should cover, among other things, your loved one's family and medical history, education, employment, living situation, social life, routines, and religion. This book provides a sample beneficiary information letter to give you an idea of how to approach it.

What to Cover in Your Diary or Beneficiary Information Letter

Family history. Provide the names of and contact information for relatives who have a good relationship with your loved one.

General medical history. Explain how the disability came to be, how the person has coped, and what you expect in the future.

Current medical care. Offer your opinions about whether it is appropriate or could be improved. List doctors and other health care providers, including physical or occupational therapists.

Education. List specific courses and teachers that bear on your loved one's present abilities.

Employment history. Note the jobs or volunteer positions your loved one has held, if any, or his or her potential for employment.

Current living situation. Explain what you think about the current situation and whether a different one might be better, especially if circumstances change. For instance, perhaps your loved one now lives alone, but you feel strongly that he or she would do better in a group home after you die. If you think the beneficiary needs day care or nursing home facilities, note this fact as well.

Social environment. Describe relationships with friends and acquaintances.

Day-to-day routines. List favorite foods, daily routines, and recreational likes and dislikes.

Religious proclivities. Offer a religious history, including any religious leaders with whom the beneficiary has a relationship, and religious activities.

Preferences for funeral arrangements. Decide what you want to happen when your loved one dies. Do you want a first-class funeral? Burial or cremation? Because the trust may be paying for a funeral and the disposition of last remains—if there is money left in the trust—you'll also want to think about the trust's remainder beneficiaries. If the trustee spends $10,000 on a funeral, that's $10,000 the remainder beneficiaries won't inherit. It's up to you.

Other relevant information. Offer whatever information you think a trustee would need to be fully responsive to your loved one's special needs.

Making the Hard Decisions

A disagreeable but essential part of a trustee's job may be to refuse the beneficiary's requests for money when they would make it impossible to provide for the beneficiary's special needs in the future. This conflict is more likely to occur when the beneficiary's powers of persuasion are intact.

> **EXAMPLE:** Johnny, a 28-year-old former athlete with paraplegia, wants to climb the famed El Capitan monolith in Yosemite National Park. The cost, including paying a highly skilled fellow climber and renting lots of special equipment, will exceed $50,000.
>
> Johnny's special needs trust currently contains assets worth $150,000 and Matthew, the person serving as trustee, has computed a rough budget of $10,000 a year. Matthew balks at spending one-third of Johnny's trust fund—and five times the annual budget—on one event, especially because Johnny may live another 50 years and will undoubtedly have many special needs over that period of time. Matthew decides to deny Johnny's request. Unfortunately, his decision causes bad feelings between him and Johnny and damages their ongoing relationship so much so that Matthew may decide to resign as trustee.
>
> However, if Matthew had decided to make the El Capitan distribution, he could do so with no liability. The trustee has full discretion to make or not make this distribution.

People with cognitive or developmental disabilities typically are less likely to confront their trustees over such issues. The trustee's role is likely to be easier when the beneficiary has few or modest needs and can be expected to be content with whatever the trustee provides.

> **EXAMPLE:** Aaron has moderate Down syndrome. He is reasonably self-sufficient, lives in a group home, and works in a sheltered workshop. He receives a partial SSI grant and Medicaid services and is the beneficiary of a special needs trust with funds valued at $200,000. Aaron loves Rolling Stones music and is always looking to add to his collection. He also enjoys visiting a nearby lake that features boat rides and likes to fly several times a year to

visit his sister, who lives halfway across the country. The person serving as trustee can pay for these expenses for many years without exhausting the trust funds.

Nonetheless, even a beneficiary with a cognitive disability may express a need that the trustee disagrees with or that threatens the fiscal health of the trust.

EXAMPLE: Freddy, who has Aspergers syndrome, is the beneficiary of a special needs trust with $150,000 worth of assets. An acquaintance wants Freddy to accompany him on a trip around the world and tells Freddy to ask the person serving as his trustee for $25,000 to finance it. Freddy's trustee honestly doesn't think that Freddy will enjoy the trip and suspects the acquaintance of trying to take advantage of Freddie's resources. The trustee refuses Freddy's request.

However, sometimes a trustee must make a disproportionately large expenditure, regardless of how severely it will deplete the trust funds. It's up to the trustee, who must decide based on the circumstances.

EXAMPLE 1: Valerie, a special needs trust beneficiary, needs a liver transplant. Medicaid may ultimately pick up the cost of the transplant through a local hospital, but Valerie wants to use the Houston Cancer Center, reputedly the best in the country. The extra cost is likely to bankrupt the trust. However, the difference in quality of treatment may be a life-or-death matter that makes Valerie's request a reasonable one.

The person serving as trustee is torn—but finally decides that Valerie's parents would want him to use the Houston clinic and let tomorrow take care of itself.

EXAMPLE 2: Kirby, a special needs trust beneficiary, is very religious and has always wanted to take a trip to the Middle East. The trip will take nearly all of the trust assets. The trustee decides to pay for the trip because even though the beneficiary will have little money left for routine special needs, the trip will be the highlight of Kirby's life and the trustee knows that Kirby's parents would have wanted him to take the trip.

TIP

Communication is key. A disbursement decision that seems perfectly reasonable to the trustee may seem arbitrary or even punitive to the beneficiary. For instance, if the beneficiary asks the trustee to buy a stereo system, and the trustee goes low-end to stay within the annual budget, the beneficiary may feel frustrated. The greater the effort the trustee makes to explain disbursement decisions to the beneficiary, the more likely it is that relations will remain cordial.

Understanding the Remainder Beneficiary's Interests

The remainder beneficiary is the person you name to inherit any assets that are left in the special needs trust when your loved one with a disability (the trust beneficiary) dies or when the trust is terminated.

Although the remainder beneficiaries will naturally be interested in how the trust is administered, the trust document you prepare with this book makes it clear that the loved one with a disability's (the trust beneficiary's) interests always come first. The person serving as trustee must provide for the trust beneficiary's special needs, even if nothing will be left and even if a remainder beneficiary complains about it.

EXAMPLE: In their wills, Carlos and his wife, Maria, leave their property to each other and provide that when the second spouse dies, $25,000 will go to their son, Ricardo, and the rest to a special needs trust they created for their daughter, Rocio, who has a developmental disability. The trust provides that Ricardo will receive any property left in the special needs trust at Rocio's death. The leftover property (if any) is the remainder, and Ricardo is the remainder beneficiary.

Carlos and Maria die together in a car accident, and their property (after the $25,000 gift to Ricardo) goes into the special needs trust. The trust property is worth about $250,000. The successor trustee who became trustee when Carlos and Maria died can spend whatever is necessary to provide for Rocio's special needs, including a trip around the world or tuition at an expensive private college.

Ricardo is resentful and thinks the trustee doesn't need to spend so much on Rocio. The trustee, obeying the terms of the trust, pays no attention to Ricardo's frustrations and concentrates on Rocio's needs.

Managing a Remainder Beneficiary's Property

If there is money left in the trust when the special needs trust beneficiary dies, the trustee's job may not be over. If a remainder beneficiary is younger than 18, an adult must manage the property for his or her benefit. Under the terms of the trust document in this book, the person serving as trustee is given that job.

The special needs trust document makes the trustee the "custodian" of the remaining property, under a law called the Uniform Transfers to Minors Act (UTMA). The UTMA, which has been adopted in all but two states (Vermont and South Carolina), sets out the custodian's duties. Basically, the job is like that of a trustee—a custodian must prudently invest and spend the money on behalf of the minor beneficiary.

The custodianship ends when the beneficiary reaches a certain age, 21 in most states. This book's trust document directs that the custodianship end when the beneficiary turns 21 unless the state's law requires distribution at age 18. When the custodianship ends, the custodian simply gives any remaining property to the beneficiary.

> **EXAMPLE:** Greta creates a special needs trust for her daughter Frieda and funds the trust through her will. In the trust document, Greta names her grandchildren, Hans and Lena, as remainder beneficiaries to inherit any funds left in the trust when Frieda dies. About a year after Greta's death, Frieda dies. At that time, Hans is 23 and Lena is 18.
>
> The person succeeding Greta as trustee gives half of the remaining money to Hans and keeps the other half in a custodial bank account for the benefit of Lena. When Lena turns 21 (the age custodianships end in her state), the trustee gives her what's left in the account outright.

If you wish to leave assets to a remainder beneficiary by using something other than an UTMA account or with outright distribution, you should consult an estate planning attorney for help. Your options may include setting up a trust for the remainder beneficiary, staging distributions (for example, leaving one-third at age 18, one-third at age 25, and balance on age 30), or leaving assets only for education of grandchildren. These decisions should be discussed with an attorney. See Chapter 10 for more on finding and working with a lawyer.

Preserving Eligibility for SSI and Medicaid

Preserving the beneficiary's eligibility for SSI and Medicaid is a crucial part of a trustee's job. That, after all, is one of the main reasons for creating the trust in the first place.

Understanding SSI and Medicaid Rules

When spending trust money, the person serving as trustee must comply with either SSI or Medicaid income and resource rules so that the beneficiary's eligibility for SSI and Medicaid is not compromised. There's a summary of these rules just below and in the Trustee's Duties Letter in Appendix B.

Trustees must have a sound understanding of these rules and must keep up to date on any changes. The current rules are set out as part of the Trustee's Duties Letter in Appendix B.

Making Reports to SSI

To remain eligible for SSI and Medicaid, your loved one (or someone authorized to act on his or her behalf, called a representative payee by the Social Security Administration) must submit an annual report to the state agency administering the SSI program, as well as report monthly on any changes in income, resources, or living arrangements. Otherwise, the beneficiary (or the representative payee, if required) will handle the job.

Medicaid and SSI Eligibility Rules: A Summary

- With some exceptions, someone who is eligible for SSI is automatically eligible for Medicaid.
- An individual who owns resources worth more than $2,000 (not counting a home, car, or furnishings) does not qualify for SSI.
- Assets in a special needs trust funded with assets other than the beneficiary's are not counted as a resource.
- If the beneficiary earns income, about half the amount earned is deducted from SSI payments. A beneficiary who earns too much loses SSI eligibility.
- After a $20 exemption, unearned income results in a dollar-for-dollar reduction of the SSI grant. Too much unearned income causes loss of SSI eligibility.
- If the beneficiary receives personal property that can be readily converted to cash, it counts as income in the month it's received and results in a dollar-for-dollar reduction of the SSI grant and possible loss of SSI eligibility for that month.
- If this property is kept, in later months it is counted as a resource and if its value—along with the value of the person's other assets— is $2,000 or more, he or she will lose SSI and Medicaid eligibility.
- If trust funds are spent for food or shelter, the SSI grant is reduced, up to one-third of the federal portion of the grant plus $20. The beneficiary does not lose SSI eligibility (unless, because of other income, the SSI grant is less than the amount deducted).
- If the trustee makes payments to third parties on the beneficiary's behalf for anything other than food or shelter, the payments are not counted as income for purposes of SSI eligibility (unless the items purchased can easily be converted to cash).

The trustee's job is to make sure that the beneficiary or guardian has accurate information about the trust activity—that is, a record of all disbursements on behalf of the beneficiary and all trust income received during the reporting period. If the trustee buys things that are countable assets under SSI rules and gives them to the beneficiary—that is, if they're not held in the trust—they must be reported monthly.

Disbursements made for property that is held in the trust don't, at least theoretically, need to be reported, because the beneficiary doesn't acquire income or resources as a result. But some SSI offices may take exception to this approach if the beneficiary actually has exclusive use and control over the property in question even if the trust owns it. The better practice is for the trustee to report all property acquired for the use of the beneficiary with an accompanying explanation that the trust owns the property.

EXAMPLE: Grace, the beneficiary of a special needs trust, wants a motorized wheelchair that has features that aren't available on the chairs that Medicaid will pay for. The person serving as trustee buys the chair in the name of the trust by making sure the receipt or bill of sale references the trust as the purchaser. The trustee also itemizes the chair as a trust asset in the trust records. Because the chair is held in trust in this manner, it probably doesn't need to be reported as an asset belonging to Grace. But the trustee decides that it's better to report the chair with an explanation that it's owned by the trust.

Terminating the Trust

Due to advances in medical technologies, people with disabilities who might have survived only until 25 or 30 in the early 20th century can now count on a fairly long life—to age 50 or beyond. For example, the average life expectancy for a child born with Down syndrome is now more than 55. This, of course, means that a special needs trust can last for decades. And, needless to say, massive—and completely unpredictable—changes in agency rules and medical treatments can occur over this period.

To take this uncertainty into account, the special needs trust you create with this book lets the person serving as trustee terminate the trust if changed circumstances warrant it. However, the trustee is not required to terminate the trust, as it may be reasonable to continue administering the trust as circumstances change. This is particulary true if the beneficiary is unsophisticated in managing money and paying bills.

If the Trust Would Interfere With Eligibility for Benefits

If the trust's continued existence would jeopardize the beneficiary's eligibility for SSI and Medicaid, the person serving as trustee has the authority to end the trust.

> **EXAMPLE:** Roberto is the beneficiary of a special needs trust created by his aunt, Mary. Years after Mary dies, changes in SSI and Medicaid eligibility rules make Roberto ineligible for those programs because of the trust assets. To get around these changes in the eligibility rules, the person serving as trustee uses his authority under the trust document to terminate the trust and disburse the funds. The trust document directs the trustee to give as much of the trust funds to Roberto as possible without disqualifying him for SSI and Medicaid, and the rest to Arturo, the remainder beneficiary Mary named in the trust.
>
> The trustee does this. Roberto continues receiving SSI and Medicaid, but no longer has the benefits of a special needs trust. Arturo might, for moral or ethical reasons, choose to use the money for Roberto's needs.

> **CAUTION**
> **This rule differs for first-party trusts.** Current rules and regulations allow early termination provisions in *third-party* special needs trusts, like the one you can create with this book. However, the rules and regulations do not permit early termination provisions for *first-party* special needs trusts—those created with the assets of the loved one with a disability. If a government employee tells you that an early termination provision is not permitted in your third-party special needs trust, it may be because that person does not understand the difference between these types of trusts.

If the Trust Is No Longer Needed

A condition that is disabling today may not be disabling in the future. It may be cured or ameliorated by advances in medical technology, or workplace demands may change, allowing someone who cannot now work to enter the job market. Or the SSI and Medicaid programs might change in a way that makes a special needs trust unnecessary.

In light of these possibilities, the trust in this book lets the person serving as trustee terminate the trust if the trust isn't necessary to preserve the beneficiary's eligibility for government benefits.

> **EXAMPLE:** Vivian uses her revocable living trust to fund a special needs trust she created for her brother Charles, who has schizophrenia. Five years after Vivian's death, a cure for schizophrenia is found, and Charles no longer needs Medicaid or the protection of the trust. Using the authority granted by the trust document, the person serving as trustee ends the trust and distributes the trust assets directly to Charles.

Paying Taxes

The person serving as trustee must file a separate tax return for the trust every year unless the income earned by the trust is below the reporting threshold (currently $300). The special needs trust you create with this book is an irrevocable trust, meaning it can't be revoked after it takes effect. The trust must have its own tax ID number, which you can get from the IRS by submitting a simple form (IRS Form SS-4) or applying online at www.irs.gov/businesses/small/index.html.

Trust income (the money earned from investing trust assets) is taxed at a special trust rate (35% for 2012) for income over $11,650. If you place only a minimal amount in the trust when you create it, you needn't worry about paying taxes. However, taxes will become a concern once significant funds land in the trust. Because the tax rate for trust income is so much higher than the rate that applies to most individuals, most types of trusts direct the trustee to distribute trust income to the beneficiary rather than keep it in the trust. But in most special needs trusts, the person serving as trustee is directed to keep all income in the trust rather than give it directly to the trust beneficiary. That's because requiring that the beneficiary receive trust income might make him or her ineligible for SSI and Medicaid, defeating the purpose of the trust.

There is a way, however, to give the beneficiary the benefit of trust income but avoid the high trust tax rate. Under IRS rules, trust income that is spent on the beneficiary's behalf is taxed at his or her individual rate, not the trust rate. So if the trustee spends the income on the beneficiary's behalf—and keeps careful records showing that trust income, not assets, was spent—the IRS should tax the income at the beneficiary's lower rate. The trust records must clearly show that the source of the disbursements was the income (interest), not the principal, and that the income was spent for the benefit of the beneficiary, not the trust itself.

> **EXAMPLE:** Joey is the trustee of a special needs trust for his sister Angela. The trust funds are invested in several funds managed by a big brokerage company, which sends Joey a monthly statement showing interest earned on the money. For the current year, the interest amounts to $5,000. In his trust accounting book, Joey records that disbursements for Angela's benefit were made out of this income, not the trust principal.
>
> When the trust taxes are computed, any money spent from the income for Angela's benefit is taxed at Angela's rate. Income that is added to the trust and not disbursed is taxed at the higher trust rate.

Going to Court

It's very unlikely, but some person or government agency might attack the validity of your special needs trust or question the trustee's actions under its terms. For example, the SSI or Medicaid program might change its rules and try to force the person serving as trustee to contribute to the beneficiary's support even though that would deprive the beneficiary of SSI and Medicaid. If this happens, this book's trust authorizes the trustee to defend the trust in whatever forum is available, including court.

Going to court is expensive. It can easily cost $10,000—possibly more—in attorney's fees. So if a special needs trust has just $10,000 worth of assets, the trustee's decision is easy: Terminate the trust. On the other hand, if the trust were worth $500,000, it would probably be worth it to hire a lawyer and challenge the government decision.

If a lawsuit is ever necessary, the trustee will generally have to hire a lawyer to handle it. In many states, the trustee cannot represent the trust in court; only a lawyer can do that. (Chapter 10 discusses finding and working with lawyers.)

The Trustee's Duties Letter

Appendix B contains a long letter that you may want to adapt and give to the people you expect to serve as trustees of the special needs trust. The letter provides an overview of the trustee's job. You may find the letter a good source of information if you're going to be the initial trustee of the special needs trust or if you want more detail about the responsibilities of the trustees who will succeed you.

The letter also explains how a successor trustee can prove his or her authority under the trust, resign as trustee, or appoint a successor trustee if all named successors are unavailable.

You can also download an electronic version of the letter, so you can tailor it to your situation. (See Appendix D.) Parts of it may not apply to you. For example, if you're appointing individual successor trustees, you'll want to delete the information about cotrustees.

Choosing Trustees

Who should you put in charge of the special needs trust? It's a hugely important question. You will probably name yourself as trustee to manage the trust while you are alive and well—although you don't have to. But who will take over the trust when you are no longer around to make sure that things go right?

Picking reliable people to manage the trust is crucial because trusts operate pretty much on the honor system. It's true that the law imposes a duty on trustees to honestly and faithfully carry out the trust's terms, but in most cases there is no court supervision. If a beneficiary (or someone acting on behalf of a beneficiary) sues the person serving as trustee, a court will examine the trustee's behavior and can remove a trustee who has failed to meet the standards set out by law. But because getting a trustee replaced usually involves at least one court filing—and possibly even a difficult lawsuit—it doesn't happen often.

After reading Chapter 5 and the letter in Appendix B outlining the trustee's duties, you should have a good idea of what trustees will be called on to do when serving as trustee. This chapter helps you make the best choice given your individual circumstances.

An Overview of Your Options

The trust in this book offers several options for naming the initial and successor trustees of your special needs trust. Here's an overview of them:

- Name yourself as initial trustee, or name yourself and a spouse or partner as initial cotrustees.
- Name someone else—perhaps the beneficiary's parent or parents.
- Name family members or friends.
- Name a professional trustee.
- Name an individual and a professional trustee to serve as cotrustees.
- Join a pooled special needs trust instead of setting up a trust yourself.

Signing Up for a Pooled Trust

If you sign up with a pooled trust, you won't have to pick a trustee—all pooled trusts offer their own trustee services. A pooled or community trust is a special needs trust, run by a nonprofit organization, that has many beneficiaries. You contribute money, which is held in a separate account but pooled with other families' funds for investing. The trustee distributes funds in the trust on behalf of the beneficiaries according to the amount in each beneficiary's separate account. (Chapter 7 discusses pooled trusts in detail, and a selected list of pooled trusts is in Appendix A.)

One way to use a pooled trust is to sign up while you are alive, if the pooled trust will allow it. This means you pay an initial fee, sign an agreement that creates an account for you with the pooled trust, and commit to paying an annual fee. You don't have to contribute money to the trust now. Rather, you can provide in your will or living trust that the trust be funded at your death. If you do it this way, your annual fees will be modest up until the trust becomes operational at your death. After that, the fees will be based on the amount of funds you contribute. Fees vary from one pooled trust to another.

Whether or not you fund the trust when you sign up or at your death, you'll have the security of knowing that your loved one's inheritance will be managed by experienced people affiliated with a nonprofit organization intended to benefit people with disabilities.

Pooled trusts are not for everybody and they come with some risks, including these:

- They are generally much more expensive to administer than naming your own trustee to serve in your own third-party special needs trust. Most pooled trusts charge a fee of 1.5% to 3.0% of assets held by the trust as an annual fee. Others charge a minimum fee that can be several thousands of dollars a year.

- If for any reason the charity loses its funding or status as a not-for-profit, the pooled trust could be shut down and the beneficiary would not have access to trust funds until the state appointed a new trust administrator.

- If the pooled trust administrators and the beneficiary do not get along there is no way to get out of the pooled trust.

- Some pooled trusts are more trustworthy than others. You'll need to do some research to find a pooled trust with a mission and structure that works for your family.

Almost all states have pooled trust programs. Most prefer to accept members only from their state. The reason for this restriction is that the trustee of the pooled trust doesn't want to take on the extra burden of keeping up to date on the laws in different states. Many pooled trusts are associated with The Arc (a national organization created to benefit people with developmental disabilities) or the National Alliance on Mental Illness (NAMI). Fortunately, their pooled trusts usually are also available to people with other physical and mental disabilities.

Instead of signing up while you are alive, you can direct the executor of your will or the successor trustee of your revocable living trust to hunt for a suitable pooled trust. If the executor or trustee can't find a suitable pooled trust, the inheritance can be routed through your will or revocable living trust to the special needs trust you create, as a backup. Read Chapter 7 for all of the details about pooled trusts.

Picking the Ideal Trustee

If a pooled trust is not right for you, and you decide to create your own special needs trust, then you must also decide who to name as initial trustee and successor trustees of that trust.

If the beneficiary of the trust is your child, you will probably name yourself to serve as the initial trustee. If you are married or partnered, you might name yourself and your spouse or partner to serve together as initial cotrustees. If the beneficiary is someone other than your child, the child's parent or parents might be the logical choice for initial trustees.

When you create your trust you will also name successor trustees—people to manage the trust when the initial trustee or cotrustees can no longer serve. The successor trustees will most likely be friends or family, but not just any friend or family member will do.

The job of trustee requires a unique balance of care for the beneficiary, fiscal responsibility, ability to understand SSI and Medicaid laws, and more. Ideally, you want your trustee to be:

- willing to serve
- able to manage the trust for your loved one's benefit
- personally acquainted with your loved one
- of roughly the same age as (or younger than) your loved one
- able to understand and apply government benefit eligibility rules
- able to maintain excellent records, and
- able to conduct financial affairs in a consistent, organized, and responsible manner.

The following subsections describe these qualities in detail. Keep them in mind when you choose your trustees.

Willingness to Serve

Every trustee and successor trustee you name must be willing to serve, so talk to all potential trustees in advance. Clearly explain under what conditions they would serve and what their duties would be. You might give them a copy of the Trustee's Duties Letter, provided by this book. The letter will help the potential trustee make an informed decision.

Before you name your trustees in the trust, make sure they accept the role you assign to them. Otherwise, when it comes time for them to serve, they might decline.

EXAMPLE: Loretta, 60 years old and recently widowed, creates a special needs trust for the benefit of her blind daughter, Luanne. She names herself as trustee and names Luanne's cousin Peter as successor trustee. Because Peter and Loretta are very close, she assumes that Peter will agree to serve as trustee but doesn't get around to mentioning it to him.

When Loretta dies ten years later, Peter learns that he has been named to succeed Loretta as trustee. Surprised and overwhelmed by the idea of taking on this responsibility, Peter refuses the appointment.

This example also highlights the importance of naming more than one level of successor trustee—so that there is always another named choice to take over if someone can't or won't serve. (See "Naming Successor Trustees," below.) If there is no named trustee able or willing to serve, the special needs trust in this book authorizes the executor of your will (if you have one) or your successor trustee of a revocable living trust (if you have one) to choose someone to serve as trustee of the special needs trust.

If any of the people you want to name as trustee or successor trustee don't want to do the job themselves, consider naming a cotrustee to serve with them. (See "Naming Cotrustees," below.) Also, you can reassure prospective trustees that as trustees they will have the authority to hire experts if and when they're needed.

TIP

Ask again later, too. Those you choose as successor trustees may not be called on to serve for years or even decades. For example, if you name yourself as trustee and are now 50 years old, the successor trustee may not be needed for 30 or more years. So even if your choice for successor trustee happily agrees to serve when you first ask, circumstances may change. Check in with your choice every few years so that, if necessary, you can exercise your authority as trustee to name a replacement.

No Conflicts of Interest

A special needs trust must be managed for the benefit of the beneficiary. This means that the person serving as trustee must not act in his or her own interests—or the interests of others—when making investment or spending decisions. Put another way, the trustee must avoid conflicts of interests. Ideally this means that the trustee should not have anything to gain from the trust, either while it is in operation or after it ends.

In real life, however, it is not uncommon to name the same person as both successor trustee and remainder beneficiary. (The remainder beneficiary is the person who gets any trust property that is left when the beneficiary dies or, in some cases, when the trust is dissolved.) This arrangement creates a direct conflict of interest when the successor trustee takes over as trustee, because every dollar of trust money spent on behalf of the beneficiary is one dollar less that the remainder beneficiary (the successor trustee) could receive at the beneficiary's death.

EXAMPLE: Jonas creates a special needs trust for his sister Clara. He names himself as trustee and names his brother Ralph as the successor trustee. The trust also provides that Ralph should receive any remaining trust property if Clara dies before Ralph. Jonas dies ten years after creating the trust. Ralph takes over as trustee and spends the money appropriately for Clara's benefit, even though every dollar he spends on her reduces the amount he will take when Clara dies. When Clara dies five years later, Ralph gets the $50,000 that remains in the trust.

There is no absolute rule against naming the same person as trustee and a remainder beneficiary. An honest and honorable trustee will make decisions based solely on the beneficiary's needs. And if you don't expect the remainder beneficiary to inherit anything—for example, if the trust funds just won't last that long—it may not be a big issue for you.

It's best, though, to name different people to serve as successor trustee and remainder beneficiary. One path that works for some families is to name a favorite charity as the remainder beneficiary—perhaps a church, senior center, or disability organization, such as The Arc or Centers for Independent Living.

Familiarity and Empathy With the Beneficiary

A special needs trust is intended to give the beneficiary goods and services in addition to the food and shelter paid for by the SSI grant. So a special needs trust functions most smoothly if the person serving as trustee has a good working knowledge of the beneficiary's needs. This relationship requires good communication that is most likely to exist if the trustee has—or is able to develop—a close personal relationship with the beneficiary. A personal relationship is especially important if the beneficiary's ability to communicate is impaired.

EXAMPLE: Douglas has schizophrenia and lives in a group home. He is the beneficiary of a special needs trust managed by his brother, Phil. Douglas has little awareness of the special needs trust or the benefits that it can provide.

Fortunately, Phil is familiar with Douglas's likes and dislikes and makes sure that his special needs are provided for within the limits of the trust funds. For instance, Phil knows that Douglas likes to play video games and so makes sure that he receives a steady supply, courtesy of the trust.

Even if the beneficiary can communicate effectively, familiarity—and empathy—between the trustee and the beneficiary are still important. A good relationship makes it easier for them to negotiate requests that the trustee may be reluctant to grant because they threaten to deplete trust assets. Also, the more familiar a trustee is with a beneficiary, the less likely it is that the trustee's decisions will be based on bias or misconceptions about people with disabilities that are, unhappily, all too common.

EXAMPLE: Angela, the beneficiary of a special needs trust, became quadriplegic after an automobile accident when she was a girl. She graduated from regular high school thanks to support she received from her family and accommodations offered by the school. Now, Angela wants to attend college and major in communications so she can pursue a career in television broadcasting.

Tomas, the trustee of Angela's trust, is her distant cousin and has not spent much time around Angela or other people with disabilities. Tomas believes that given Angela's physical condition she is chasing a pipe dream and rejects her request for tuition and other expenses of college. Tomas thinks he is being reasonable. Angela believes he is making unwarranted assumptions about what she can accomplish. Because the trustee has full authority to make decisions, Angela will not be able to use trust funds for her education.

While serious disagreements between the beneficiary and the trustee are rare, they can be devastating to the purpose of the trust. For that reason, even if you choose a trustee who has an ideal relationship with the beneficiary, it's wise for the trust to name someone who can remove and replace the trustee, if necessary. See "Naming a Trust Protector or Trust Advisory Committee," at the end of this chapter.

Closeness in Age to the Beneficiary

Special needs trusts can last for months, years, or decades. In many instances, their duration is very hard to predict. Today, many people with disabilities live much longer than their doctors or families originally expected. Such dramatic increases in life span are due both to medical advances and shifting attitudes toward people with disabilities. Institutionalization used to be the norm for people with many kinds of disabilities, but now they often live at home and are integrated into mainstream educational and social activities—and live a lot longer as a result.

When you're choosing a trustee, you should do your best to estimate your loved one's likely life span, despite the inherent uncertainty. You need to think about how long you can expect the trustee to be able to manage the trust.

It's best, of course, if the trustees will be around as long as the beneficiary is alive. So if you are creating a special needs trust for your child, who may outlive you by decades, your choice for successor trustee should be someone closer to your child's age than to yours. On the other hand, if your loved one's disability makes a long life very unlikely, it's reasonable to choose a successor trustee who is closer to your age.

Keep in mind that the special needs trust you create is likely to be fully funded at your death through a will, revocable living trust, or life insurance policy. If you're in your 40s or 50s, you likely have several decades to live, and it is wise to choose a successor trustee who is likely to live even longer.

You could also consider allowing your named trustee the ability to appoint his or her own successor if you are no longer able to do it. Another option is to name a trust protector, as described at the end of this chapter.

TIP

Keep your estate planning documents current. You can amend your will or revocable living trust—and the money you are leaving to the special needs trust you created—right up until your death or until you lose legal capacity to handle your affairs. So, if it appears that a special needs trust is appropriate when you create it, but it later becomes unnecessary because of changes in your loved one's disability or in the laws governing SSI and Medicaid, you can make changes to your estate plan. Also, if you've named yourself initial trustee and your choices for successor trustee die before you, you can use your position as the trustee to name new successor trustees. See Chapter 8.

Willingness to Get Help With Government Rules

Each trustee you name will need to become familiar with the rules that determine eligibility for SSI and Medicaid—and how the special needs trust can be used to supplement the beneficiary's needs without violating these rules. Some of the basic rules can be understood fairly easily. However, unless the trustee already has some experience with the rules of the public benefits programs, it may be best to get help from a professional—either a special needs planning lawyer or a nonlawyer with an expertise in public benefits counseling—at least until the trustee is comfortable that he or she understands the rules.

While it is important to name someone with basic common sense, common sense alone will not be enough to administer a special needs trust because SSI and Medicaid eligibility rules and regulations rarely make sense. A trustee who does not get professional help may believe he or she is doing the right thing by doing things that might actually destroy the beneficiary's public benefits eligibility. This is particularly worrisome because often the problem isn't caught for many years, and the beneficiary could be required to pay back any benefits he or she was not entitled to receive during that time.

In addition to hiring a professional for help, some resources that will help the trustee keep up to date are listed in this book's Trustee's Duties Letter.

Guidance for Successor Trustees

The initial trustee will write checks out of the special needs trust to supplement your loved one's needs. The record of that spending will provide valuable guidance to the successor trustee about the types of expenses the trust can meet within the SSI guidelines. Also, when significant assets are added to the special needs trust, you may want to give a copy of the trust to the local Social Security Administration (SSA) office to see if it will qualify as a third-party special needs trust. See Chapter 9.

Financial Knowledge and Competence

Using trust money to provide for the special needs of a beneficiary is usually the fun part of being a trustee. Not so much fun is the business side of trust management: making reports, keeping records, filing tax returns, and making appropriate investment decisions. There are plenty of people who are quite comfortable with these tasks, but you may not know any among the group of people who you would naturally choose to serve as trustee.

In this situation, you have several options. You could name cotrustees, one of whom has financial expertise, name a professional or corporate trustee or cotrustee, or join a pooled trust. Each of these options is discussed in this chapter.

Also keep in mind that a trustee who does not have the financial knowledge required to manage the trust can always get help. A trustee who isn't savvy in business matters is authorized, by the trust document, to hire experts for financial advice. For instance, an accountant or a tax service could help prepare the trust tax returns, while a financial planner could give advice on investment strategies.

Of course, the fact that the trustee gets help from experts doesn't mean that the trustee is off the hook for managing the trust. The trustee's ultimate responsibility for carrying out all the terms of the trust cannot be outsourced (delegated) to anyone else.

It may be hard to know now just how much of the trust property will be spent on these experts to support the trustee. It could end up costing the trust more for your trustee to rely on experts than it would cost to hire a professional trustee with whom you could negotiate the fee up front. (See "Naming a Professional or Corporate Trustee," below.) If you do stick with a relative or friend as your choice for trustee, you'll want that person to understand that he or she should do as much of the work as possible and use outside experts only when necessary.

Using Trust Protectors

Some special needs trusts name people to serve as "trust protectors" or "trust advisers" on various issues, such as investment strategies or compliance with SSI and Medicaid rules. These advisers have no legal authority over the trust, but the trustee is asked to consult them in certain matters.

This may sound like an ideal solution if your choice for trustee lacks expertise in certain areas. However, having to consult advisers may add to the trustee's burden and be the thing that drives a trustee to resign. If you prefer this option, you can include a trust protector provision in the trust you make with this book. Or you can have a lawyer help you to include a trust protector in your trust. Read more about using a trust protector or trust advisory committee in the last section of this chapter.

Naming the Initial Trustee

When you create your special needs trust, you will name someone as the initial trustee or cotrustees to manage the trust. If the trust starts out with just a small deposit in a bank account, there won't be much for the initial trustee to do until the trust is fully funded. However, if you (or friends or relatives) deposit a sizable sum in the trust account, the initial trustee's job will get more complex, as described in Chapter 5.

Most people who create a special needs trust will name themselves as initial trustee and then name others as successor trustees.

EXAMPLE 1: Lona Clark, age 43, creates a special needs trust for her autistic daughter, Julie Clark. She names herself as the initial trustee and her nephew David as the first successor trustee. She also names her niece Maya as second successor trustee, in case David is unable or unwilling to serve. She deposits $500 in a bank as trustee of the Julie Clark Special Needs Trust. From time to time Lona deposits her own money in the account and writes checks against the account to provide for Julie's special needs.

When Lona dies at the age of 63, there is $750 left in the trust. However, Lona had paid for a $50,000 term life insurance policy payable to the "trustee of the Julie Clark Special Needs Trust." David takes over as trustee and receives the life insurance payment. The account now has $50,750 for David to manage. Maya will take over if David becomes unavailable.

EXAMPLE 2: Now, assume instead that when Lona creates the trust, she has a domestic partner Ken who is also Julie's father. Lona names herself and Ken as initial cotrustees, David as first successor trustee, and Maya as second successor trustee. Ken survives Lona by 20 years and serves as sole trustee during that time. When he dies, David is unwilling to serve, so Maya becomes the trustee.

Under some conditions, you may want to name someone other than yourself as initial trustee. For example, if the beneficiary of the trust is not your child, it might make more sense to name the beneficiary's parent or parents as initial trustee or cotrustees. Also, even if the beneficiary is your child, if you don't expect to be able to manage the trust for very long—for example, if you are near the end of your own life—you may choose to name someone other than yourself as initial trustee.

EXAMPLE: Deborah creates a special needs trust for her son, Billie. Deborah does not expect to live much longer because she has advanced lung cancer. Instead of naming herself as initial trustee, Deborah names her sister, Catherine, as initial trustee and her brother, Eugene, as successor trustee.

> ### Initial Cotrustees
>
> If you are married or otherwise partnered, you may name yourself and your partner as cotrustees. See "Naming Cotrustees," below. If you choose this option and one cotrustee becomes unavailable, the survivor will serve as an individual trustee.

Naming Successor Trustees

In your trust you will name one or more people to take over when the initial trustee (probably you) can no longer serve. Unfortunately, the person you name to serve as successor trustee may not be available when the moment arrives. Things happen—people may become ill or die, move to another part of the country, or simply get too busy to serve because of their own responsibilities. Whatever the reason, it's important to name a short list of subsequent successor trustees who can take over, if necessary.

> **EXAMPLE:** Edward creates a special needs trust for his domestic partner Sam, who has three siblings, Drew, Kai, and Chris. Any of them would do just fine as trustee. Edward names himself as trustee and Drew as first successor trustee. He also decides to name Kai as the second successor trustee, to serve if Drew can't or won't serve. He also names Chris as third successor trustee, to serve if neither Drew nor Kai is available.

The successor trustee who takes over for the initial trustee is called the "first successor" trustee. The successor trustee who takes over for the first successor trustee is called the "second successor" trustee, and so on. You can name as many levels of successor trustees as you wish. You should name as many people as you feel comfortable naming. As long as you name several people who are relatively close in age to the beneficiary, you should be fine.

Even if you name an agency or institution, rather than an individual, as trustee, you'll still want to name successor trustees. Companies do go out of business. And even though you expect to leave enough money in the trust to make it feasible to hire a corporate or professional trustee, there may not be enough when the trust goes into effect years from now. If a problem such as this does come up, you'll want someone to step in to carry out the terms of the trust. If no person is able and willing to serve as trustee, a court will have to appoint a successor.

If the unlikely happens and none of the people you named as successor trustee are available, the terms of the trust allow the executor or administrator of your estate to name a trustee to manage the trust.

TIP

Name qualified successor trustees. When naming successor trustees, keep in mind the critical qualities for all trustees discussed earlier in this chapter and in Chapter 5. Consider each potential successor trustee as if he or she will eventually manage the trust. Do not name someone just to be nice or out of obligation—naming an unqualified person will put the trust, and your loved one's benefits, in jeopardy.

Naming Cotrustees

You can name cotrustees for any level of trustee. For example, you can name two or more people to serve as initial cotrustees, first successor cotrustees, second successor cotrustees, and so on.

EXAMPLE: Marla is ten and has Down syndrome. Her parents create a special needs trust, naming themselves as initial cotrustees. Marla's older sister Beth is willing to be named as successor trustee for Marla's special needs trust. However, Marla's parents are hesitant to put Beth in charge of all the record keeping, investments, trust disbursements, and tax obligations. So they name Marla's cousin Paul, who is a CPA, to serve as a cotrustee with Beth.

You might consider naming cotrustees if:

- You want a couple to serve together.
- You want to pair one trustee who knows the beneficiary well with another who has stronger financial skills.
- You want two or more people to share the burden of managing the trust.

But if you go this route, keep in mind that naming cotrustees creates additional questions and concerns. Will the cotrustees cooperate? Should each be able to act for the trust alone, or must all agree to every action? These issues are discussed next.

Picking People Who Work Well Together

As you can probably imagine, naming cotrustees can cause difficulties. Record keeping, investment decisions, and tax reporting all become problematic unless there is excellent communication among the cotrustees.

Just finding people willing to work with each other and commit to trustee obligations over a period that might last decades can be difficult. Don't name more than one trustee to serve at a time unless you're confident that they can work together well, on issues that are both financial and emotional, over the long term.

Also, keep in mind that all cotrustees are legally responsible to the trust. So if, one cotrustee acts negligently, all costrustees could be held legally responsible for those actions, even if they had nothing to do with it. This is another reason to name cotrustees who will work well together and who won't act without consulting the others.

There is no legal limit to the number of cotrustees you can appoint to manage a special needs trust. For example, if your loved one has four siblings all of whom want to be involved in the management of the trust, you could legally name all of them to serve as cotrustees. However, it is in your loved one's best interest to keep the number of cotrustees to the absolute minimum. The more trustees serving at any one time, the harder it will be for them to make unified decisions. Disharmony among the cotrustees could seriously affect trust management and even risk legal problems, including the loss of SSI eligibility.

Some Alternatives to Cotrustees

Pay a professional. If the trust contains enough money to pay the fees charged by professional and corporate trustees, this may be the preferable option. (See "Naming a Professional or Corporate Trustee," below.)

Let one trustee name cotrustees. Why not let your successor trustee name cotrustees if needed? This might seem sensible, but it can get messy. For example, it may be hard to get rid of a new trustee if the original one decides the arrangement isn't working. You'll need to see a lawyer if you want your trustee to have this authority.

Name more levels of successor trustees. If you are blessed with a number of good candidates for trustee, consider naming them as subsequent successor trustees rather than as cotrustees. That way, if one person becomes unable to shoulder the burden, the next person in line can take over. (See "Naming Successor Trustees," above.)

May Cotrustees Act on Their Own?

Cotrustees—and the people, businesses, and institutions they deal with—need to know whether each of them can act independently or whether they must sign off on everything jointly. For example, if you name cotrustees, and one of them wants to write a check from the trust account to pay for a plane ticket for your loved one, must the other one sign the check, too?

In your trust document, you must state whether cotrustees should act jointly or independently. Each way has its pros and cons. If you require that all cotrustees must agree before they can act on behalf of the trust, it may be tough to get any decisions made. There may be gridlock because the cotrustees disagree or simply because one or more of them is not available when decisions need to be made.

On the other hand, if you let each cotrustee act independently, you are increasing the chances that mistakes will be made that impair the beneficiary's eligibility for SSI and Medicaid. This is because the more people who have to understand and follow the benefit program eligibility rules, the more likely it is that a misunderstanding will occur.

EXAMPLE: Melissa creates a special needs trust for her daughter Penelope and names Penelope's two siblings as successor trustees to take over at Melissa's death. Each trustee has authority to act independently. Penelope's brother, John, takes his duties seriously, learns the income and resource rules for SSI eligibility, and is judicious in the disbursements he makes from the trust.

Penelope's sister, Gwen, however, is very loving but has little sense of money or program rules. Gwen sees no harm in slipping Penelope cash as needed. When making her report to SSI, Penelope mentions the cash—which, because of its amount, makes her temporarily ineligible for SSI and Medicaid.

Assigning Specific Duties to Each Cotrustee

The trust document in this book does not spell out specific duties for each cotrustee. Instead, the trustees work out a division of labor on their own.

It's possible, however, to give each trustee specific responsibilities. For example, you could give one trustee financial responsibility (investment, spending, taxes, and so on), make another responsible for communicating the beneficiary's needs to the money person, and charge a third trustee with monitoring the other two and doing anything that falls between the cracks.

See a lawyer if you want your trust document to be structured in this way.

Naming a Professional or Corporate Trustee

If you don't want to put the special needs trust funds into the hands of a family member or friend, and a pooled trust doesn't seems like the right choice either (see Chapter 7), you have another option: You can hire an expert—a professional or corporate trustee.

The advantage of using a professional trustee—an individual who administers the trust for a professional fee—is his or her knowledge about and experience with administering trusts. It is a professional trustee's job to understand the trust rules, keep excellent records, make appropriate disbursements, pay all taxes, and prudently invest trust assets. Further, if a mistake is made, a professional trustee generally carries liability insurance or has sufficient assets to pay back the trust—whereas a family member or friend may not. While hiring a professional may seem expensive, ultimately, it may be cheaper than paying to fix problems created by a well-intentioned friend or family member who made a simple mistake.

Corporate trustees are financial institutions such as banks, savings and loan institutions, and some brokerage houses that will administer a trust for a fee. However, for many trusts, corporate trustees aren't really an option because most corporate fiduciaries will assume responsibility only for very large trusts—for example, trusts worth more than $250,000, or even $1,000,000.

TIP
Find an experienced professional. Not all corporate or professional trustees have experience in running special needs trusts. Make sure the bank or professional you name is experienced.

If you do decide to hire a professional or corporate trustee, you may have to do a lot of shopping to find a trustee you are comfortable with. Talk to at least two or three people before you settle on someone. Here are some questions to ask during your search:

- Is the trustee located close to the beneficiary?
- How much experience does the trustee have in managing special needs trusts?
- Does the trustee have direct experience working with individuals with disabilities?
- Does the trustee have expertise in the Social Security Administration and state Medicaid rules and regulations, or access to this expertise?
- What is the trustee's investment experience?
- Is the trustee open to working with a family member or friend as cotrustee or adviser?
- What are the trustee and investment fees? Are these charged separately or bundled? Are there any hidden transaction or other fees? For example, in addition to a monthly fee measured by a percentage of the trust assets, is there a charge for each disbursement or for issuing reports of trust activity?
- Do the fees suddenly increase when a particular threshold is crossed? For example, do they charge one fee for ten or fewer disbursements and a higher fee for more than ten?
- Exactly what services are included? For example, is the trustee prepared to take care of all the functions discussed in Chapter 5 or will you have to make separate arrangements for one or more of them?
- How will the trustee keep current on the beneficiary's needs?

Some uncertainty is always involved in naming a corporate or professional trustee as successor trustee. Most likely, the special needs trust will not be fully funded until your death—and by that time, the trustee's fees may have gone way up. The minimum value of trusts that the trustee will accept may have risen as well.

> **EXAMPLE:** Bonnie creates a special needs trust for her grandchild Stacey. In addition to the small amounts of money that Bonnie puts in the trust during her life, the trust will be funded with the proceeds of a $300,000 life insurance policy. Bonnie names Stacey's mother, Francine, as successor

trustee, but has great reservations about Francine's ability to manage the trust appropriately. So she shops around and finds a corporate trustee that is willing to serve as a cotrustee with Francine as long as the trust has at least $300,000 in assets when the corporate trustee is called on to serve. Based on that information, Bonnie names that corporate trustee and Francine as successor cotrustees.

Bonnie lives for another 20 years. When she dies, the corporate trustee accepts only trusts worth at least $600,000. The result? Francine will be sole trustee, in complete charge of the trust.

To avoid this problem, it's wise to name one or more successor trustees to take over if the professional trustee doesn't work out. Or you can add a trust protector, as described below.

Using a Trust Protector or Trust Advisory Committee

When naming a trustee for a special needs trust, it's important to remember that the trustee will have absolute authority over the assets in the trust. The trustee must be given this authority to meet the legal definition of a special needs trust; however it gives the trustee broad power to make both good and bad decisions. For example, a trustee could refuse to make disbursements that are perfectly acceptable or make mistakes managing trust assets. If there is no procedure for removing a poorly performing trustee and the trustee refuses to resign, there may be no way to get rid of the trustee unless he or she does something really bad to harm the trust, like stealing trust money or refusing to follow the trust's terms.

EXAMPLE: Ryan is the trustee of a special needs trust set up for the benefit of Amir by his parents. Amir has asked that Ryan make a distribution to pay for monthly Internet service. Normally, this is a great type of disbursement that will enhance the quality of life for Amir at a modest cost. However, Ryan believes that using the Internet is morally wrong and refuses to pay for it. Even though Amir's parents left a letter to Ryan saying they wished to encourage Amir to use the Internet, no one (not even

Amir) can force Ryan to pay for Amir's Internet. Further, if Amir tried to get Ryan removed as trustee, Ryan's refusal to pay for Internet might be an insufficient reason to have him removed by a court.

One way to provide a check and balance against a poorly performing trustee is to add a role in the trust called a "trust protector." (If you want to name more than one person to this role, the trust can name those people to serve as an "advisory committee.") If this role is included, the trust gives the trust protector or trust advisory committee the right to fire and replace the trustee at any time for any reason. The beneficiary of the special needs trust cannot serve in these roles.

> **EXAMPLE:** In the above example, if Amir's special needs trust named Sean as the trust protector with the right to remove the trustee at any time for any reason, then Sean could remove Ryan as trustee. The trust can also empower Sean to name a successor trustee. This is an all or nothing power of removal, so Sean cannot force Ryan to pay for the Internet, he can only remove Ryan as trustee.

The use of a trust protector can work particularly well when you want a friend or family member to oversee a professional or corporate trustee. That said, while most trust protectors are friends or family members, if there is no one close to the beneficiary who can serve this role, a financial advisor, CPA, or special needs planning attorney may be willing to do the job.

Deciding who to name trust protector may be easier than naming a trustee because the trust protector does not generally have day-to-day responsibilities and is often only needed when something is not going well with the trust administration. However, still take care in who you name as trust protector—bad trust protectors can cause big problems for trusts if they can use their power to remove and replace trustees without good reason.

When choosing who to name for this role, consider that a good trust protector will:

- stay in contact with the beneficiary
- be able to review and understand trust financial statements
- be willing to confront a poorly performing trustee
- listen reasonably when a trustee explains his or her decisions, and
- make thoughtful and reasoned decisions about removing a trustee.

There are other good reasons to name a trust protector (or an advisory committee). You can provide the trust protector with additional rights—such as the right to amend the trust if changes to the law make it prudent to do so. Or you could give the trust protector the right to interpret "ambiguous provisions," a provision that could be interpreted in more than one way. If you don't name a trust protector, the solution to these issues is to ask a court to fix the trust, which requires court costs and attorney's fees.

Rules about including trust protectors in special needs trusts may vary from state to state. This book's trust includes a simple trust provision that you can include in your trust. If you want a more robust trust provision, or one that is tailored to your specific circumstances, see an experienced special needs planning lawyer in your state for help. See Chapter 10 for tips on finding a good lawyer. ●

Joining a Pooled Trust

Instead of naming a trustee to handle the special needs trust you create, you may be able to have your loved one's inheritance managed as part of a group trust. These pooled trusts, also known as community or master trusts, are managed by nonprofit organizations.

Pooled trusts are an alternative to doing your own special needs trust if you can't come up with a logical choice for trustee. Just sign up with a pooled trust, and you can let them handle the rest.

> **EXAMPLE:** Mildred's daughter Cassie will need SSI and Medicaid for the rest of her life. Mildred wants to leave Cassie $50,000 cash, without jeopardizing Cassie's benefits. A special needs trust is perfect for this purpose, but Mildred can't think of anyone she can count on to assume the role of successor trustee.
>
> Mildred decides to join a pooled trust and have it act as successor trustee. Because many pooled trusts are run by people dedicated to serving an entire community of disabled persons, Mildred has faith that Cassie will be well taken care of and that her special needs will be met by the pooled trust as she continues to receive SSI and Medicaid benefits.

TIP

Pooled trusts can also be used for funds owned by the beneficiary. This book focuses on third-party special needs trusts—trusts in which the trust funds originate from third parties and not from funds owned by the beneficiary. However, if your loved one does have money of his or her own, you can use a pooled trust to shelter those funds from consideration as a resource when qualifying for SSI and Medicaid.

This chapter gives you a general description of pooled trusts and how they work. If you think a pooled trust might work for you, check Appendix A for one in your loved one's state (there are also several national pooled trusts).

An Overview of Pooled Trusts

Pooled trusts are run by nonprofit organizations set up to expertly and efficiently administer master special needs trusts on behalf of individual beneficiaries with disabilities. Assets are combined and invested together; funds are spent on beneficiaries in proportion to their share of the total amount.

No two pooled trusts are exactly alike. Each has its own fees, menu of available services, and contracts under which it operates. Some offer many options, complicated contracts, and complex fee schedules. Others offer a single agreement and an easy-to-understand fee schedule. Some are organized to provide complete care of beneficiaries while others just manage the money in an appropriate manner.

But whatever their differences, all pooled trusts share some basic features that make them worth considering:

- The people managing a trust and its assets will be knowledgeable about agency rules regarding income and resources and will be able to deal with any questions from the SSI or Medicaid programs.

- The trust directors usually are relatives of people with disabilities and are attuned to that community.

- Even if you don't have a lot of money to leave to your loved one, a pooled trust can give your loved one the benefits of a special needs trust.

If you find a pooled trust that looks like it might work for you, give it a call or visit its website. The information in this chapter should help you understand what you learn from the program itself.

As a general rule, if you plan on using a pooled trust, it is good to set up an account for your loved one during your life, even if you don't put much money into it. It gives you an opportunity to see how the program works and get to know the people who will be caring for your loved one after your death. In fact, some pooled trusts insist on this approach so that they can become fully conversant with your loved one's background and needs and your experiences as a caregiver.

Some pooled trusts let you establish an account without funding it immediately. You will be required to pay a small annual renewal fee to keep the account active. Then, you can use your will, a living trust, or another estate planning tool, such as life insurance, to leave property to the account at your death.

EXAMPLE: Craig creates an account for his daughter Ashley with the ABC Pooled Trust. Although he doesn't have to, Craig transfers a $10,000 CD into Ashley's account to avoid paying renewal fees. He also plans to leave $25,000 to the account through his living trust and another $25,000 through a term life insurance policy payable at his death.

If you don't set up an account with a pooled trust during your life, you can direct your executor or successor trustee of your revocable living trust to join a pooled trust after your death, if one is available. However, this approach deprives you of control over which pooled trust to use and makes it more difficult for the pooled trust to arrange a smooth continuity from your care of the beneficiary to theirs.

EXAMPLE: Billie, a Tennessee resident, creates a special needs trust for her developmentally disabled granddaughter Kai. Billie names Kai's brother Thom to serve as trustee when Billie dies, but she's uneasy about whether Thom can do the job.

A few years later Billie learns that Tennessee has a pooled trust that would give Kai the same benefits as the special needs trust she created. Billie visits the pooled trust's website and learns that the trust program offers all the services that, in Billie's opinion, Thom might be unable to handle. Billie can sign up for the trust and introduce the program's staff to Kai right away.

Billie decides to use the pooled trusted instead. She creates an account with the pooled trust and changes her will to leave Kai's inheritance directly to the pooled trust account. Then, to end the special needs trust that she had previously created, she uses her power as trustee to spend the trust funds and terminate the trust.

How Pooled Trusts Came About

Many pooled trusts were created in response to a 1993 change in the Social Security Act. The change authorized persons with disabilities to shelter their own money (from consideration as a resource by SSI and Medicaid) by placing it with a nonprofit organization for management. The new law also allowed the nonprofits to keep a portion of any funds remaining in the trust after the beneficiary's death—creating a lucrative fundraising opportunity. (Not all pooled trusts impose this requirement.) Existing organizations such as The Arc and the National Association on Mental Illness (NAMI), which in some states already operated pooled trusts, were well placed to expand their trust operations.

Can You Use a Pooled Trust?

A pooled trust might not be an option for you. It all depends on where your loved one lives, what kind of disability he or she has, and the amount of funds you have available to place in the trust.

The Beneficiary's Residence

Pooled trusts currently exist in almost every state. (See Appendix A for a state-by-state list of pooled trusts.) Most of them accept only beneficiaries who live in the state where the trust is established.

EXAMPLE: Ralph's mother Charlene wants to join a pooled trust on Ralph's behalf. Ralph lives in Vermont; his mother lives in California. Even though there are several pooled trusts in California, Charlene can't use them; it is the beneficiary's state of residence that counts. If no pooled trust has been established in Vermont, the only option for Charlene is to try to make arrangements with a pooled trust that is willing to operate across state lines.

If you don't find a pooled trust in your loved one's state, consider one of the national pooled trusts or call one in an adjoining state. The other state's pooled trust program may be able to steer you in the right direction.

Why Most Pooled Trusts Stick Close to Home

Most pooled trusts accept only beneficiaries in their own states because these trusts are experts about the state laws that apply to self-settled trusts (trusts funded with the beneficiary's own property). Because every state has its own Medicaid rules, rules governing self-settled trusts vary from state to state—and it's very difficult to keep up with them in all states. So most pooled trusts have become expert on the rules of their own state and prefer not to venture into uncharted territory.

Kind of Disability

Virtually all pooled trusts require their beneficiaries to meet Social Security disability standards set for SSI and SSDI eligibility. They may also require that the beneficiary have the type of disability for which the pooled trust was created in the first place. For instance, a pooled trust intended primarily to help people with developmental disabilities may not accept a person with quadriplegia as a beneficiary.

The reason for this "discrimination" is not sinister. Most pooled trusts are dedicated to providing a broad range of services to people with a certain disability. Staff members trained to deal with autism, for example, may not be comfortable or familiar with the needs of the physically disabled or the blind.

On the other hand, most pooled trusts are willing to at least consider each applicant on a case-by-case basis—which means there is no harm in asking a particular program what its disability requirements are, if any.

This potential hitch in acceptance of your loved one by a pooled trust is another good reason to sign up while you are alive rather than leave this important step to your executor or successor trustee.

Advantages and Disadvantages of Pooled Trusts

Advantages	Disadvantages
• If you don't know someone who is willing and competent to be trustee, a pooled trust program can provide one. • Pooled trust staff or volunteers often have expertise and experience with people who have disabilities. • You can get professional management for trusts that are too small (less than about $250,000) for most banks and trust companies. • Pooled trusts usually work closely with banks and trust companies and can tap their investment expertise. • Experts manage the trust assets and make the required reports after the fund starts disbursing money. • You don't have to worry about what might happen if an individual trustee died or couldn't serve. With a pooled trust, there will likely be a trustee. • Management fees are generally much lower than those of banks and trust companies. • You don't have to draft and maintain your own special needs trust document; the program will provide one. It may have been reviewed by Medicaid and SSI to make sure it complies with their rules. • The program will probably be overseen by volunteers who likely include legal and financial experts, family members of people with disabilities, and disability advocates.	• Pooled trusts can be much more expensive than an individual trust set up by you and run by a friend or family member. • If you change your mind after joining a pooled trust and withdraw, you may forfeit some or all of the enrollment fee you've already paid. • If the person with a disability does not like the pooled trust program he or she generally cannot move assets to a different trust. • Your agreement with the pooled trust program may give it the right to keep part of any assets that remain in a trust after the beneficiary dies—a result you may not want. • If the pooled trust requires that it be allowed to keep a portion of any remainder, an unethical program could refuse to disburse funds to your loved one in an attempt to keep more money for itself. • Unless you pay extra fees, the trust may operate in a remote and bureaucratic manner, far removed from your loved one's actual needs. • The pooled trust program could cease to operate because the charity is out of business. (Many program contracts address this possibility.) • Investment decisions are beyond your control and might not be as conservative as you would provide in your own special needs trust. • Pooled trusts may not be as responsive as personal or professional trustees and disbursements may be delayed.

Kinds of Property

Most pooled trust programs accept only cash, which can be invested to earn more money for the beneficiary. They don't want to be in charge of tangible items that actually cost money because they must be stored, insured, and maintained. So you probably don't want to use a pooled trust if you are leaving tangible property—for example, jewelry, heirlooms, vehicles, or collections—that you would want preserved in its tangible form. If you leave that type of property to a pooled trust, it will be sold for cash.

Some pooled trusts, however, accept a beneficiary's home as a trust asset. But because a home is not counted as a resource by SSI or Medicaid, regardless of its value, you could leave it directly to your loved one and leave the cash part of your loved one's inheritance to the pooled trust.

Amount of Property

All pooled trusts require a minimum level of funding. The "buy-in" amount for a pooled trust is surprisingly affordable, usually between $5,000 and $25,000. That's about 1% to 5% of the minimum amount many banks and trust companies require. A few pooled trusts require more—much more—than these amounts, but, in turn, offer a higher level of service. (See "Extra Services," below.) Keep in mind, however, that in many states another option is to hire an individual professional trustee who may require no minimums at all.

Funding requirements change over time. If you fund the pooled trust while you are alive, you will be sure to meet the minimum funding requirement. However, if you plan to leave money to the pooled trust at your death, you risk having less in your estate than is necessary.

EXAMPLE: Trudy joins the ABC Pooled Trust for her daughter Emily. At that time, the buy-in is $15,000. Instead of depositing money in Emily's account then, Trudy decides to wait and fund the account with the proceeds of a $25,000 life insurance policy payable at her death.

When Trudy dies 15 years later, however, the buy-in amount has gone up to $50,000. Because Emily will not qualify for that pooled trust, she will likely receive the $25,000 outright and lose SSI and Medicaid eligibility.

Limitations of Pooled Trusts

While pooled special needs trusts work for many people, they do have some important limitations that you should consider before joining one. For example:

- A pooled trust is only as good as the nonprofit that is managing it. Some may do a good job for a while, but in the face of financial problems or management changes, may end up doing a terrible job or even going out of business altogether.

- Some pooled trusts distribute assets only at certain times of the month. This can be a problem for a beneficiary who may need distributions more frequently.

- Pooled trusts can be very expensive. Find out exactly how much a pooled trust charges before you join. Generally, there is a one-time setup fee that can run from a few hundred dollars to several thousand dollars. Plus, there is an annual fee—based on a percentage of the assets that are put into the trust—that can be several thousand dollars a year. If you're only putting a modest amount of assets into the trust, the fees of the pooled trust can seriously deplete these assets. In contrast, a friend or family member may not charge anything to serve as the trustee of an individual trust.

- Pooled trust are inflexible. Once the assets are in the pooled trust, it is difficult if not impossible to move the assets to another trust. Your beneficiary is then stuck with this pooled trust even if the trustee does not do a good job.

- Many pooled trusts will not agree to own real estate or authorize other nontraditional investments. If your inheritance will include these types of investments, an individual special needs trust would serve you better.

How Pooled Trusts Work

Most pooled trust programs have similar structures and work in similar ways.

How Pooled Trust Programs Are Organized

The typical pooled trust program is overseen by a board of directors. Directors are commonly volunteer nonprofit organization leaders, members of the charity, parents and relatives of the disabled, and professional and business leaders. The board sets the direction for the organization.

A trustee who is knowledgeable about the resource and income rules of the SSI and Medicaid programs is responsible for managing the trust. The trustee usually works with an independent bank trust department responsible for managing trust funds and making the actual distributions for the benefit of the trust beneficiaries. A professional money manager will be responsible for managing the money.

Finally, often a pooled trust has a social services component dedicated to providing individualized services for each beneficiary of the trust.

Your Contract With the Trust

If you want to put assets into a pooled trust on behalf of a loved one, you sign an agreement—called a joinder agreement—authorizing the program or trustee to manage the account as part of the pooled trust.

Typically, the contract also:

- authorizes the program to provide typical special needs services— such as making disbursements appropriate to the beneficiary's needs on a timely basis
- authorizes specific life services, and
- sets the fees, if any, for those services.

The joinder agreement is discussed in more detail in "Joining a Pooled Trust," below.

Basic Trustee Services Under a Pooled Trust

A pooled trust program usually takes on all the responsibilities of a regular trustee (discussed in Chapter 5). The trustee and program staff hired by the program will:

- invest trust property
- handle requests for disbursements
- keep up to date on government rules regarding eligibility for SSI, Medicaid, and other benefits
- keep records for each beneficiary's account, including your loved one's
- prepare necessary reports for the beneficiary and other interested parties, and
- prepare tax returns.

Extra Services

For many people, it's enough that the pooled trust manages the trust fund and makes disbursements to meet the beneficiary's special needs. But some pooled trusts do much more.

Some beneficiaries, for example, can't make appropriate decisions for themselves and need somebody on the scene to act as a substitute parent. If a court has appointed a guardian or conservator, that person will do the job. (See Chapter 1.) But many adult beneficiaries have no court-appointed guardian.

In that situation, the pooled trust may furnish, for an additional fee, someone who will provide a wide range of services. This person might frequently visit the beneficiary, attend meetings with SSI and Medicaid officials about the beneficiary, and be the beneficiary's advocate in dealings with benefit agencies. This unofficial guardian might also:

- periodically evaluate the beneficiary's health and health care
- evaluate the suitability of living arrangements
- promote and improve social contacts and recreational opportunities

- monitor daytime activities by making random visits and obtaining feedback from the beneficiary

- assist the beneficiary with daily money management

- provide help and support in emergencies, and

- identify and find solutions for problems that affect the beneficiary's quality of life (for example, obtaining psychological help if the beneficiary seems depressed).

If you want these personal one-on-one services, which are often called "life services" or "care coordination," you'll need to meet with the appropriate program personnel to complete a plan and arrange for payment. But be careful. As with any social service program, the services delivered may be less than what were promised. If these services are a major reason you are choosing a pooled trust, ask for some references of people currently receiving the services and get their opinion. Also, use your common sense. The longer and more detailed a plan is, the less likely it is to be read, let alone followed.

As you would expect, highly personalized services cost extra. Each pooled trust offering these services sets its own fees. If there are several pooled trusts available to you, do some comparison shopping; the cost of the services you need will help you determine which trust is the best fit for you and your family. If only one pooled trust is available, you'll have to decide whether the services are worth the price.

How Your Funds Are Managed

In a pooled trust, the funds you contribute stay in a separate "subaccount" for accounting purposes, but are combined with other trust funds for investment purposes. This, naturally, saves on investment fees.

The nonprofit administrator keeps records of the amount of each beneficiary's subaccount and the amount spent for that person. These figures are reported to the beneficiaries, to interested members of the beneficiary's family, and to the remainder beneficiaries.

How the Trustee Spends Trust Funds

Like the trustee of an individual special needs trust, the trustee of a typical pooled trust has complete discretion over spending—provided, of course, that disbursements don't make the beneficiary ineligible for SSI, Medicaid, or similar government benefits.

Some trusts require beneficiaries or their representatives to ask for disbursements in writing; other trusts are more informal. Family members have no control over how trust assets are spent, but are encouraged to give the trustee information that will help the trustee make good decisions

When you enroll your loved one in a pooled trust program, you'll probably be asked for lots of information about him or her and how you would like to see the trust funds used. Some programs gather this information in an interview. Others will give you a questionnaire to fill out, probably something called a "needs and resource assessment."

If the pooled trust you choose is oriented toward a type of disability that is different than your loved one's, it will be up to you to provide the necessary information in an interview or in your own letter. (Chapter 5 discusses writing a "beneficiary information" letter; a sample is in Appendix C.)

The trust will also want to know whom to consult when questions come up about the beneficiary's needs and personal situation. Of course, the more completely you document your wishes and desires regarding care of your loved one, the less likely such consultations will be necessary. But because it's impossible to predict what may happen, the more people you can line up to be available for the trust to confer with, the better.

EXAMPLE: Phil's father joins a pooled trust to handle the inheritance he plans to leave Phil, who needs a wheelchair. Phil gives the trust program personnel lots of information about his needs as a wheelchair user.

After his father dies, Phil develops a severe mental illness and is unable to direct his own needs. The trust is uncertain about what type of treatment to obtain for Phil. Fortunately, Phil's father gave the trust a list of relatives he trusted to act in Phil's best interest. The trust finds a relative

Typical Questions for the Family

Here is some of the information requested by a pooled trust that is geared toward beneficiaries with mental illness. An entirely different set of questions would be appropriate for a person with cerebral palsy or paraplegia.

- Contact information for you and the beneficiary
- SSI and Medicaid eligibility status
- SSDI, SSA, or Medicare eligibility status
- History of hospitalization over last five years
- Status of current medications, if any
- Cooperativeness in taking meds
- Mental health services received currently
- Contact information for psychiatrist and case manager
- History of conservatorship or guardianship
- Type of crisis beneficiary is most likely to experience
- History of suicide or violence ideation, if any
- History of substance abuse, if any
- History of unannounced departures, if any
- Does relative manage his/her own money?
- What expenses family currently pays for on relative's behalf
- Is family considering making a condo/house available for the beneficiary?
- Beneficiary's private insurance, if any
- Does family desire that relative receive living skills training, recreation, vacations, travel, and/or quality of life enhancement out of trust resources? If so, prioritize.
- What are your relative's interests and pastimes, and which does the family wish to support/promote via the trust?
- Anything else you think the social services staff or trustee should know.

who is eager to help and becomes an important liaison between Phil and the pooled trust.

Fees

Generally, pooled trust programs charge the same or higher management fees than do private professional fiduciaries or the trust departments in banks and other financial institutions. As discussed above however, many pooled trusts offer additional life services, while corporate trust departments generally deal just with the money end of things. Obviously, these charges are much more than a family member would typically charge for doing these services. If the assets to fund the trust are small then it is nearly always better to find a trusted friend or family member to serve as trustee.

Fee amounts, and when and how they are charged, vary from organization to organization. Some fees are due when you join the trust program. Others are paid out of the funds you leave the trust at your death.

Most programs have four types of fees:

- a one-time nonrefundable enrollment or setup fee

- an annual renewal fee for unfunded accounts

- a management (or "consulting") fee for funded accounts based on the amount of funds, and

- fees for specific life services.

An enrollment or setup fee can run as little as $500 and as much as $3,000, but most are between $500 and $1,500. If you join the trust and leave it without any money, annual renewal fees for unfunded trusts are typically $75 to $500. The management or consulting fees tend to be based on the amount you have deposited in the account; they are often between 1% and 3% of the funds in the account. Most pooled trusts also have a minimum annual charge for when the percentage fee doesn't provide sufficient funds. This fee is generally $1,500 a year to $2,500 a year and only charged when the percentage fee isn't more.

Some pooled trusts charge an hourly or flat fee for specific services. These also vary among programs; there is really no typical amount.

Program fees are likely to increase from year to year, so you'll want to get a written statement of fees and payment schedules when you're investigating different pooled trust programs.

Pooled Trust Fees	
Type of Fee	Typical Amount
Enrollment	$500 to $1,500
Renewal fees for unfunded trusts	$75 to $100 per year
Management	1% to 3% of the funds in the account
Specific services	Hourly rate or flat fee

EXAMPLE: Katie sets up in her will that her daughter Val's inheritance will be sent to the DEF Pooled Trust. Katie dies and leaves Val $100,000. The trust charges a $1,000 enrollment fee plus annual 2% management fee or a minimum fee of $1,800 a year whichever is greater. To join the trust, Val must pay $3,000 of the assets for the enrollment fee plus the first year's management fee. In addition, there are specific services that incur an additional charge like $25 for each check after the first five checks a month; $50 fee for rush service on checks; and an hourly rate of $100 per hour for care management consulting. Val needs to use ten checks a month to pay for her budgeted items, costing her an additional $1,500 each year. So, Val will pay at least $4,500 in fees the first year. Each year thereafter, the fees will be based on the amount of assets being held in trust and how many additional services Val requires.

Joining a Pooled Trust

If you find a pooled trust that you're really interested in, it's time to ask some detailed questions about how the trust will provide for your loved one.

Investigating Your Options

No government agency oversees pooled trusts to make sure they are managing assets wisely and honestly. In other words, they are unregulated. There is currently no certification or accreditation process for pooled trust programs.

As discussed above, pooled trusts vary considerably in terms of the services they offer. All offer trust management, investment services, and expertise in federal benefit resource and eligibility rules. The programs tend to differ in:

- the nature of the supplementary services offered (see "Extra Services," above)
- the relationship between a beneficiary and the trust manager
- fees, and
- what happens to money in the account when the beneficiary dies.

For this reason, it's very important to read the materials from any program you are considering and meet with a program representative to discuss the details of the program. Before you sign any papers, the program representative should carefully explain the process, including fees and the scope of services.

In the course of this process, you'll want to pay close attention to your feelings about the place you're dealing with and the people you encounter. For instance, if you get a polished presentation, you may be put off if you are more comfortable with "just plain folks"—or you may be impressed by the professionalism. If you are more confused than enlightened, it may be a sign to shop for a different program.

Here are some questions to ask before entrusting your loved one's inheritance to the program:

- Does the trust program have the financial or volunteer support of one or more well-known disability organizations?

- Does the board of directors include people with expertise or experience in disability, legal, and financial matters?

- Does the program use the services of a reputable bank, a trust company, or another financial institution as a trustee or for account management?

- Does the trustee's investment strategy make sense to you?

- Does the program give you clear and comprehensive information about how the trust operates, including its fees and services, or do you feel confused?

- Are you satisfied that the program will always know about your loved one's special needs?

- Do program staffers answer your questions in easy-to-understand language?

- Are staff members knowledgeable about federal and state benefits, laws that affect planning, and the reporting requirements imposed by SSI and Medicaid after the trust is active?

- How happy are other families who use the pooled trust? Ask the program for evaluations it's received, and talk to other families directly if possible.

- Does the trust document provide for a trust protector or trust advisory committee who has the power to replace the trustee, if necessary?

- Does the program's annual report make it clear that the program is operated in a businesslike manner? (If you're not comfortable deciphering the report, ask someone who is.)

- Is the trust financially self-sufficient, or does it depend on third-party funding that might decrease or, in the case of government funding, be withdrawn altogether? You want to be sure that the program could continue in the absence of those funds.

Signing the Agreement

Every pooled trust operates under a master trust document, which creates the special needs trust to which you'll be contributing. Master trusts contain provisions very similar to those of the special needs trust in this book, plus provisions unique to pooled trusts.

When you join the pooled trust, you sign a joinder agreement and pay the one-time nonrefundable enrollment fee described above. The joinder agreement links your loved one to the master trust provisions, describes your duties as the person supplying the money (the grantor), explains what happens if you wish to withdraw the funds later, and specifies what will be done with any funds left in your loved one's account when it terminates. Some joinder agreements also let you describe your preferences for disbursements once the trust is funded and goes into effect.

After you die, the joinder agreement becomes irrevocable, which means any funds that have been put in the account will stay there. The trustee will manage and disburse them for your loved one's benefit under the terms of the trust.

Making an Appropriate Estate Plan to Fund the Trust

You may want to sign an agreement with a pooled trust during your lifetime but wait until your death to have money go into the trust. To make that happen, all you have to do is use your will or living trust to route the property you are leaving your loved one to that pooled trust. Chapter 9 tells you how to do this.

There is, however, a risk that the trust won't in fact get funded.

EXAMPLE: Paula joins the Greater Springfield Community Trust on behalf of her sister Annabelle. She does this by signing a joinder agreement, paying a $500 setup fee, and agreeing to pay an annual renewal fee of $75 until the trust is funded with at least $25,000. Paula's plan is to fund the trust through her will when she dies.

Paula makes the renewal payments while she is alive but dies broke. When the renewal payments stop and the trust is not funded, the account is closed.

If you don't want to sign up with a pooled trust now but would like the executor of your will or the successor trustee of your living trust to explore the possibility of using a pooled trust, you can provide for this in your will or living trust. As a backup measure, as part of your estate plan you should also establish your own special needs trust to take the property if a suitable pooled trust isn't available when the time comes. (See Chapter 9.)

> **EXAMPLE:** Joe creates a special needs trust for his niece Sophie. In his will, Joe directs his executor (Sophie's sister Catherine) to try to join the ABC Pooled Trust and to place Sophie's inheritance in it. If the ABC Pooled Trust doesn't work out, he directs Catherine to place Sophie's inheritance in the special needs trust he created as a backup.

If the Pooled Trust Changes for the Worse

When selecting a pooled trust, keep in mind that the quality of the trust may change over time, For example, perhaps at the time you investigate a pooled trust it provides all the services you want, has an active and diverse volunteer board, and its fees meet your expectations. However, years later when you die, the pooled trust may have withdrawn most services, the volunteer board may have lost most of its members and might only meet twice a year, and the fees might have increased.

In this situation, there are not a lot of options for the beneficiary or his or her legal representatives. It will be difficult, if not impossible, to change pooled trusts or to move out of a trust that no longer is performing adequately. The beneficiary can end up stuck in a pooled trust that at one time did great work but by the time of funding has become a terrible institution.

After naming a pooled trust for the person with a disability in your will or living trust, you should periodically check to make sure it still meets your requirements. If not, you can change the pooled trust recipient in your will or living trust documents. However, if assets have already been transferred to the trust, you may have no way of changing the pooled trust. This will depend on the terms of the pooled trust document.

What Happens When the Trust Ends

Eventually, the pooled trust account for your loved one will no longer be necessary. The most likely scenario is that the account will end when your loved one dies. But it could also happen if Congress changes benefit laws, the pooled trust itself quits operating, or the trust runs out of money.

When the Beneficiary Dies

You may fully expect that all trust property will have been spent on your loved one by the time he or she dies. But your loved one may die sooner than expected, or if the trust account is quite large, some money may remain at the time of your loved one's death.

If there is money left, some or all of it will go to beneficiaries you name in the joinder agreement. Some of it may stay in the trust, usually to help it provide services that other trust beneficiaries might not be able to afford. This arrangement is required by many pooled trusts.

EXAMPLE: Joyce signs a joinder agreement with the XYZ Pooled Trust. The agreement provides that at her loved one's death, $300 of any money left in the trust account will be kept by the pooled trust. The rest will be paid to the beneficiaries Joyce names.

If the Pooled Trust Stops Operating

All corporations—profit and nonprofit—have the potential for eternal life, and most nonprofits have boards of directors who feel strongly about their organizations and want to keep them going if at all possible. But it's certainly possible that a particular pooled trust program will someday cease operations. There are many possible causes—financial difficulties, a failure of management, or lack of adequate membership, to name a few.

What happens to your money if the pooled trust goes out of business? Most if not all states require defunct nonprofits to distribute any remaining assets to another suitable nonprofit organization. The contract you sign with the pooled trust will probably address this question.

Pooled Trusts vs Individual Special Needs Trusts

The chart below shows some of the important differences between a pooled trust and an individual special needs trust. As you can see, in most circumstances, an individual trust will be a better fit for you and your loved one than joining a pooled trust. Pooled trusts really only make sense when there is no one in your life that you trust enough to manage money set aside for the person with a disability.

Issue	Pooled Trust	Individual Trust
Setup	You must sign a joinder agreement and the trust is provided by the organization.	You draft a trust yourself or with the help of a lawyer.
Trustee	The trustee is provided by the pooled trust.	You name a trustee to serve. This may be a trusted friend or family member, or a private professional or corporate trustee.
Costs and fees	Costs and fees include enrollment fees, ongoing management fees, and sometimes fees for specific services.	There are no fees if you name a trusted family member or friend. You will pay professional fees if you hire a private professional or corporate trustee.
Trust remainder	The pooled trust may keep some or all of the trust remainder.	The assets go to whomever you name.
Flexibility	The beneficiary most likely will have to stay with the trust, even if the trustee is doing a bad job.	You can set up terms in trust to have trustee removed or replaced if he or she is not doing a good job.
Administration	The beneficiary is stuck with trust's management team, who are often paid professionals or volunteers.	A family member, friend, or paid professional will manage the trust. A family member or friend may have to hire professional help.
Administrator dies or charity goes out of business	The agreement may cover this—if not, the state's attorney general may decide where assets go to be managed.	If the trustee dies, then the successor named in the trust takes over. If no successor is named or if the successor is not available, a court will appoint one.

Creating Your Special Needs Trust

This chapter shows you how to create a valid special needs trust. During your life, you can hold property in the trust and you can use your will, living trust, or other estate planning device—such as a life insurance policy or a transfer-on-death designation—to route property to the trust at your death.

If you want a peek at what your finished document might look like, there is a sample trust at the end of this chapter. Of course, your trust will look a little different because of the choices you make to fit your own circumstances.

SEE AN EXPERT

Get help with other kinds of special needs trusts. If you want to create a trust that will be funded with the beneficiary's own money, such as a personal injury recovery or direct inheritance (a "self-settled" trust), you'll need to hire a lawyer. You'll also need a lawyer if you want to create a special needs trust that is part of your will or living trust and that takes effect when you die. See Chapter 10 for tips on finding and working with a lawyer.

Drafting the Trust Document

Now you're ready to start. We'll go through the clauses (called "articles") in order, explaining what each one means and letting you know whether or not you need to make any choices or fill in any information.

Much of the trust document is "boilerplate," language that you must include but that you don't have to fuss with. Every special needs trust requires certain language to ensure that the SSI or Medicaid programs won't count property held in the trust as a resource of the beneficiary.

For some articles you must fill in a blank. We provide instructions and also give you a cross-reference to the chapter that discusses the particular issue. If you need some help making the decision, just flip back and read more about your options.

The easiest way to assemble your special needs trust is to use the downloadable eForms that come with this book (see Appendix D). Just modify the clauses to fit your situation. You will sign the finished product in front of a notary public. (Instructions for doing that are in Chapter 9.)

CAUTION

Don't change trust language. The trust in this chapter is designed to comply with the minimum legal requirements so that the trust doesn't interfere with the person with a disability's public benefits. To keep the trust drafting process manageable, this book doesn't offer all potential options. If you want something more than a bare-bones trust, you should consult an attorney. Otherwise, your changes might:

- interfere with the purpose of the trust
- create an inconsistency within the trust document, or
- change the numbering of the trust clauses (because of the extensive cross-referencing within the trust document).

Chapter 10 has some advice on how to go about finding a lawyer.

Naming Your Trust

The name of your special needs trust should include the name of the beneficiary.

What you need to do: Replace "[*Name of Beneficiary*]" with the name of your loved one.

Name of the Trust
The [*Name of Beneficiary*] Special Needs Trust

Article 1. Creation of the Trust

The first clause of your trust document makes it irrevocable (that is, it can't be changed). It also identifies both you (the "Grantor") and your loved one (the "Beneficiary").

This trust is designed to have just one grantor, but if you are creating the trust with another person—for example, your child's other parent—you can alter the trust to name more than one grantor. Doing so names both of you as the creators of the trust, but it doesn't give either of you any power to manage the trust; only the trustees have that power. So, while you should feel free to name more than one grantor here in Article 1, your more critical decision will be whether or not to name yourselves cotrustees in Article 4.

To name more than one grantor, put the grantors' names here in Article 1. Then go through the rest of the trust, add an "s" to every instance of "grantor" (Warning: there are a lot of them!), and make the following verb agree. For example, you would change Section 1 of Article 3 from "Grantor intends this trust…" to "Grantors intend this trust…."

What you need to do: Fill in your name(s) and the name of the beneficiary.

ARTICLE 1. Creation of Trust

[*Your name(s)*], Grantor, is creating this special needs trust for the benefit of [*name of beneficiary*], Beneficiary. This trust shall become irrevocable upon execution.

Article 2. Purpose of the Trust

Next, you state the central purpose of the trust: to provide for your loved one's special needs over and above the support and medical assistance provided by government programs. Should an agency or court be called on to interpret any part of this trust document, the purpose stated here will serve as the overarching guideline. It makes clear beyond any doubt that the trust property may never be considered available as a resource for the purpose of determining eligibility for SSI and Medicaid.

What you need to do: Decide whether or not to include a description of your loved one's disability. If you want to, use the first alternate article (shown below in Option 1), fill in the description and then delete the second alternate article. If you don't want to include a description, use the second alternate article (shown below in Option 2) and delete the first one.

Option 1: If you wish, include here a brief description of the beneficiary's disability. This will inform anyone who reads the trust document about the nature of the beneficiary's disability and clarify why the trust is being created. However, describing a disability is not legally required. Here are some examples:

- The nature of the disability is: major mental illness diagnosed as schizophrenia.
- The nature of the disability is: Down syndrome.
- The nature of the disability is: cystic fibrosis.

OPTION 1

ARTICLE 2. Purpose of Trust

Beneficiary has a disability and will likely require government assistance during Grantor's life and after Grantor's death. The nature of the disability is: _____.

Grantor creates this special needs trust to enhance Beneficiary's quality of life while at the same time preserving Beneficiary's eligibility for government support and medical assistance programs, including SSI, Medicaid, or other similar programs. Grantor intends this Declaration of Trust to be interpreted in light of this purpose.

Option 2: If you don't want to describe the disability, simply omit the second sentence of the paragraph, as shown below.

OPTION 2

ARTICLE 2. Purpose of Trust

Beneficiary has a disability and will likely require government assistance during Grantor's life and after Grantor's death. Grantor creates this special needs trust to enhance Beneficiary's quality of life while at the same time preserving Beneficiary's eligibility for government support and medical assistance programs, including SSI, Medicaid, or other similar programs. Grantor intends this Declaration of Trust to be interpreted in light of this purpose.

Article 3. Defining Special Needs

This clause explains the types of goods and services you want the trustee to be able to provide for your loved one.

The fact that something isn't mentioned in this list doesn't preclude your trustee from providing it, as long as it doesn't interfere with your loved one's eligibility for government assistance.

What you may want to do: Add items not included and delete ones that you're sure aren't necessary in your circumstances. Or you can just leave the clause as is.

ARTICLE 3. Examples of Special Needs

1. Grantor intends this trust to provide Beneficiary with goods and services to meet Beneficiary's special needs, which are needs that are not provided for by any government programs.

2. Special needs include but are not limited to: out-of-pocket medical and dental expenses; medical equipment not provided by Medicaid or similar programs; eyeglasses; exercise equipment; annual independent checkups; transportation; vehicle maintenance; vehicle insurance premiums; life insurance premiums; physical rehabilitation services not covered by Medicaid or similar programs; essential dietary needs; materials for hobbies; tickets for recreational or cultural events; musical instruments; cosmetics; home furnishings; home improvements; computer or electronic equipment; cable television; telephones; televisions; radios; cameras; trips; vacations; visits to friends; entertainment; membership in book, health, record, video, or other clubs; newspaper and magazine subscriptions; athletic training or competitions; personal care attendant or escort; vocational rehabilitation or habilitation; professional services; costs of attending or participating in meetings, conferences, seminars, or training sessions; and tuition and expenses connected with all types of technical degree programs and higher education.

Article 4. Identification of Trustees

Here you state who you want to serve as trustee of the trust. You can name one or more persons in each role as trustee or successor trustee. If you do name cotrustees, you will also need to decide whether you want them to act jointly or independently as they administer the trust. If you decide that they must work jointly, then the cotrustees will have to agree on all decisions. If you decide that they can work independently, then each may make decisions without the approval of the other cotrustee or cotrustees. (See Chapter 6 for a full discussion of the pros and cons of allowing cotrustees to act jointly or independently.)

EXAMPLE 1: When creating a special needs trust for her daughter Susan, Nora names herself and her partner, Mick, as cotrustees. Nora believes that she and Mick are both very responsible and good at communicating with each other, so in the trust document she indicates that they can act independently to administer the trust for Susan's benefit.

EXAMPLE 2: Nora names Susan's two brothers David and Mark to serve as first successor cotrustees. They will serve as cotrustees when she and Mick can no longer serve. Even though Nora thinks that she and Mick can administer the trust independently, she has her doubts about David and Mark, so she requires that all cotrustees act jointly. This means that Nora and Mick (and later, Mark and David) must make every decision about the trust together.

 SEE AN EXPERT

If you want some cotrustees to act jointly and others to act independently, you will need to hire a lawyer to draft a trust with more flexibility.

Article 4 gives the executor of your will (or the successor trustee of your living trust) the power to name a trustee for this special needs trust if none of the people you named to serve are available when you die.

This article also gives the trustee the power to resign at any time and states that if you (the grantor) have named the same person to be both a trustee or successor trustee and a remainder beneficiary, that you are aware of the potential conflict of interest. (See Chapter 6.)

What you need to do: Decide who you want to name as initial trustees and successor trustees, then fill in the blank lines of Article 4. If you're not naming any cotrustees, delete the unnecessary sections and renumber the remaining sections. To do all of this, read and follow the instructions below.

Naming the initial trustee. After the word "Trustee(s)," insert the name or names of the initial trustee or cotrustees for the trust. Most grantors serve as the initial trustee, but there are circumstances in which you might want to name someone else. See Chapter 6.

Naming successor trustees. After you've named your initial trustee or cotrustees, name the people who will take over if the initial trustee or cotrustees cannot serve. The successor trustees that you name to take over for the initial trustees are called "first successor" trustees. You can name one or more persons to serve as first successor trustee. In the clause, fill in the name or names after "First Successor Trustee(s)."

If possible, you should also name one or two additional successor trustees who will step in if your first choices for successor trustee cannot serve. The "second successor" trustee will take over, if necessary, for the first successor trustee and the "third successor" trustee will take over for the second successor trustee. Insert the names of your additional successor trustees on the corresponding lines of Section 1.

Specifying how cotrustees will act. If you decide to name more than one trustee to serve together, you must also decide how you want those cotrustees to work together to make decisions. They'll either need to act jointly or independently. (See Chapter 6.) Mark your choice on Section 3.

If you do not name cotrustees. If you decide not to name any cotrustees to serve together, remove the sections that refer to cotrustees —Sections 2, 3, 4, and 6. Then renumber the remaining sections.

ARTICLE 4. Trustees

1. The following persons or entities shall serve, in the order listed, as trustee(s) of this special needs trust:

   Trustee(s): _____

   First Successor Trustee(s): _____

   Second Successor Trustee(s): _____

   Third Successor Trustee(s): _____

2. If any person or entity named as a cotrustee or successor cotrustee is unable to serve, the trust shall be managed by the remaining cotrustees or successor cotrustees.

3. All cotrustees shall act: ☐ jointly ☐ independently.

4. Cotrustees shall cooperate with each other to carry out the trust purpose set out in Article 2, to prevent harmful and costly duplication of activities and to avoid unnecessary delay in making disbursements to Beneficiary.

5. If no successor trustee named here is available to serve, the trust protector named in this trust may name a trustee to manage the special needs trust. If there is no trust protector, the personal representative of Grantor's estate may name a trustee to manage this special needs trust. If there is no personal representative, the successor trustee of Grantor's revocable living trust, if any, may name a trustee to manage this trust. In the event there is no successor trustee of Grantor's revocable living trust, then, on petition of any interested person, a court of competent jurisdiction shall designate the successor trustee. In no event shall a court obtain jurisdiction over this trust by exercise of this provision.

6. All references to trustee in this trust document include each cotrustee named in this Article.

7. Any trustee may resign at any time. The resigning trustee shall give written notarized notice of the resignation to Beneficiary, Beneficiary's legal guardian or conservator, all affected agencies, and all persons and entities named in the trust as successor trustees or remainder beneficiaries.

8. If a remainder beneficiary is also named as a trustee or successor trustee, Grantor is aware of the potential conflict of interest and intends for the trustee or successor trustee to serve as provided for in this Declaration of Trust.

Article 5. Powers of Successor Trustees

This article puts any successor trustee in the same position as the original trustee, once a successor trustee takes over. It lets the successor trustee show third parties—banks, for example—that he or she has power to act on behalf the trust.

What you need to do: Nothing. This is just boilerplate.

ARTICLE 5. Powers of Successor Trustees

All authority and powers, including discretionary powers, conferred upon a trustee or cotrustee shall pass to all successor trustees.

Article 6. Trust Protector

This provision allows you to name an individual or a group of individuals to oversee the trustee's actions and make changes to the trust, if necessary. Whether to include this provision is up to you.

A trust protector provides flexibility when you are no longer there to manage the trust. For example, you may want to give someone the right to remove and replace a trustee who does not work out. Other common provisions allow the trust protector to modify the terms of the trust or to interpret ambiguous language in the trust document. The last section of Chapter 6 details the benefits of naming someone to look after the trust.

When choosing a trust protector, name people whom you trust completely, but whom might not be right to serve as trustee—perhaps because they are too busy or live too far away, or for another reason.

What you need to do. Decide whether you want to name a trust protector. If you decide not to, remove this clause and renumber the clauses that follow.

If you do want to name a trust protector, you will need to tailor your trust document to reflect your wishes. In Section 2, insert the name or names of the people you want to serve as a trust protector or as a trust advisory committee. Include your backup choices as "successors."

ARTICLE 6. Trust Protector

1. The function of the trust protector is to assist, if needed, in protecting the interests of Beneficiary and in achieving the objectives and intent of this trust agreement.

2. The following persons or entities shall serve, in the order listed, as trust protector of this special needs trust:

    Trust Protector: _____

    First Successor: _____

    Second Successor: _____

    Third Successor: _____

3. The trust protector shall have the authority to remove any Trustee [*choose one:* only for cause/with or without cause] and appoint a Trustee under this agreement. Whenever the office of Trustee is vacant and no successor Trustee is effectively named, the trust protector shall appoint an individual or a corporate fiduciary to serve as Trustee familiar with the administration of special needs trusts.

    A trust protector may not appoint himself or herself as a Trustee and a trust protector may not simultaneously serve as both trust protector and Trustee. This is in keeping with the intent and purpose that the trust protector's only interest will be to protect the financial resources governed by this agreement and the intent that the assets of this trust agreement not be considered income or resources for all needs-based and entitlement benefits from any government agency.

4. The trust protector may amend any provision of this agreement to:

    (a.) Add or modify terms of the trust so that the trust will protect the financial resources governed by this agreement and to comply with the intent of this trust that trust assets shall not be considered income or resources for all needs-based and entitlement public benefits from any government agency for which the trust beneficiary is eligible;

    (b.) Alter the administrative and investment powers of Trustee to comply with any changes in the law;

ARTICLE 6. Trust Protector

(c.) Reflect tax or other legal changes that affect trust administration; and

(d.) Correct ambiguities, including scrivener errors that might otherwise require court construction or reformation.

Notwithstanding the foregoing, our trust protector shall not amend this agreement in any manner that would limit or alter the rights of Beneficiary in any trust assets held by the trust before the amendment, unless the purpose of the amendment is to modify an existing provision in the trust that defeats the trust's intent of preserving public benefits.

An amendment made by the trust protector in good faith shall be conclusive on all persons interested in the trust and the trust protector shall not be liable for the consequences of any amendment or for not having amended the trust. An amendment to this agreement shall be made in a written instrument signed by the trust protector. The trust protector shall deliver a copy of the amendment to the trust beneficiary, the trust beneficiary's legal representative, and the currently serving Trustee.

5. The books and records of this trust agreement, including all documentation, inventories and accountings, shall be open and available for inspection by the trust protector at all reasonable times.

6. Any trust protector (including successors) shall have the right to appoint a successor trust protectors in writing. Such appointment shall take effect on the death, resignation, or incapacity of the appointing trust protector. If there are successor trust protectors named in this agreement, the appointment of a successor trust protector under this subsection shall take effect only if and when all trust protectors named fail to qualify or cease to act.

7. A trust protector may resign by giving notice to Beneficiary and to the trustee then serving. Such resignation shall take effect on the date set forth in the notice, which shall not be earlier than 30 days after the date of delivery of the notice of resignation, unless an earlier effective date shall be agreed to by the trustee.

Next, decide which of the optional powers you want to include. Here are your choices:

- Section 3, the power to remove and replace a trustee
- Section 4, the power to amend the trust, or
- Section 5, the power to review the trustee's records.

Delete any section that you don't want to include, and then renumber the remaining sections, if necessary.

Also, if you decide to give the trust protector the power to remove and replace a trustee in Section 3, you must decide whether the trust protector needs to have a good reason to do so. In the first sentence, include "only for cause" if you want the trust protector to be able to remove a trustee only for a justifiable reason. Or include "with or without cause" if you want the trust protector to be able to remove the trustee for any reason, regardless of the trustee's performance.

Article 7. Contributions to the Trust

This provision requires the person serving as trustee to keep the trust as a third-party trust—that is, one funded exclusively with property from someone other than the beneficiary. None of the beneficiary's own assets may be added to the trust.

It's fine, though, to accept property from other third-party sources. For example, once the trust is operational, a relative or friend may wish to throw some money the beneficiary's way. Because a gift made directly to the beneficiary might interfere with the beneficiary's eligibility for SSI and Medicaid, the friend or relative could instead put the money in the special needs trust by giving it to the trustee.

 CAUTION

This is crucial: If the beneficiary comes into some money—for instance, wins the lottery or a lawsuit, or receives a gift or inheritance— those funds may not be put into this trust. If any of the beneficiary's property were added to the trust, all the trust assets might be considered the beneficiary's property—and the trust would no longer serve its purpose.

Instead, a separate trust should be established for the beneficiary's own funds, with the help of a lawyer. (See Chapter 10 for tips on finding a lawyer.)

What you need to do: Nothing. This is just boilerplate.

ARTICLE 7. Contributions to the Trust

Trustee shall accept contributions to the trust from any person or entity. However, Trustee shall not accept any assets that are owned by Beneficiary, including public assistance, Social Security benefits, or any other earned or unearned income.

Article 8. Use of Principal and Income

This article requires that income earned by trust assets be kept in the trust and not be distributed to the beneficiary. The reason is that income distributed to the beneficiary would be deducted from the beneficiary's SSI grant and would interfere with the beneficiary's eligibility for SSI and Medicaid.

For bookkeeping purposes, the retained income must be used first when the trustee spends trust money for the beneficiary's benefit. This way, the income spent for the beneficiary can be taxed as the beneficiary's income (even though he or she doesn't actually get it). That's desirable because typically the beneficiary's income tax rate is much lower than the trust income tax rate. (See Chapter 5 for more on the rules governing income earned by a special needs trust.)

What you need to do: Nothing.

ARTICLE 8. Use of Principal and Income

Income earned from trust property shall be retained in the trust to be used for trust purposes. When making disbursements for Beneficiary's benefit, Trustee shall keep adequate records to show that current and accumulated trust income is used first, and then trust principal.

Article 9. Trustee's Duty to Cooperate in Seeking Government Benefits

This part of the trust document requires that the person serving as trustee cooperate with the beneficiary (or his or her legal representative) to secure all possible government benefits for the beneficiary. The greater the benefits, the longer the trust funds will last.

What you need to do: Nothing.

ARTICLE 9. Trustee's Duty to Cooperate in Seeking Government Benefits

Trustee shall cooperate with Beneficiary by providing information that is necessary for Beneficiary to obtain or maintain eligibility for needs-based public benefits and entitlement programs, including, but not limited to, Social Security payments, Supplemental Security Income, Social Security Disability Insurance, Veterans Administration benefits, HUD housing benefits, Medicare, and Medicaid. However, Trustee shall not be responsible to Beneficiary to obtain or maintain Beneficiary's eligibility for these programs.

Article 10. Trustee's Discretion Over Disbursements

This provision is the heart and soul of your special needs trust. It gives the person serving as trustee unlimited discretion to make disbursements, as long as the distributions:

- are consistent with the trust purpose described in Article 2
- are made for the benefit of the beneficiary (though it's okay for others to benefit indirectly), and
- won't deprive the beneficiary of eligibility for SSI, Medicaid, or similar programs.

What you need to do: Nothing.

ARTICLE 10. Trustee's Discretion Over Disbursements

Trustee shall have complete discretion in how the trust property is used, provided that the property is used only for the purpose of helping Beneficiary by providing Beneficiary with goods and services that supplement those provided by SSI, Medicaid, or similar programs, and never for a purpose that will eliminate Beneficiary's eligibility for those programs unless it is in the best interests of Beneficiary to do so. All actions of Trustee shall be directed toward carrying out the primary purpose of this trust to supplement Beneficiary's public benefits. Trustee's discretion to carry out this purpose is absolute. Hence, while Trustee is to be guided by the needs of Beneficiary, as determined by Trustee, in Trustee's sole and absolute discretion, Trustee is not obliged to make any specific distributions under the terms of this trust. Because Trustee shall be solely responsible for determining what discretionary distributions may be made from this trust, Beneficiary does not have access to principal or income of the trust or authority to direct distributions from the trust for any purpose.

Article 11. Trustee's Duty to File Tax Returns and Make Reports

This article requires the person serving as trustee to:

- prepare and file all required trust tax returns
- assemble all information necessary to prepare reports required by government agencies as a condition of eligibility for SSI and Medicaid
- submit all information required by government agencies as a condition of eligibility for SSI and Medicaid or, alternatively, turn over the information to the beneficiary if he or she wants to submit it, and
- share basic information about trust activity with the beneficiary, a guardian or conservator if any, and other interested parties such as a person or an entity who has been designated by a government agency to receive funds on the beneficiary's behalf (a representative payee).

The required information about trust activity includes:

- income and contributions (for example, money contributed by a relative) received by the trust
- what trust income and assets were spent on, and
- the current amount of money in the trust.

This work must be done anyway to compute annual taxes and make reports required by SSI and Medicaid. This article requires that the people most interested in the trust be included in the information loop.

What you need to do: Nothing.

ARTICLE 11. Trustee's Duty to File Tax Returns and Make Reports

1. Trustee shall prepare and file all required trust tax returns.

2. Trustee shall provide to Beneficiary, or Beneficiary's legal guardian, conservator, representative payee, or agent, if any, all information necessary for the reports required by a government agency as a condition of Beneficiary's continued eligibility for SSI, Medicaid, and other similar benefits.

3. Trustee shall annually provide Beneficiary, Beneficiary's legal guardian, conservator, representative payee, or agent, if any, and the remainder beneficiaries named in Article 13, with written information about trust activity, including an accounting of current trust assets, income earned by the trust, contributions from outside sources made to the trust, disbursements made to meet Beneficiary's special needs, and an accounting of all purchases by Trustee.

4. Upon request, Trustee shall provide the persons named in Section 3 of this article with copies of the trust's annual income tax returns.

Article 12. Termination of the Trust

At some point, the person serving as trustee will have to end the trust. This part of the trust document describes what circumstances justify ending the trust and what the trustee should do with any money left in the trust. (Wrapping up the trust is discussed in Chapter 1.)

What you need to do: Nothing.

ARTICLE 12. Termination of the Trust

1. Trustee shall terminate this trust if:
    - in his or her sole discretion, the Trustee determines that the value of the trust property makes it impractical to administer the trust, or
    - in his or her sole discretion, the Trustee determines that changes in Beneficiary's disability make a special needs trust unnecessary, or
    - Beneficiary dies.

2. If Trustee terminates the trust for any reason other than Beneficiary's death, upon termination of the trust, and after all debts and taxes legally owed by the trust have been paid, Trustee shall distribute the trust property and accumulated income to Beneficiary or Beneficiary's legal guardian, conservator, representative payee, or agent, if any, unless such distribution would deprive Beneficiary of needed government benefits. In that event, Trustee shall distribute as much of the property as possible to Beneficiary consistent with maintaining the benefits and distribute the rest of the property to the remainder beneficiaries named in Article 13.

3. If Trustee terminates the trust because of Beneficiary's death, the trust property and accumulated income shall be distributed to the remainder beneficiaries as set out in Article 13 after all debts and taxes legally owed by the trust have been paid.

4. Any termination of the trust shall be in writing and notarized. Trustee shall provide copies of the termination to Beneficiary, Beneficiary's legal guardian or conservator, and all persons and entities named in the trust as successor trustees or remainder beneficiaries.

Article 13. Remainder Beneficiaries

Here, you name someone to inherit any property left in the trust after it's terminated. This "remainder" beneficiary can be one or more people or organizations. You can also name alternate remainder beneficiaries.

Usually, the trust ends when the beneficiary dies. But the remainder beneficiary could also inherit if the trust ends for another reason but some trust property can't be given to the beneficiary because it would interfere with eligibility for SSI or Medicaid.

If the remainder beneficiary is under 18 when he or she inherits trust property, an adult must manage the property. It's the trustee's job to act as "custodian" under the Uniform Transfers to Minors Act or pick someone else to do it. A custodian, like a trustee, must manage, invest, and spend the money on behalf of the young beneficiary. Generally, the custodianship ends when the remainder beneficiary reaches age 21. (See Chapter 5 for more on this.)

Finally, this article restates that the person serving as trustee must act in the beneficiary's best interest and always put that interest ahead of the remainder beneficiary's interest. Because every disbursement from the trust for the beneficiary's benefit means there is less money left over for the remainder beneficiaries, a natural conflict of interest exists. This conflict is most evident if the trustee is also the remainder beneficiary, which is common but best avoided. (See Chapter 6.) Regardless of any such conflict, the trustee is duty-bound to always put the interests of the primary beneficiary first.

What you need to do: Fill in the names of the remainder beneficiaries (Section 1) and alternates (Section 2). If there's a chance that any of these people could inherit trust property before they're adults, in Section 5 fill in the state in which you (or the beneficiary) lives. If not, you can delete all of Section 5.

CAUTION

Special rules for South Carolina and Vermont residents. These two states have not adopted the Uniform Transfers to Minors Act, so you cannot direct your trustee to serve as a custodian for a young remainder beneficiary. You'll need to omit Section 5 of Article 13. If you want to name a minor as residuary beneficiary, see a lawyer for help.

ARTICLE 13. Remainder Beneficiaries

1. If Trustee terminates this special needs trust, and there are trust assets that Trustee does not distribute to Beneficiary under the terms of Article 12, Trustee shall distribute the remaining trust principal and accumulated income, after all debts and taxes legally owed by the trust have been paid, to [*names of remainder beneficiary(ies)*].

2. If the remainder beneficiary or beneficiaries named in Section 1 of this article fails or fail to survive Beneficiary by 30 days, Trustee shall distribute the property to [*names of alternate remainder beneficiary(ies)*].

3. If the remainder beneficiary or beneficiaries named in Section 2 of this article fails or fail to survive Beneficiary by 30 days, Trustee shall distribute property to Beneficiary's heirs at law.

4. While administering this special needs trust, Trustee shall in all cases exercise discretion in accordance with Article 10 and without regard to the interests of any remainder beneficiary named in this article.

5. If, when a remainder beneficiary inherits property under this article, he or she is not yet 18 years old, or, in the opinion of Trustee, is unable to prudently manage the property to be distributed and is under the age of 21, Trustee shall either (a) retain that beneficiary's share as a custodian under the Uniform Transfers to Minors Act of [*state*] , or (b) name another person to serve as custodian for the property under that Act and distribute the property to that custodian. The custodianship shall end when the remainder beneficiary turns 21 unless the law requires it to end at age 18. When the custodianship ends, the custodian shall distribute any remaining custodial property to the beneficiary.

Article 14. Trustee Powers

This long clause spells out the powers that the person serving as trustee will have while administering the trust. The idea here is to give the trustee maximum authority to deal with the trust and trust property in a way that will provide the most benefit for the beneficiary, consistent with Article 2 (which states the purpose of the trust, to benefit your loved one and preserve eligibility for SSI and Medicaid) and Article 10 (which gives the trustee unfettered discretion over how trust funds are spent).

What you need to do: Nothing.

ARTICLE 14. Trustee Powers

Trustee shall, in addition to the powers given by law, have the following powers applicable to all property held in trust, whether principal or income, and exercisable without order of any court that has jurisdiction over Beneficiary:

1. To retain any property transferred to this trust, and to make such investments and reinvestments and in such proportions as Trustee considers beneficial and prudent in light of the trust purposes set out in Article 2.

2. To (1) participate in any merger or reorganization affecting securities held hereunder at any time; (2) deposit stock under voting agreements; (3) exercise any option to subscribe for stocks, bonds, or debentures; and (4) grant proxies, discretionary or otherwise, to vote shares of stock, provided that the trustee's investment decisions shall be guided by the Prudent Investor Act as enacted by the state where this trust is administered, or if it has not been so enacted, by the Uniform Prudent Investor Act as originally published by the National Conference of Commissioners on Uniform State Laws.

3. To manage, operate, or repair real estate or other property and to lease real estate and other property upon such terms and for such period as Trustee deems advisable.

4. To buy or sell (and to grant options for the sale of) any real or personal property at public or private sale for such prices and upon such terms as Trustee thinks proper.

5. To purchase, maintain, improve, or replace a residence, or any interest in it, where Beneficiary may reside, including any portion of the residence that may be owned by a family member.

ARTICLE 14. Trustee Powers (cont'd)

6. To permit any person to reside at any real property held in this trust at which Beneficiary is residing, on such terms as Trustee deems proper, for the purpose of providing care, supervision, or simple companionship to Beneficiary.

7. To seek court permission to amend the trust only if necessary to fulfill the trust purposes set out in Article 2.

8. To make loans, but not gifts, for Beneficiary's benefit, provided the loans do not interfere with the trust purposes set out in Article 2.

9. To pay premiums to provide supplementary health insurance for Beneficiary or life insurance policies that may be owned or acquired by the trust. If Trustee is also the insured of any life insurance policy owned by the trust, then Trustee may exercise all rights and incidents of ownership with respect to such policy only in a fiduciary capacity, including the power to change the beneficiary, to surrender or cancel the policy, to assign the policy, to revoke any assignment, to pledge a policy for a loan, or to obtain a loan against the surrender value of the policy from the insurer.

10. To start or defend such litigation with respect to the trust or any property of the trust as Trustee deems advisable, at the expense of the trust.

11. To carry, at the expense of the trust, insurance of such kinds and in such amounts as Trustee deems advisable both to protect the trust property against any damage or loss and to protect Trustee against liability with respect to third persons.

12. To prepare and file returns and arrange for payment with respect to all local, state, federal, and foreign taxes incident to this trust, to prepare all necessary fiduciary income tax returns, and to make all necessary and appropriate elections.

13. To prepare and, if necessary, file all reports required of providers of government benefits received by Beneficiary, and to prepare and distribute annual reports of trust activity to Beneficiary and any named remainder beneficiaries.

14. Upon termination of the trust, to pay all debts and taxes determined by the trustee to be legally owed by the trust.

15. To hire attorneys, accountants, investment advisers, financial advisers, tax preparation services, and any other experts should Trustee, in Trustee's unfettered discretion, determine such expertise to be necessary for proper management of the trust.

ARTICLE 14. Trustee Powers (cont'd)

16. To appoint one or more persons or agencies to serve as successor trustee in case no other trustees or successor trustees named in this trust are available to serve. Such appointment shall be made in writing and notarized. Trustee shall provide copies of the appointment to Beneficiary, Beneficiary's legal guardian or conservator, and all persons and entities named in the trust as successor trustees or remainder beneficiaries.

Article 15. Trustee Compensation

The issue of compensation is most problematic when you choose a friend or relative to handle the trustee chores.

Although your choice for successor trustee may initially turn down your offer of compensation, this may change down the road; serving as a trustee can be a time-consuming job. So this trust document entitles the person serving as trustee to reimbursement for out-of-pocket costs and reasonable payment for services rendered. The trustee determines what is "reasonable."

There is no easy way to define reasonable fees. You just need to trust your trustee—and given that you are asking him or her to take on such an important job, you surely do.

 SEE AN EXPERT

If you'd rather set out a definite fee, see a lawyer. If you have concerns about this arrangement, consult an attorney about customizing your trust document to address the issue of the trustee's compensation.

If you choose a corporate or professional successor trustee, you will be told about the trustee's fee. Most charge a flat rate—usually a percent of the property in the trust. (See Chapter 6.) Some add extra fees for particular actions, such as $50 per disbursement or $25 per phone conversation with the beneficiary. If you're paying a professional trustee, you can add this to the end of the last sentence of the clause: "unless the compensation has been set out in a written agreement between Grantor and Trustee."

What you need to do: Nothing. Unless you're using a professional trustee, in which case, add the clause described in the paragraph above.

ARTICLE 15. Trustee Compensation

Trustee shall be entitled to reasonable compensation, from trust assets, commensurate with the services actually performed, and to reimbursement for expenses properly incurred. Trustee shall determine what compensation is reasonable by referring to the fees charged for similar services in the community where Trustee is serving.

Article 16. Spendthrift Provisions

This clause puts the trust property off-limits to everyone but the person serving as trustee, including the beneficiary. It prevents the beneficiary from transferring his or her interest in the trust to a third party, and protects trust assets from being grabbed by a creditor if the beneficiary is on the losing end of a lawsuit or files for bankruptcy. It also makes clear to SSI, Medicaid, and similar benefit programs that the trust property and income are unavailable to the beneficiary and that the trustee may use them only for the purposes stated in the trust document.

What you need to do: Nothing.

ARTICLE 16. Spendthrift Provisions

1. Beneficiary has no right or power, whether alone or in conjunction with others in whatever capacity, to amend, revoke, or terminate this special needs trust. No interest in the income or principal of this trust may be anticipated, assigned, encumbered, or subject to any creditor's claim or legal process.

2. Because trust funds will be conserved and maintained for Beneficiary's special needs, no part of the income or principal shall be construed as part of Beneficiary's "estate" or be subject to the claims of voluntary or involuntary creditors for the provision of care and services (including residential care) to or for Beneficiary by any city, county, or state government; the federal government; or any public or private agency except as otherwise provided in this trust instrument.

Article 17. Bond

This article states that the person serving as trustee does not need to obtain a bond. In the world of trusts, a bond is a kind of insurance policy that would cover losses to the trust if the trustee embezzled trust funds or otherwise violated the duty of trust owed to the beneficiary.

With a special needs trust, there is rarely need for a bond. Here's why:

• You should have full faith in the person you've chosen as trustee and successor trustee.

• Bonds will be paid with trust money.

• Something in the successor trustee's background—a bankruptcy, perhaps, or an old criminal conviction—might make it difficult or even impossible to obtain a bond except at an exorbitant cost. This could prevent your choice from serving, a result you might not want.

SEE AN EXPERT

If you want a bond, get help from an attorney. If you would gain peace of mind by requiring a bond and you're not concerned about the cost, see a lawyer.

What you need to do: Nothing.

ARTICLE 17. Bond

Unless required by a court of competent jurisdiction or a trust protector, Trustee and Successor Trustees are not required to post a bond.

Article 18. Photocopies

This provision makes it clear that a copy of the trust carries the same legal weight as the original. Because there is only one original, it's possible that somewhere down the line a successor trustee will have only a copy and will need to use it to do business in the name of the trust.

What you need to do: Nothing.

ARTICLE 18. Photocopies

All photocopies of this Declaration of Trust shall carry the same legal weight as the original.

Article 19. Trustee Not Liable for Good-Faith Actions

This clause states that a trustee who acts in good faith won't be personally liable for losses caused by his or her actions. (See Chapter 6 for more on the trustee's fiduciary duty.)

What you need to do: Nothing.

ARTICLE 19. Trustee Not Liable for Good-Faith Actions

A trustee of any kind nominated by this document shall not be liable to any beneficiary for the trustee's acts or omissions, except in cases of willful misconduct, bad faith, or gross negligence.

Certification by Grantor

A few legal formalities remain. You, any trustees other than yourself, and the notary will sign the trust. Your signature certifies that you are the maker of the trust. The signatures of any trustees other than yourself certify their willingness to serve in the role of trustee. When you sign the certification in front of a notary, your trust becomes legal.

What you need to do: First, in the section labeled "Certification by Grantor," insert your name under the signature line. Then, if you named yourself as trustee, remove the italics and brackets so that after your name are a comma and the words "Grantor and Trustee." If you named someone other than yourself as initial trustee, after your name, remove the brackets and the word "Trustee" so that only a comma and the word "Grantor" appear after your name. If there is another grantor, repeat this line for the second grantor. Do not sign the trust yet.

Certification by Grantor

I certify that I have read this Declaration of Trust and that it correctly states the terms and conditions under which the trust property is to be held, managed, and disposed of by Trustee, and I approve the Declaration of Trust.

Dated: _____

[*Your Name*], Grantor [*and Trustee*]: _____

Certification of Trustee

This section documents that the person you name as initial trustee (if other than yourself) agrees to serve in that role. Legally, this section isn't required, but it's a good way to show that the trustee has agreed to serve.

What you need to do: If you named only yourself as initial trustee, delete this entire section. Otherwise, insert the name of the initial trustee or cotrustee under the signature line. If you named only one initial trustee (other than yourself), change every instance of "I/we" to "I." If you named more than one person (other than yourself) to serve as cotrustees, change all instances of "I/we" to "we" and insert a signature line for each cotrustee.

Certification of Trustees

[*I/We*] certify that [*I/we*] have read the [*Name of Beneficiary*] Special Needs Trust, and, having been appointed as Trustee(s) by Grantor, [*I/we*] agree to serve as Trustee(s) and to manage the trust property under the trust's terms and conditions.

Dated: _____

_____

[*Name of Trustee*], Trustee

_____

[*Name of Trustee*], Trustee

CAUTION

Special rules for Florida trusts. If you're finalizing your trust in Florida, you must have two witnesses sign it. See Chapter 9 for details.

Notary's Acknowledgment

In this section, the notary public will certify that he or she watched you sign the trust.

What you need to do: The notary will probably have a form for this, but you may want to bring the form we've appended to the trust, just in case. If you do bring it, keep it on a separate page from the rest of the trust.

Making the Trust Legal and Effective

Congratulations! If you've worked your way through all of those clauses, you should now have the special needs trust language you want. To make your trust legal, you (and any other initial trustees) now need to sign the trust document in front of a notary. After that you will obtain a taxpayer ID number and open a bank account for the trust. Read Chapter 9 for details about each of these tasks.

Keeping the Special Needs Trust Up to Date

Make it a point to review the special needs trust every few years. Changes in the law or in your loved one's condition may require you to make a change. For example, if a new SSI rule makes the special needs trust obsolete or if your loved one no longer needs government aid, you, as trustee, would need to terminate the trust under its termination clause (Article 12) or seek a court's permission to amend it. Or, if you can no longer serve as trustee and none of your named successor trustees are available, you can choose new successor trustees.

The good news is that SSI and Medicaid rules regarding third-party special needs trusts (the kind covered in this book) have not changed significantly over the past 20 years. SSI and Medicaid rules regarding the treatment of income and resources have changed somewhat more frequently, but these changes have had little effect on third-party special needs trusts.

Of course, the fact that this area of the law has been stable in the past doesn't mean that a cash-strapped federal or state government won't change the rules in the future. Chapter 10 tells you how to stay current on the rules affecting third-party special needs trusts.

Hiring a Lawyer to Keep You Up to Speed

Most lawyers who specialize in drafting special needs trusts offer updating services as part of their overall package. The lawyers periodically notify their clients to come in for a checkup—often for a fee. Clients are also notified if important changes in SSI and Medicaid rules occur. These update services are intended to give the clients peace of mind that comes with having a knowledgeable professional looking out for their interests. You'll have to decide whether or not this service is worth the price to you. See Chapter 10 for more information on finding lawyers who specialize in this area.

Sample Special Needs Trust

Here is a sample of a special needs trust. It was made for someone else, so it won't match your trust exactly, but it should give you a good idea of what your final document will look like.

The Bessie Escobar Special Needs Trust

ARTICLE 1. CREATION OF TRUST

Gloria C. Escobar, Grantor, is creating this special needs trust for the benefit of Bessie Escobar, Beneficiary. This trust shall become irrevocable upon execution.

ARTICLE 2. PURPOSE OF TRUST

Beneficiary has a disability and will likely require government assistance during Grantor's life and after Grantor's death. Grantor creates this special needs trust to enhance Beneficiary's quality of life while at the same time preserving Beneficiary's eligibility for government support and medical assistance programs, including SSI, Medicaid, or other similar programs. Grantor intends this Declaration of Trust to be interpreted in light of this purpose.

ARTICLE 3. EXAMPLES OF SPECIAL NEEDS

1. Grantor intends this trust to provide Beneficiary with goods and services to meet Beneficiary's special needs, which are needs that are not provided for by any government programs.

2. Special needs include but are not limited to: out-of-pocket medical and dental expenses; medical equipment not provided by Medicaid or similar programs; eyeglasses; exercise equipment; annual independent checkups; transportation; vehicle maintenance; vehicle insurance premiums; life insurance premiums; physical rehabilitation services not covered by Medicaid or similar programs; essential dietary needs; materials for hobbies; tickets for recreational or cultural events; musical instruments; cosmetics; home furnishings; home improvements; computer or electronic equipment; cable television; telephones; televisions; radios; cameras; trips; vacations; visits to friends; entertainment; membership in book, health, record, video, or other clubs; newspaper and magazine subscriptions; athletic training or competitions; personal care attendant or escort; vocational rehabilitation or habilitation; professional services; costs of attending or participating in meetings, conferences, seminars, or training sessions; and tuition and expenses connected with all types of technical degree programs and higher education.

ARTICLE 4. TRUSTEES

1. The following persons or entities shall serve, in the order listed, as trustee(s) of this special needs trust:

   Trustee(s): Gloria C. Escobar and Richard Sanchez

   First Successor Trustee(s): Jaime L. Sanchez

   Second Successor Trustee(s): Lola S. Sanchez

2. If Gloria C. Escobar is unavailable to serve, Rafael M. Escobar shall serve as a cotrustee instead.

3. All cotrustees shall act: [X] jointly [ ] independently.

4. Cotrustees shall cooperate with each other to carry out the trust purpose set out in Article 2, to prevent harmful and costly duplication of activities, and to avoid unnecessary delay in making disbursements to Beneficiary.

5. If no successor trustee named here is available to serve, the trust protector named in this trust may name a trustee to manage the special needs trust. If there is no trust protector, the personal representative of Grantor's estate may name a trustee to manage this special needs trust. If there is no personal representative, the successor trustee of Grantor's revocable living trust, if any, may name a trustee to manage this trust. In the event there is no successor trustee of Grantor's revocable living trust, then, on petition of any interested person, a court of competent jurisdiction shall designate the successor Trustee. In no event shall a court obtain jurisdiction over this trust by exercise of this provision.

6. All references to trustee in this trust document include each cotrustee named in this article.

7. Any trustee may resign at any time. The resigning trustee shall give written notarized notice of the resignation to Beneficiary, Beneficiary's legal guardian or conservator, all affected agencies, and all persons and entities named in the trust as successor trustees or remainder beneficiaries.

8. If a remainder beneficiary is also named as a trustee or successor trustee, Grantor is aware of the potential conflict of interest and intends for the trustee or successor trustee to serve as provided for in this Declaration of Trust.

ARTICLE 5. POWERS OF SUCCESSOR TRUSTEES

All authority and powers, including discretionary powers, conferred upon a trustee or cotrustee shall pass to all successor trustees.

ARTICLE 6. TRUST PROTECTOR

1. The function of the trust protector is to assist, if needed, in protecting the interests of Beneficiary and in achieving the objectives and intent of this trust agreement.

2. The following persons or entities shall serve, in the order listed, as trust protector of this special needs trust:

    Trust Protector: Stephen Brust
    First Successor: Roger Zelazny
    Second Successor: Patrick Rothfuss

3. The trust protector shall have the authority to remove any Trustee with or without cause and appoint a Trustee under this agreement. Whenever the office of Trustee is vacant and no successor Trustee is effectively named, the trust protector shall appoint an individual or a corporate fiduciary to serve as Trustee familiar with the administration of special needs trusts.

    A trust protector may not appoint himself or herself as a Trustee and a trust protector may not simultaneously serve as both trust protector and Trustee. This is in keeping with the intent and purpose that the trust protector's only interest will be to protect the financial resources governed by this agreement and the intent that the assets of this trust agreement not be considered income or resources for all needs-based and entitlement benefits from any government agency.

4. The trust protector may amend any provision of this agreement to:

    (a) Add or modify terms of the trust so that the trust will protect the financial resources governed by this agreement and to comply with the intent of this trust that trust assets shall not be considered income or resources for all needs-based and entitlement public benefits from any government agency for which the trust beneficiary is eligible;

(b) Alter the administrative and investment powers of Trustee to comply with any changes in the law;

(c) Reflect tax or other legal changes that affect trust administration; and

(d) Correct ambiguities, including scrivener errors that might otherwise require court construction or reformation.

Notwithstanding the foregoing, our trust protector shall not amend this agreement in any manner that would limit or alter the rights of Beneficiary in any trust assets held by the trust before the amendment, unless the purpose of the amendment is to modify an existing provision in the trust that defeats the trust's intent of preserving public benefits.

An amendment made by the trust protector in good faith shall be conclusive on all persons interested in the trust and the trust protector shall not be liable for the consequences of any amendment or for not having amended the trust. An amendment to this agreement shall be made in a written instrument signed by the trust protector. The trust protector shall deliver a copy of the amendment to the trust beneficiary, the trust beneficiary's legal representative, and the currently serving Trustee.

5. The books and records of this trust agreement, including all documentation, inventories and accountings, shall be open and available for inspection by the trust protector at all reasonable times.

6. Any trust protector (including successors) shall have the right to appoint a successor trust protector in writing. Such appointment shall take effect on the death, resignation, or incapacity of the appointing trust protector. If there are successor trust protectors named in this agreement, the appointment of a successor trust protector under this subsection shall take effect only if and when all trust protectors named fail to qualify or cease to act.

7. A trust protector may resign by giving notice to Beneficiary and to the trustee then serving. Such resignation shall take effect on the date set forth in the notice, which shall not be earlier than 30 days after the date of delivery of the notice of resignation, unless an earlier effective date shall be agreed to by the trustee.

ARTICLE 7. CONTRIBUTIONS TO THE TRUST

Trustee shall accept contributions to the trust from any person or entity. However, Trustee shall not accept any assets that are owned by Beneficiary, including public assistance, Social Security benefits, or any other earned or unearned income.

ARTICLE 8. USE OF PRINCIPAL AND INCOME

Income earned from trust property shall be retained in the trust to be used for trust purposes. When making disbursements for Beneficiary's benefit, Trustee shall keep adequate records to show that current and accumulated trust income is used first, and then trust principal.

ARTICLE 9. TRUSTEE'S DUTY TO COOPERATE IN SEEKING OF GOVERNMENT BENEFITS

Trustee shall cooperate with Beneficiary by providing information that is necessary for Beneficiary to obtain or maintain eligibility for needs-based public benefits and entitlement programs, including, but not limited to, Social Security payments, Supplemental Security Income, Social Security Disability Insurance, Veterans Administration benefits, HUD housing benefits, Medicare, and Medicaid. However, Trustee shall not be responsible to the Beneficiary to obtain or maintain Beneficiary's eligibility for these programs.

ARTICLE 10. TRUSTEE'S DISCRETION OVER DISBURSEMENTS

Trustee shall have complete discretion in how the trust property is used, provided that the property is used only for the purpose of helping Beneficiary by providing Beneficiary with goods and services that supplement those provided by SSI, Medicaid, or similar programs, and never for a purpose that will eliminate Beneficiary's eligibility for those programs unless it is in the best interests of Beneficiary to do so. All actions of Trustee shall be directed toward carrying out the primary purpose of this trust to supplement Beneficiary's public benefits. Trustee's discretion to carry out this purpose is absolute. Hence, while Trustee is to be guided by the needs of Beneficiary, as determined by Trustee, in Trustee's sole and absolute discretion, Trustee is not obliged to make any specific distributions under the terms of this trust. Because Trustee shall be solely responsible for determining what discretionary distributions may be made from this trust, Beneficiary does not have access to principal or income of the trust or authority to direct distributions from the trust for any purpose.

ARTICLE 11. TRUSTEE'S DUTY TO FILE TAX RETURNS AND MAKE REPORTS

1. Trustee shall prepare and file all required trust tax returns.

2. Trustee shall provide to Beneficiary, or Beneficiary's legal guardian, conservator, representative payee, or agent, if any, all information necessary for the reports required by a government agency as a condition of the Beneficiary's continued eligibility for SSI, Medicaid, and other similar benefits.

3. Trustee shall annually provide Beneficiary, Beneficiary's legal guardian, conservator, representative payee, or agent, if any, and the remainder beneficiaries named in Article 13, with written information about trust activity, including an accounting of current trust assets, income earned by the trust, contributions from outside sources made to the trust, disbursements made to meet Beneficiary's special needs, and an accounting of all purchases by Trustee.

4. Upon request, Trustee shall provide the persons named in Section 3 of this article with copies of the trust's annual income tax returns.

ARTICLE 12. TERMINATION OF THE TRUST

1. Trustee shall terminate this trust if:

   • in his or her sole discretion the Trustee determines that the value of the trust property makes it impractical to administer the trust, or

   • in his or her sole discretion Trustee determines that changes in Beneficiary's disability make a special needs trust unnecessary, or

   • Beneficiary dies.

2. If Trustee terminates the trust for any reason other than Beneficiary's death, upon termination of the trust, and after all debts and taxes legally owed by the trust have been paid, Trustee shall distribute the trust property and accumulated income to Beneficiary or Beneficiary's legal guardian, conservator, representative payee, or agent, if any, unless such distribution would deprive Beneficiary of needed government benefits. In that event, Trustee shall distribute as much of the property as possible to Beneficiary consistent with maintaining the benefits and distribute the rest of the property to the remainder beneficiaries named in Article 13.

3. If Trustee terminates the trust because of Beneficiary's death, the trust property and accumulated income shall be distributed to the remainder beneficiaries as set out in Article 13 after all debts and taxes legally owed by the trust have been paid.

4. Any termination of the trust shall be in writing and notarized. Trustee shall provide copies of the termination to Beneficiary, Beneficiary's legal guardian or conservator, and all persons and entities named in the trust as successor trustees or remainder beneficiaries.

ARTICLE 13. REMAINDER BENEFICIARIES

1. If Trustee terminates this special needs trust, and there are trust assets that Trustee does not distribute to Beneficiary under the terms of Article 12, Trustee shall distribute the remaining trust principal and accumulated income, after all debts and taxes legally owed by the trust have been paid, to Lola S. Sanchez.

2. If the remainder beneficiary or beneficiaries named in Section 1 of this article fails or fail to survive Beneficiary by 30 days, Trustee shall distribute the property to Maria S. Sanchez.

3. If the remainder beneficiary or beneficiaries named in Section 2 of this article fails or fail to survive Beneficiary by 30 days, Trustee shall distribute property to Beneficiary's heirs at law.

4. While administering this special needs trust, Trustee shall in all cases exercise discretion in accordance with Article 10 and without regard to the interests of any remainder beneficiary named in this article.

5. If, when a remainder beneficiary inherits property under this article, he or she is not yet 18 years old, or, in the opinion of Trustee, is unable to prudently manage the property to be distributed and is under the age of 21, Trustee shall either (a) retain that beneficiary's share as a custodian under the Uniform Transfers to Minors Act of Kentucky, or (b) name another person to serve as custodian for the property under that act and distribute the property to that custodian. The custodianship shall end when the remainder beneficiary turns 21 unless the law requires it to end at age 18. When the custodianship ends, the custodian shall distribute any remaining custodial property to the beneficiary.

ARTICLE 14. TRUSTEE POWERS

Trustee shall, in addition to the powers given by law, have the following powers applicable to all property held in trust, whether principal or income, and exercisable without order of any court that has jurisdiction over Beneficiary:

1. To retain any property transferred to this trust, and to make such investments and reinvestments and in such proportions as Trustee considers beneficial and prudent in light of the trust purposes set out in Article 2, provided that the trustee's investment decisions shall be guided by the Prudent Investor Act as enacted by the state where this trust is administered, or if it has not been so enacted, by the Uniform Prudent Investor Act as originally published by the National Conference of Commissioners on Uniform State Laws.

2. To (1) participate in any merger or reorganization affecting securities held hereunder at any time; (2) deposit stock under voting agreements; (3) exercise any option to subscribe for stocks, bonds, or debentures; and (4) grant proxies, discretionary or otherwise, to vote shares of stock.

3. To manage, operate, or repair real estate or other property and to lease real estate and other property upon such terms and for such period as Trustee deems advisable.

4. To buy or sell (and to grant options for the sale of) any real or personal property at public or private sale for such prices and upon such terms as Trustee thinks proper.

5. To purchase, maintain, improve, or replace a residence, or any interest in it, where Beneficiary may reside, including any portion of the residence that may be owned by a family member.

6. To permit any person to reside at any real property held in this trust at which Beneficiary is residing, on such terms as Trustee deems proper, for the purpose of providing care, supervision, or simple companionship to Beneficiary.

7. To seek court permission to amend the trust only if necessary to fulfill the trust purposes set out in Article 2.

8. To make loans, but not gifts, for Beneficiary's benefit, provided the loans do not interfere with the trust purposes set out in Article 2.

9. To pay premiums to provide supplementary health insurance for Beneficiary or life insurance policies that may be owned or acquired by the trust. If Trustee is also the insured of any life insurance policy owned by the trust, then Trustee may exercise all rights and incidents of ownership with respect to such policy only in a fiduciary capacity, including the power to change the beneficiary, to surrender or cancel the policy, to assign the policy, to revoke any assignment, to pledge a policy for a loan, or to obtain a loan against the surrender value of the policy from the insurer.

10. To start or defend such litigation with respect to the trust or any property of the trust as Trustee deems advisable, at the expense of the trust.

11. To carry, at the expense of the trust, insurance of such kinds and in such amounts as Trustee deems advisable both to protect the trust property against any damage or loss and to protect Trustee against liability with respect to third persons.

12. To prepare and file returns and arrange for payment with respect to all local, state, federal, and foreign taxes incident to this trust, to prepare all necessary fiduciary income tax returns, and to make all necessary and appropriate elections.

13. To prepare and, if necessary, file all reports required of providers of government benefits received by Beneficiary, and to prepare and distribute annual reports of trust activity to Beneficiary and any named remainder beneficiaries.

14. Upon termination of the trust, to pay all debts and taxes determined by the trustee to be legally owed by the trust.

15. To hire attorneys, accountants, investment advisers, financial advisers, tax preparation services, and any other experts should Trustee, in Trustee's unfettered discretion, determine such expertise to be necessary for proper management of the trust.

16. To appoint one or more persons or agencies to serve as successor trustee in case no other trustees or successor trustees named in this trust are available to serve. Such appointment shall be made in writing and notarized. Trustee shall provide copies of the appointment to Beneficiary, Beneficiary's legal guardian or conservator, and all persons and entities named in the trust as successor trustees or remainder beneficiaries.

ARTICLE 15. TRUSTEE COMPENSATION

Trustee shall be entitled to reasonable compensation, from trust assets, commensurate with the services actually performed, and to reimbursement for expenses properly incurred. Trustee shall determine what compensation is reasonable by referring to the fees charged for similar services in the community where Trustee is serving.

ARTICLE 16. SPENDTHRIFT PROVISIONS

1. Beneficiary has no right or power, whether alone or in conjunction with others in whatever capacity, to amend, revoke, or terminate this special needs trust. No interest in the income or principal of this trust may be anticipated, assigned, encumbered, or subject to any creditor's claim or legal process.

2. Because trust funds will be conserved and maintained for Beneficiary's special needs, no part of the income or principal shall be construed as part of Beneficiary's "estate" or be subject to the claims of voluntary or involuntary creditors for the provision of care and services (including residential care) to or for Beneficiary by any city, county, or state government; the federal government; or any public or private agency except as otherwise provided in this trust instrument.

ARTICLE 17. BOND

Unless required by a court of competent jurisdiction or the trust protector, Trustee and Successor Trustees are not required to post a bond.

ARTICLE 18. PHOTOCOPIES

All photocopies of this Declaration of Trust shall carry the same legal weight as the original.

ARTICLE 19. TRUSTEE NOT LIABLE FOR GOOD-FAITH ACTIONS

A trustee of any kind nominated by this document shall not be liable to any beneficiary for the trustee's acts or omissions, except in cases of willful misconduct, bad faith, or gross negligence.

CERTIFICATION BY GRANTOR

I certify that I have read this Declaration of Trust and that it correctly states the terms and conditions under which the trust property is to be held, managed, and disposed of by the trustee, and I approve the Declaration of Trust.

Dated: _____ June 15, 20xx _____

Gloria C. Escobar
Gloria C. Escobar, Grantor and Trustee

CERTIFICATION OF TRUSTEE(S)

I certify that I have read The Bessie Escobar Special Needs Trust and, having been appointed as Trustee by Grantor, I agree to serve as Trustee and to manage the trust property under the trust's terms and conditions.

Dated: _____ June 15, 20xx _____

Richard Sanchez
Richard Sanchez, Trustee

Finalizing and Funding Your Special Needs Trust

I f you have finished drafting your trust, congratulations! Now you have just a few more steps to finish it up. First, you'll take your trust to a notary, sign it, and have it notarized. Then you'll apply to the IRS for a taxpayer ID number, set up a trust bank account, and modify your estate plan to transfer money into the trust at your death. This chapter discusses each of these final steps.

Making Your Trust Legal

Your signature and the signature and seal of the notary make your special needs trust legal. Getting your trust notarized will be a straightforward task. Here are some tips.

Make Your Final Changes

Before you take your trust document to the notary, check it over carefully to make sure everything is as you want it to be. Here are some things to go over:

- Do you understand all of the clauses and why they're there?
- Are all of the names spelled correctly?
- Are the clauses numbered sequentially?
- Have you deleted all extraneous instructional text?

It's important that you double-check every part of the trust because after you sign it and have it notarized, it becomes irrevocable. In other words, you can't make any changes to it other than to name a new successor trustee to replace one who becomes unable to serve.

Take Your Trust Document to the Notary

When you're satisfied with your document, take it to a notary public where you (or you and your initial trustee or cotrustee) will sign it. You can find a notary public online or though the yellow pages. Most title insurance companies and banks also have notaries on site. Bring some identification to show the notary you are who you say you are. Usually your driver's license or passport will do—the notary can tell you what to bring. You will sign the trust in front of the notary, who will then notarize the document to show that he or she witnessed your signing it. At that time, your special needs trust will be legal and final.

> **CAUTION**
>
> **Florida requires witnesses.** Florida requires that you sign your trust in front of two witnesses. Use the special Florida Witness Statement, provided to you as a downloadable eForm. (See Appendix D.) Bring the witnesses with you to the notary. You will all sign the document there together. Trustees, successor trustees, or trust protectors of the trust may be witnesses, but the beneficiary of the trust may not.

What If You Want to Change Your Special Needs Trust?

You cannot legally amend an irrevocable trust without the permission of a court, except for those few exceptions you may have set forth in the document for the trust protector. If other changes need to be made, the person serving as trustee (presumably you, while you are alive) can terminate the trust under certain conditions. For example, the trust allows the trustee to terminate the trust for lack of adequate funding. After terminating the trust, you can create a new trust with a new taxpayer ID number that incorporates the changes you wish to make. If, acting as trustee, you do terminate the trust, make sure you notify the beneficiary, all successor trustees, all remainder beneficiaries, the beneficiary's guardian or conservator, and any affected agencies, such as SSI and Medicaid. If possible, also retrieve all copies of the terminated trust you have distributed.

Copies

After you sign your special needs trust and have it notarized, you should make copies to distribute to all the people who should know about it. For example, you may want to give copies to the people you have named as successor trustees, guardians or conservators of the beneficiary, remainder beneficiaries, and relevant agencies.

Keep the original in a safe place, perhaps with your estate planning documents. Make sure the successor trustees know where you keep the original in case someone needs to see it when you are no longer available.

Taxes

The trustee must file a federal income tax return (Form 1041) for the trust if the trust generates more than $600 of gross income or any taxable income during the taxable year. Income generated by the trust is taxed at a special high tax rate for trusts. However, if income earned by the trust is used for the beneficiary's benefit, it can be claimed by the beneficiary and taxed at the beneficiary's rate which is commonly a lower rate even though the beneficiary never actually receives the income. So, when making disbursements from the trust for your loved one's benefit, use trust income before using the principal.

The trustee may also have to file state tax returns. Look for state-specific tax information on the state tax board's website or consult with a local tax professional.

See Appendix B (Letter to Trustee) for more information on filing trust taxes. If you have concerns about filing tax returns or about how trust income taxes work, see a tax professional who is knowledgeable about special needs trusts.

Obtaining an Employer Identification Number

Your special needs trust must have a taxpayer ID number. The IRS refers to this number as an Employer Identification Number (EIN) even though in your case it has nothing to do with employers.

Use IRS Form SS-4 to apply for an EIN. You can get your number immediately with a successful application by phone or online at www .irs.gov. If you send the form through the mail or by fax, it may take you several weeks to get your EIN number. The IRS will send you an official hard copy of your EIN after it processes your application.

Form **SS-4** (Rev. January 2010) Department of the Treasury Internal Revenue Service	**Application for Employer Identification Number** (For use by employers, corporations, partnerships, trusts, estates, churches, government agencies, Indian tribal entities, certain individuals, and others.) ▶ See separate instructions for each line. ▶ Keep a copy for your records.	OMB No. 1545-0003 EIN

<table>
<tr><td rowspan="13">Type or print clearly.</td><td colspan="3">1 Legal name of entity (or individual) for whom the EIN is being requested</td></tr>
<tr><td colspan="2">2 Trade name of business (if different from name on line 1)</td><td>3 Executor, administrator, trustee, "care of" name</td></tr>
<tr><td colspan="2">4a Mailing address (room, apt., suite no. and street, or P.O. box)</td><td>5a Street address (if different) (Do not enter a P.O. box.)</td></tr>
<tr><td colspan="2">4b City, state, and ZIP code (if foreign, see instructions)</td><td>5b City, state, and ZIP code (if foreign, see instructions)</td></tr>
<tr><td colspan="3">6 County and state where principal business is located</td></tr>
<tr><td colspan="2">7a Name of responsible party</td><td>7b SSN, ITIN, or EIN</td></tr>
</table>

8a Is this application for a limited liability company (LLC) (or a foreign equivalent)? . . . . ☐ Yes ☐ No	**8b** If 8a is "Yes," enter the number of LLC members . . . . ▶

8c If 8a is "Yes," was the LLC organized in the United States? . . . . ☐ Yes ☐ No

9a Type of entity (check only one box). **Caution.** If 8a is "Yes," see the instructions for the correct box to check.

☐ Sole proprietor (SSN) ___ : ___
☐ Partnership
☐ Corporation (enter form number to be filed) ▶___
☐ Personal service corporation
☐ Church or church-controlled organization
☐ Other nonprofit organization (specify) ▶___
☐ Other (specify) ▶

☐ Estate (SSN of decedent) ___
☐ Plan administrator (TIN) ___
☐ Trust (TIN of grantor) ___
☐ National Guard   ☐ State/local government
☐ Farmers' cooperative   ☐ Federal government/military
☐ REMIC   ☐ Indian tribal governments/enterprises
Group Exemption Number (GEN) if any ▶

9b If a corporation, name the state or foreign country (if applicable) where incorporated	State	Foreign country

10 **Reason for applying** (check only one box)

☐ Started new business (specify type) ▶ ___
☐ Hired employees (Check the box and see line 13.)
☐ Compliance with IRS withholding regulations
☐ Other (specify) ▶

☐ Banking purpose (specify purpose) ▶ ___
☐ Changed type of organization (specify new type) ▶ ___
☐ Purchased going business
☐ Created a trust (specify type) ▶ ___
☐ Created a pension plan (specify type) ▶ ___

11 Date business started or acquired (month, day, year). See instructions.	**12** Closing month of accounting year
	14 If you expect your employment tax liability to be $1,000 or less in a full calendar year **and** want to file Form 944 annually instead of Forms 941 quarterly, check here. (Your employment tax liability generally will be $1,000 or less if you expect to pay $4,000 or less in total wages.) If you do not check this box, you must file Form 941 for every quarter. ☐

13 Highest number of employees expected in the next 12 months (enter -0- if none).

If no employees expected, skip line 14.

Agricultural	Household	Other

15 First date wages or annuities were paid (month, day, year). **Note.** If applicant is a withholding agent, enter date income will first be paid to nonresident alien (month, day, year) . . . . ▶

16 Check **one** box that best describes the principal activity of your business.
☐ Construction ☐ Rental & leasing ☐ Transportation & warehousing
☐ Real estate ☐ Manufacturing ☐ Finance & insurance
☐ Health care & social assistance ☐ Wholesale-agent/broker
☐ Accommodation & food service ☐ Wholesale-other ☐ Retail
☐ Other (specify)

17 Indicate principal line of merchandise sold, specific construction work done, products produced, or services provided.

18 Has the applicant entity shown on line 1 ever applied for and received an EIN? ☐ Yes ☐ No
If "Yes," write previous EIN here ▶

Third Party Designee	Complete this section **only** if you want to authorize the named individual to receive the entity's EIN and answer questions about the completion of this form.	
	Designee's name	Designee's telephone number (include area code) ( )
	Address and ZIP code	Designee's fax number (include area code) ( )

Under penalties of perjury, I declare that I have examined this application, and to the best of my knowledge and belief, it is true, correct, and complete.

Name and title (type or print clearly) ▶	Applicant's telephone number (include area code) ( )
Signature ▶ Date ▶	Applicant's fax number (include area code) ( )

For Privacy Act and Paperwork Reduction Act Notice, see separate instructions.   Cat. No. 16055N   Form **SS-4** (Rev. 1-2010)

Tips for SS-4

Be sure to read the instructions that accompany Form SS-4. Here are our instructions, which assume that you are the initial trustee. If you're not, substitute the trustee's information for yours (except on Line 7; see below).

SS-4 Line Number	What to Write
Line 1—Legal name of entity (or individual) for whom the EIN is being requested.	Name of the trust, usually "The [*Name of Beneficiary*] Special Needs Trust."
Line 2—Trade name of business.	Leave blank.
Line 3—Executor, administrator, trustee, "care of" name.	Your name, as initial trustee.
Lines 4a–b—Mailing address.	Your mailing address, as initial trustee.
Lines 5a–b—Street address.	Your street address, as initial trustee, if different from Line 4. Otherwise leave blank.
Line 6—County and state where principal is located.	The county and state where the trust bank account will be located.
Lines 7a–b—Name of responsible party.	Your name and Social Security number.
Lines 8a–c	Mark "No" in 8a; leave 8b and 8c blank.
Lines 9a–b—Type of entity.	Check "other" and enter "Special needs trust" and your SSN on the line. Leave 9b blank.
Line 10—Reason for applying.	Mark "Created a trust" and write "special needs trust" on the line.
Line 11—Date business started or acquired.	Date the trust was notarized.
Line 12—Closing month of accounting year.	Write "December."
Line 13—Highest number of employees expected in the next 12 months.	Write "0."
Line 14—Employment tax.	Mark "No."
Line 15—First date wages or annuities were paid.	Write "Not Applicable."
Line 16	Mark "Other" and write "Special Needs Trust."
Line 17	Write "Special needs trust services."
Line 18	Check "No" unless you've applied before for an EIN. If you have, write in your previous EIN.

Third Party Designee. Fill out this section only if someone other than the grantor is doing the paperwork and should be contacted if the IRS has any questions.

Name and Signature. Print your name, then sign and date on the line below. Write your phone number and fax number (if you have one).

Opening the Trust's Deposit Account

Once you have a hard copy of your EIN number, you can open a deposit account for the trust. Take the EIN number and a copy of the trust to your institution of choice (bank, credit union, or brokerage firm) and tell an officer you want to open an account for the trust. They will probably want to see a copy of the trust and will take it from there.

Make a Small Initial Deposit

Depository institutions differ in the amounts they require to open and maintain trust accounts—usually in the low hundreds. You'll probably benefit from depositing the minimum, at least at first. The main reason to open a bank account now is to create a place to route property when you die. There is no particular reason to keep lots of money in the trust's bank account while you are alive. On the other hand, you may need to put money in the trust's bank account for other reasons. For example, you may choose to use this account to receive gifts from other benefactors or to minimize the assets in your estate if you're concerned about eventual estate tax.

Keep in mind, however, that the less you deposit, the less you'll have to worry about taxes. As long as the trust produces less than $600 a year in income, you won't have to file a federal tax return. So you may want to keep the deposit less than the amount it would take to produce that amount of interest (roughly $12,000, at a 5% rate of return.)

> ! **CAUTION**
>
> **Keep the beneficiary's funds separate from trust funds.** Never put the beneficiary's own funds in this special needs trust account. Doing so would put the beneficiary's SSI or Medicaid benefits at risk because it might prompt those programs to treat all trust assets as a resource available to the beneficiary. If you want to shelter your loved one's own savings or other property in a special needs trust, see a lawyer. Do not use the trust in this book.

Notifying Appropriate Agencies

If the beneficiary of the trust receives need-based benefits through programs such as SSI and Medicaid, contact the office that runs that program and tell them about the trust. They will probably want you to send them a copy of the trust document so they can make sure it really is a third-party trust and that the trust property is not available to the beneficiary as a countable resource. (See Chapter 3.)

Incorporating the Trust Into Your Estate Plan

To protect your loved one's benefits after you die, you'll need to leave property as a gift to the trust, not directly to your loved one. You must do this through your will, living trust, life insurance, deposit account, securities, or another estate planning tool.

If you die without legally specifying who should receive your property, the probate court will distribute it following "intestacy" laws. These laws give property to the deceased's closest relatives. Property passing to your loved one through intestate laws (rather than going directly to the special needs trust) will be owned by him or her. Medicare and SSI will consider that property your loved one's resource, seriously jeopardizing eligibility for benefits.

Avoid this problem by leaving property to the special needs trust through a will or revocable living trust, or by designating the trust as the beneficiary to inherit a deposit account, insurance policy, or securities.

Using a Living Trust or Will to Fund the Special Needs Trust

If you use a will or revocable living trust to provide for the beneficiary of your special needs trust, in the will, name the trustee of the special needs trust as the beneficiary of the property you want to leave.

EXAMPLE: Carlos wants to provide for his three children in his will. One child, Jose, has a disability and will likely need SSI and Medicaid for the rest of his life. Carlos leaves two-thirds of his property directly to the other children and leaves the last third to Jose through the special needs trust. Carlos uses this language: "I leave one-third of my property (subject to this will) to the Trustee of the Jose Esparza Special Needs Trust created on January 20, 20xx." When Carlos dies, that third will go to whoever is serving as trustee at that time and will be placed in the trust's bank.

Funding a Trust Through a Beneficiary Designation

You can also leave money or property to a special needs trust through a beneficiary designation, used with a life insurance policy, deposit account, or securities.

Many people use insurance policies to fund their special needs trusts. To do this, you would name the trustee of the special needs trust as the policy beneficiary. You don't need to name the actual person, because you don't know who that will be. Rather, you name the "Trustee" of the trust. The proceeds will go to the person who holds that position when the time comes.

EXAMPLE: Shirley creates a special needs trust for her son Richard, naming herself as trustee and her daughter Nan and nephew Ken as successor cotrustees. She designates the "Trustee of the Richard Jones Special Needs Trust" as the beneficiary of her $25,000 life insurance policy. When Shirley dies, Ken is unable to serve as trustee because of illness, so Nan receives the benefits as sole trustee of the trust. The money is held in the special needs trust, managed by Nan.

You can do the same with a bank account, certificate of deposit (CD), money market account, or stock brokerage account. Simply name the "Trustee" of the trust on the account's payable-on-death beneficiary designation form, which you can get from the company that administers the account.

Leaving Property to a Pooled Trust

If you decide you want to join a pooled trust (discussed in Chapter 7), use your will, revocable living trust, insurance policy, or beneficiary designation to route property to the pooled trust.

Fortunately, most pooled trusts will tell you exactly how to leave property to the trust through your will, revocable living trust, or beneficiary designation. If they don't, they can usually put you in touch with a lawyer who can help you draft the right language. Here are some general instructions to give you an idea about the process.

If You Sign Up With a Pooled Trust Now

If you sign up with a pooled trust during your life and want to fund it with property you leave at your death, name the trustee of the pooled trust to receive any property you want to go to your loved one. This will authorize the successor trustee of your revocable living trust or the executor of your will to distribute the property to the pooled trust. For this to work, you'll need to know the identity of the trustee of the pooled trust—usually either a bank or an individual who coordinates with a bank.

> **EXAMPLE:** Michael's daughter Annie has a developmental disability and receives SSI benefits. Michael signs a joinder agreement with a local pooled trust operated by The Arc. He plans to fund the trust when he dies by leaving money through his revocable living trust.
>
> Michael finds out that the trustee of the pooled trust is Bank of America, but that the pooled trust wants him to use the name of an individual cotrustee instead of the bank. So he names "John C. Parcival, Trustee of the Arc of Ohio Pooled Trust" to receive property left by Michael to Annie in his living trust.
>
> Here is how this would appear in a revocable living trust document:

> **V. BENEFICIARIES**
>
> All trust property left to Anne L. Casey shall be given to John C. Parcival, Trustee of the Arc of Ohio Pooled Trust, to be used for Anne L. Casey's benefit under the joinder agreement signed by Grantor on January 3, 20xx.

If You Don't Sign Up Now

If you want to use a pooled trust but can't find a suitable one that's available to you, create a special needs trust and direct the executor of your will or the successor trustee of your living trust to look for a suitable pooled trust after your death. (See Chapter 7.) With luck, by then there will be a pooled trust that will work for your loved one.

If this option sounds right for you, here is the language you can insert into your will or revocable living trust.

> **PART __. [NAME OF BENEFICIARY] SPECIAL NEEDS TRUST**
>
> [Testator/Grantor] has created a special needs trust on [date trust was notarized] in the name of [name of beneficiary]. However, [Testator/Grantor] directs the [executor/trustee], before placing property in that trust, to explore the possibility of joining a pooled trust for the purpose of managing all property left to [name of beneficiary]. If after such exploration a suitable pooled trust is found, the [executor/trustee] shall join the trust and transfer property to that trust. If no suitable pooled trust is located and joined, all [property left through this will/trust property] left to [name of beneficiary] shall be placed in the [name of beneficiary] Special Needs Trust and managed according to its terms.

Where to Get More Help

I n the course of using this book, you may find yourself in need of some expert advice, or at least some additional information. This chapter steers you to resources available online or in the library and offers some tips on working with professionals.

TIP

The Internet is a great resource. Getting answers can be as simple as using a search engine to look up "special needs trust" or other words that describe your questions, such as "Illinois pooled trust," or "SSI eligibility standards." (Google works great for this.) You'll quickly get a lot of hits. Be patient and perseverant and you likely will find what you need.

Robert Berring, a well-known law professor, always advises that the first step in all research is: Talk to a human being who knows something about the subject. The humans you will want to talk to about your special needs trust are:

- lawyers who specialize in special needs planning law, elder law, or Medicaid issues and who can give you individualized advice, and
- financial planners with a background in assisting persons with disabilities, who can help you figure out how much property you'll need to put in the trust and how to set up a sensible budget.

Lawyers

You can't beat lawyers for good legal advice. In fact, they are the only people permitted to give it. Other professionals such as financial planners, insurance agents, Social Security Administration (SSA) personnel, and paralegals may incidentally dole out information related to special needs trusts as part of their overall services. Lawyers, however, are the only people you can go to for legal advice tailored to your individual situation.

When to See a Lawyer

First and foremost, you'll want to talk to a lawyer if you feel discomfort about doing this important task yourself.

Even if you are comfortable with drafting your own trust, it's important to keep in mind that special needs trusts are intended to last for many years. Questions may arise that weren't anticipated in this book, such as big changes in the SSI and Medicaid rules. Knowing a lawyer whose job it is to keep track of new legislation might save you and your loved one with special needs a lot of grief due to loss of public benefits and potential fines down the line.

Finally, this book tries to cover the situations that most people encounter, but it doesn't contain details that might be important to you if your situation is unusual. For example, if two of your children have disabilities and you want to provide for them in a single special needs trust, you'll need help beyond this book. On the other hand, if you create a separate trust for each child, then there is no problem. The point is, if you have questions that aren't answered between these covers, a lawyer can help.

Why You May Have Difficulty Getting Help From a Lawyer

If you want to draft your own special needs trust but just need some additional information, ideally you should be able to have a short consultation with a special needs trust lawyer, pay a reasonable fee, and get all your questions answered. Even better, for an additional fee, the lawyer would review your trust, make helpful suggestions, and give you the peace of mind that comes from having a knowledgeable professional looking over your shoulder. Unfortunately, this scenario is unlikely for two reasons:

- Many special needs trust lawyers think people shouldn't create special needs trusts themselves because of the complexity and ever-changing rules and regulations on public benefits.
- A lawyer maybe concerned that if he or she gives you piecemeal advice or services, and down the road something goes wrong that had

nothing to do with the lawyer's review, you or your heirs will still sue him or her for malpractice.

Why Lawyers Think Special Needs Trusts Are Too Complex for Nonlawyers

Most attorneys who believe that only lawyers should draft special needs trusts are mainly concerned about the impact that the trust will have on the person with a disability. Attorneys worry that if a nonlawyer drafts the trust incorrectly or without taking into consideration the complexity of the situation, it may have a disastrous effect on the beneficiary's eligibility for SSI and Medicaid. They recognize that for a person with severe disabilities, a poorly drafted trust could have drastic (even fatal) consequences if mistakes in the trust result in the loss of health care or monthly check. Because the stakes are so high and because the rules can be complicated, most attorneys are uncomfortable trusting that a nonlawyer will be able to do all that is necessary to create a qualifying special needs trust.

Those attorneys are correct about the complexities of the benefit rules and the risks of making mistakes. However, we believe that in some circumstances—if you cannot afford an attorney, or if the trust will be relatively small—the benefits of making a simple do-it-yourself special needs trust outweigh the risks of not having one at all. And in those situations, a nonlawyer can safely create a "bare-bones" special needs trust like the one in this book.

The trust in this book is designed to meet the minimum requirements of a third-party special needs trust. We call it a "bare-bones" trust because it contains just the very basics required by the law and does not take into account your unique circumstances. Working with an attorney would result in a much more complex and detailed trust that would address all of your family's unique factual situations. In contrast, the trust in this book is like a car that meets the minimum safety requirements but doesn't provide any of the extras (like power steering or antilock brakes) that may be necessary for some people. If your loved one doesn't require an individualized plan or if your financial situation is such that you cannot afford an attorney, and if you are willing to spend the time to carefully review this book and draft the trust with thought and precision, then the trust you make will protect your loved one's eligibility for SSI and Medicaid.

TIP

Hire a lawyer if you need a trust for your loved one's own money. Remember that the third-party trust provided by this book can only be funded with assets that do not belong to your loved one with special needs. If your loved one with special needs has assets of his or her own (or is receiving a litigation recovery or inheritance from someone else) then you need a first-party special needs trust and you cannot use the trust provided by this book. (See Chapter 1.)

Why Lawyers Try to Avoid Giving Piecemeal Services

Even a lawyer who is comfortable with the idea of your using this book may be reluctant to get involved on a piecemeal basis. Lawyers learn early that the only way to make sure something is done right is to do it all themselves. They are worried that if you end up doing something that messes up your trust, they will be held responsible.

Additionally, most states' laws require that if a lawyer has reviewed one part of a document then he or she is taking responsibility for the entire document. If something is wrong with another part of the document that was not reviewed by the lawyer, he or she can still be sued for malpractice.

It's also difficult for a lawyer to analyze someone else's trust document —even one created by another lawyer. They much prefer to simply use the one they're familiar with.

This being said, an experienced special needs lawyer may be willing to go over the trust document from this book and give you advice. For experienced special needs planning attorneys, the trust in this book should not be too difficult to review and to give you advice on. In searching for a lawyer who will do this work, we recommend that you find one who has experience in drafting special needs trusts (not all estate planning attorneys will have that experience) and, if a lawyer agrees to provide this advice, that the fees for doing so are put in writing.

How to Find Special Needs Trust Lawyers

The world is full of lawyers—but finding one who has the expertise you need and a manner you like can take some shopping around.

General Estate Planning Lawyers

If you are already working with an estate planning lawyer—perhaps for your will or revocable living trust—that lawyer will most likely be able to help you or refer you to a special needs trust specialist. Be careful though—many estate planning lawyers will try and draft these trusts themselves even if they don't have the necessary experience. Use this book to educate yourself so that you can ask questions to see if your lawyer has the expertise to understand how to plan for your loved one with special needs.

Special Needs Planning Attorneys

The best way to find an attorney who specializes in this area is to go to the website for the Academy of Special Needs Planners. This is a national organization of attorneys devoted to doing planning for persons with disabilities. The organization has attorneys in just about every state with multiple attorneys in most states. You can search for an attorney in your state by going to www.specialneedsanswers.com/professionals.

You might also try to get a recommendation from someone in your own informal network of friends and acquaintances. You undoubtedly know people with a family member who has the same or similar disability as your loved one—they may have already found a lawyer who could also help you.

You can also check in with any local or national group that concerns itself with a particular disabled population. There are hundreds of groups that focus on specific disabilities, such as spina bifida, paraplegia, cystic fibrosis, and autism. Chances are these groups work with lawyers who are adept at special needs trusts. Often, these lawyers have a child or relative of their own with a disability and have both practical and legal insights to offer.

Organizations that create pooled trusts (discussed in Chapter 7) can be an excellent place to obtain a referral. Appendix A contains contact information for pooled trusts.

TIP
Let Nolo take the guesswork out of finding a lawyer. Nolo's Lawyer Directory provides detailed profiles of attorney advertisers, including information about each lawyer's education, experience, practice areas, and fee schedule. Go to www.lawyers.nolo.com or Nolo's main website at www.nolo.com.

What to Look for in a Lawyer

First and foremost, you want a lawyer who has experience in drafting special needs trusts. But you'll also want a lawyer you feel comfortable with.

In many parts of the country, you may have little choice of special needs trust lawyers. If so, as the old song goes, "Love the one you're with." But if you have several lawyers to pick from, here are a few questions to consider after an initial meeting:

- Does the lawyer seem interested in helping you resolve your specific questions and issues?
- Is the lawyer respectful of your self-help efforts?
- Does the lawyer seem confident of having the skills and knowledge to do the job well?
- Does the lawyer understand the disability and state benefits that your loved one with special needs is receiving?
- Are you willing and able to pay the lawyer's fee?
- Does the lawyer carry professional liability insurance?

• Perhaps most important, is the chemistry right? Do you feel reassured that you'll get exactly the services you need, no more and no less?

Paralegals

Social Security regulations explicitly authorize nonlawyer paralegals to represent clients in administrative proceedings dealing with benefit disputes. So if you have questions about your state's SSI and Medicaid income and resource rules, a paralegal may be just the ticket.

You can find paralegals in your area by searching online or using the yellow pages. In your area they might be called "document preparers" or "legal document assistants." Look for a paralegal who specializes in SSI and Medicaid matters, and compare fees.

Paralegals who work in the Social Security area are largely unregulated. If you want recourse in case you get bum advice, hire a paralegal who carries "errors and omissions" insurance—many do. Of course you may have to pay more if your paralegal is insured, but it may well be worth it.

If you need information about customizing your special needs trust or your options for a different type of trust—for instance, one that takes effect at your death—you'll need to see a lawyer. Paralegals are limited to advice and information about Social Security matters.

Certified Financial Planners

Special needs trusts often involve financial planning over a long period of time. Financial planners are people with accounting, investment, and insurance knowledge who can help you compute how much money you will need to accomplish your general estate planning goals and adequately fund your special needs trust.

Financial planners are not licensed professionals, but a central board certifies them. (For information about the certification process, visit www.cfp.net.)

Financial planners can provide a wealth of information on:

- how much money the special needs trust will need to accomplish your goals for your loved one

- a budget for the trustee who will manage the trust, and

- the best sources of funding for the trust, including advice on insurance options.

Just like attorneys, not all financial planners understand the unique financial requirements of a person with special needs. Make sure that the financial planner you select understands the financial needs that your loved one will have. Be sure to ask all of them how many times they have planned for a person with a disability and how they will incorporate public benefits into their planning. If they cannot answer these questions to your satisfaction, find another planner.

To find a local certified financial planner, visit these websites (or enter "certified financial planner" and your city's name into your favorite search engine):

- www.fpanet.org

- www.paladinregistry.com

- www.wiseradvisor.com.

Also some large financial institutions have planners who specialize in this area of financial planning:

- MassMutual Financial Group has a program called SpecialCare, dedicated to special needs financial planning. In order to be a part of the program, MassMutual agents are required to take a week-long course on special needs planning. Call 800-272-2216 or visit the company's website at www.massmutual.com.

- Merrill Lynch & Co. has set up a program that focuses on financial planning for special needs families and has a training program for its brokers. Call 877-456-7526 or visit the company's website at www .wealthmanagement.ml.com.

- MetLife Inc. has created a special needs unit to help families design financial plans and to refer people to groups that direct families to government benefits and services. Call 877-MetDESK (638-3375) or visit the company's website at www.metlife.com.

> **CAUTION**
> **Financial planners aren't always disinterested advisers.** Many financial planners are affiliated with one or more insurance companies. Their advice may be sound, but they also have interest in selling insurance at rates that might not be in your best interest. Especially when you are exploring insurance options, make sure you ask the right questions. See Chapter 4.

SSA and Medicaid Personnel

A special needs trust is designed to preserve your loved one's SSI and Medicaid benefits. If you need more information about those benefits than this book provides, ask someone at your local SSA office. You may get lucky and get your question answered. However, even SSA and Medicaid personnel don't always know the rules, so be sure to get a second opinion before following their advice.

If there is a program near where you live that delivers legal services to the poor, you might visit it and see what materials it has. You may find written resources explaining various aspects of the SSI and Medicaid programs, and the staff may be able to answer your questions.

Keeping Up to Date

Many years may pass between the time you create the trust and the time when it is fully funded (probably at your death). For example, if you are in your 40s or 50s when you create a special needs trust, at least 30 or 40 years will probably go by before you die. During that time, things that may happen include:

- SSI and Medicaid rules change in ways that require you to revoke or amend the trust.

- SSI and Medicaid rules change and make your loved one ineligible for benefits—which would eliminate the need for a special needs trust.

- Your loved one develops additional needs that you want to specifically provide for in the trust.

- Your loved one is no longer disabled and can inherit the property outright.

- A single-payer health care system is implemented (don't hold your breath), making a special needs trust unnecessary in many cases.

Obviously, you need to stay on top of such developments.

Subscribe to the Author's Monthly Online Newsletter

Author Kevin Urbatsch sends out a monthly online newsletter called the "Special Needs News." The newsletter provides updates on public benefits and issues that involve persons with disabilities. To receive the newsletter, go to www.MyersUrbatsch.com and follow the instructions for signing up.

Disability Groups' Newsletters and Websites

One excellent way to keep up to date on changes is to hook up with a group that cares about disabilities and check its newsletters and website. Such an organization will pick up on any changes in government regulations. Some groups are listed below. You can also get information from groups that focus on a specific condition, such as autism or Down syndrome.

Some Sources of Information About Disability Benefits and Laws

Academy of Special Needs Planners, www.specialneedsplanners.com

Disability Resources, www.disabilityresources.org

Exceptional Parent magazine, www.eparent.com

Federal government agencies that provide services to persons with disabilities, www.disabilityinfo.com

National Alliance on Mental Illness (NAMI), www.nami.org

The Arc, www.thearc.org

Federal Statutes and Regulations

If you want to be connected directly to the source of SSI and Medicaid regulation changes, you can read the government regulations themselves. Some of the language is dense, but the regs can be helpful if you are willing to take some time to read and digest them. Most of them are in Volume 20 of the Code of Federal Regulations (C.F.R.), Section 416. Online sources are listed below.

The particular areas of interest to you at all these sites are:

• how the SSI and Medicaid programs view special needs trusts funded by third parties

• what property the SSI and Medicaid programs consider the recipient's countable resources for eligibility purposes

• what the SSI and Medicaid programs consider to be income, and

• what the SSI and Medicaid programs consider to be income in kind, including in-kind support and maintenance (ISM).

Topic of Regulation or Statute	Citation	Website
Regulations issued by the Social Security Administration	20 C.F.R. §§ 416.101–416.2227	www.gpo.gov/fdsys
SSI resource rules	20 C.F.R. §§ 416.1210–416.1238	www.gpo.gov/fdsys
SSI in general	20 C.F.R. §§ 416.101–416.2227	www.gpo.gov/fdsys
Medicaid	42 C.F.R. §§ 430–456.657	www.gpo.gov/fdsys
Medicaid eligibility	42 C.F.R. §§ 435.700–435.740	www.gpo.gov/fdsys
Guidelines relied on by workers at the Social Security and local district offices	POMS (*Program Operations Manual System*)	http://policy.ssa.gov
State rules for Medicaid		www.medicaid.gov
How local SSI and Medicaid offices must treat special needs trusts	42 U.S.C. § 1396r-5 (Medicare Catastrophic Coverage Act of 1998), 42 U.S.C. § 1396p(d)(4) (A–C)(a–e)	www.ssa.gov

CAUTION

Help with legal research. Legal research, like other types of specialized research, has its own logic and terminology. Finding appropriate cases, knowing how to read them, and knowing how to find out whether a case you find is still good law are beyond the scope of this book. But there's help. *Legal Research: How to Find & Understand the Law*, by Stephen Elias and Susan Levinkind (Nolo), will get you where you need to go.

Books

Needless to say, a fair number of books discuss special needs trusts. Most deal with raising children with special needs and address the entire subject, from cradle to grave. Special needs trusts are but one subject of many.

To find these books, simply go to a good bookstore and look in the special needs or parenting sections. Or try an online bookstore and search for "special needs." You may be surprised at how many titles appear.

A few books provide a more detailed discussion of special needs trusts, both self-settled and third-party trusts. Many of them were written for lawyers, and you're most likely to find them in a law library. Law libraries accessible to the general public typically are located in courthouses, civic center buildings, or public law schools.

All law libraries have reference librarians, who are generally most helpful and willing to get you started. Just ask for materials on special needs trusts and you'll probably be given more than you can comfortably deal with.

RESOURCE

Learn about administering a special needs trust. *Administering the California Special Needs Trust,* by Kevin Urbatsch (iUniverse) explains to trustees how to administer a special needs trust. You can find this book through Amazon.com or Barnes and Noble.

Glossary

Antitransfer laws. Laws that penalize people who, in order to become eligible for means-tested benefits, such as SSI and Medicaid, have transferred their assets to others for less than fair market value.

Asset. Anything of value, including cash, promissory notes, tangible and intangible personal property, and real estate.

Beneficial interest. A type of property ownership held by people who are expected to benefit from trust assets in some way but who currently have no legal claim to them. The beneficiary of a special needs trust has a beneficial interest in the trust assets.

Beneficiary. Any person or entity entitled to inherit or receive property under a will or trust. The person for whom a special needs trust is created and whose needs will be paid for under the terms of the trust is the trust beneficiary.

Beneficiary designation. A document in which the owner of a deposit, retirement, or brokerage account names a beneficiary to receive any funds left in the account at the owner's death.

Burial policy. An insurance policy that covers the cost of disposing of a person's remains.

Code of Federal Regulations (C.F.R.). A set of publications containing regulations issued by federal agencies and organized by subject. Regulations for the SSI program are found in 20 C.F.R. §§ 416.101 and following.

Community trust. See Pooled trust.

Conditional SSI payments. Temporary SSI payments made on the condition that the recipient get rid of certain assets in an appropriate manner. They are made if an applicant for SSI has too many assets to qualify for that program.

Conservator. A person appointed by a court to make personal and/or financial decisions for another person (the conservatee) who is not able to make them.

Conservatorship. The relationship between a conservator and conservatee.

Corporate trustee. A bank or another financial institution that provides trustee services for various types of trusts. Many special needs trusts expected to be funded with $250,000 or more have a corporate trustee, instead of a family member, manage trust assets.

Corpus. A Latin term for the assets held in a trust.

Cotrustee. One of two or more persons or institutions named to manage trust assets together.

Countable resource. Property that the SSI and Medicaid programs consider available to an applicant or a recipient when determining that person's eligibility for benefits. Assets held in a properly drafted third-party special needs trust are not countable assets.

Custodianship. An arrangement created under a state law called the Uniform Transfers to Minors Act, under which a person may name an adult (the custodian) to manage property left to a minor until the minor turns an age between 18 and 25, depending on the state.

Direct inheritance. Property left outright to someone. SSI and Medicaid benefits may be reduced or eliminated if a recipient receives a direct inheritance, since the inheritance will be counted as income in the month received and as a resource in the following months. Property left to a special needs trust is not counted as a direct inheritance.

Disability. In general, a physical, sensory, psychiatric, learning, or intellectual impairment that affects daily living activities. Disabilities may be either temporary or permanent; they may arise from illness or injury or be present from birth. For the purpose of obtaining SSI and Medicaid, a disability is a mental or physical condition that leaves someone permanently unable to "do any substantial gainful activity."

Disabled. Having a disability. Many people with disabling conditions prefer to be identified according to their specific disability, such as "a person with paraplegia" or "a person with cerebral palsy."

Disbursements. Payments of trust funds by the trustee. In a special needs trust, the trustee typically makes disbursements to pay for the beneficiary's needs that aren't covered by SSI or Medicaid, such as a companion, school tuition, books, or hobby equipment.

Earned income. Wages paid by an employer or income from self-employment. Earned income can result in a reduced SSI payment.

Elder law. Legal issues typically faced by the elderly, including government benefits, nursing home care, and elder abuse.

Estate planning. Creating documents necessary to carry out your wishes for what should happen to your property and children after your death. Often, estate planning involves strategies designed to minimize probate fees so that more is left for inheritors.

Estate tax. Federal and state taxes imposed on the value of a person's net worth at death. For deaths in 2013, federal estate taxes apply only to estates with a net worth greater than $5.25 million, but some states tax smaller estates.

Executor. The person named in a will to carry out the will's provisions, including filing the will in the proper court, inventorying the deceased person's property, paying debts and taxes, and distributing the remaining property to the beneficiaries named in the will. Called personal representative in some states.

Exempt asset. See Noncountable resource.

Federal benefit rate. The share of the SSI grant paid by the federal government. Many states add a supplementary grant to the federal benefit rate.

Fiduciary. A person who owes a special duty of trust to another person or entity. In a special needs trust, the trustee owes a fiduciary duty to the beneficiary of the trust to strictly comply with the trust's terms and to manage the trust solely for the beneficiary's benefit.

Financial planner. A person skilled in assessing people's financial needs and the various options for meeting them, including various types of insurance and investments. Many financial planners are certified by a central trade organization, but governments don't license them.

Food. Ordinary food—that is, food that isn't necessary because of special medical needs—is supposed to be paid for by SSI. If the trustee of a special needs trust pays for the beneficiary's food, the amount paid is considered income to the beneficiary and deducted from the grant, up to a certain amount.

Funding a trust. Putting property in trust by assigning the property to the trust or changing title documents to reflect the trust's ownership. Technically, the trustee owns the trust property, subject to the trust's terms and the trustee's fiduciary duty.

Furniture and personal effects. As defined by the SSA, just about any property typically used in a home. Furniture and personal effects are not counted as resources for the purpose of determining a person's eligibility for SSI and Medicaid.

Gift. Property permanently transferred to someone without receiving anything in return. Property transferred to an irrevocable living trust while the giver is alive is considered a gift because the property can't be taken back. However, property transferred to a revocable living trust is not a gift, because the giver does not give up control over it and can revoke the trust at any time. Finally, property left at death under a will or living trust is commonly called a gift.

Gift tax. A federal tax on gifts over $14,000 made by one person to a single recipient in one calendar year. The tax is not payable when the gift is made, but rather when the person giving the gift dies. Those who die in 2013 can make taxable gifts (during life and at death) that total up to $5.25 million before owing gift tax. These exemption amounts will increase with inflation.

Good faith. The honest belief that one's actions are correct and appropriate. Most special needs trusts provide that trustees are not liable for losses caused by actions taken in good faith.

Grantor. Someone who creates a trust. Also called settlor or trustor.

Group home. For purposes of the Medicaid program, a home in which two or more SSI recipients live and receive food and shelter for one overall price.

Guardian. A person appointed by a court to handle the personal and financial affairs of a child, or of an adult who has been judged to be unable to handle these matters alone. In many states, the term conservator is used when the incompetent person is an adult.

Independent trustee. A trustee who is not related to the beneficiary of the trust and does not stand to inherit any property under the trust.

Independent trustees are preferred when family members are likely to disagree over management of the trust. However, independent trustees' fees are usually higher than those charged by a family member.

Inheritance. Property received as a result of another person's death. Typically, a person receives an inheritance under the terms of a will, revocable living trust, or state law (termed the law of intestate succession).

In-kind income. See In-kind support and maintenance.

In-kind support and maintenance (ISM). Shelter or food provided to an SSI recipient. The value of ISM is considered income. An SSI recipient's monthly grant is reduced dollar for dollar by the total value of the ISM received in a month, up to a certain amount. Also called in-kind income.

Inter vivos trust. A trust created by a person during his or her lifetime (inter vivos is Latin for "between the living"). The most popular form of inter vivos trust is the revocable living trust. However, an inter vivos trust may also be irrevocable—for example, a special needs trust that is created and immediately put into effect by a living grantor.

Joinder agreement. The written contract between a person who contributes funds to a pooled trust on behalf of a disabled loved one and the nonprofit organization operating the pooled trust. The joinder agreement "joins" the beneficiary's funds with the other funds in the pooled trust.

Letter of intent. A term commonly used to describe a letter in which the creator of a special needs trust provides personal details about the trust beneficiary for the guidance of future trustees of the trust.

Living trust. A trust created during the grantor's lifetime, usually to avoid probate. The grantor is usually the trustee during his or her life; then the successor trustee takes over and distributes the trust property to beneficiaries named in the trust document. Sometimes called inter vivos trust or revocable living trust.

Long-term care. Nursing home care that lasts more than two months. Nursing home care typically is paid for by long-term care insurance, or by Medicaid if the patient meets strict income and resource limitations.

Master trust. A special needs trust under which a nonprofit organization operates a pooled trust on behalf of many individual beneficiaries.

Medicaid. A health care delivery program intended to serve people with limited income and resources. Medicaid is paid for with state and federal funds. It is administered by the states, which, under federal rules, determine who is eligible for benefits.

Medically needy. People whose income is too high for regular Medicaid eligibility but who are eligible for benefits if they contribute part of their income (called their share of cost) toward their medical care.

Medicare. A health care delivery system available to people who qualify because of age or disability and work history. Medicare eligibility does not depend on a person's income or resources. People who qualify for Medicare may still need Medicaid to pay for prescriptions and long-term care, and many people with limited income and resources receive benefits under both programs.

Negligence. Failure to act in a way in which a reasonable and prudent person would act under similar circumstances.

Noncountable resource. Property that is not considered as a resource by the SSI and Medicaid programs for purposes of determining program eligibility.

OBRA. The federal Omnibus Budget Reconciliation Act, a law that, among other things, describes the circumstances under which property in a special needs trust may be considered the trust beneficiary's resource for the purpose of determining eligibility for SSI and Medicaid. (42 U.S.C. §§ 1395 and following.)

Payback provision. A provision in a special needs trust requiring that, after the beneficiary dies, the trustee must use any property left in the trust to reimburse Medicaid for benefits the beneficiary received. Special needs trusts containing property originally belonging to the beneficiary (self-settled trusts) must have a payback provision to avoid having the property considered the beneficiary's resource for program eligibility purposes. Third-party trusts, like the one in this book, do not have a payback provision.

Personal representative. See Executor.

Plan for Achieving Self-Support (PASS). A plan (approved by SSI) that allows an SSI recipient to own otherwise countable resources as part of an effort to become self-supporting.

POMS. *Program Operations Manual System*, a set of guidelines issued by the Social Security Administration to help lower-level employees interpret the federal statutes and regulations that govern the SSI and Medicaid programs.

Pooled trust. A special needs trust operated by a nonprofit organization for the benefit of several beneficiaries. Assets are jointly managed and invested. SSI does not consider pooled trust funds donated by a third party for a beneficiary to be a resource available to the beneficiary.

Presumed maximum value (PMV). The presumed value of food or shelter provided to an SSI recipient by a third party. The PMV is the amount of the federal portion of the SSI grant plus $20. In 2013, this amount is $256.67. The recipient can prove that the value is, in fact, less.

Principal. Property held in trust. Income generated by the trust principal is considered income in the year received and principal if retained in the trust after that time. Also called trust corpus.

Principal residence. A person's home and the land on which it is situated. SSI does not consider a person's principal residence a resource, regardless of its value.

Probate. A court proceeding in which (1) the authenticity of a will (if any) is established, (2) the person whose responsibility it is to handle the person's estate (executor or administrator) is appointed, (3) the deceased person's debts and taxes are paid, (4) the people who inherit are identified, and (5) the property is distributed to them. Probate happens only if someone petitions the court to open a probate proceeding, and only affects property that hasn't been disposed of in some other way—for example, through a trust.

Prudent Investor Act. A law containing investment principles articulated by a group of nationally respected judges and law professors. Most states apply these principles to trustees in the absence of contrary investment instructions in the trust document. As a whole, the law requires trustees to make commonsense investment decisions that will best serve the purposes of the trust.

Remainder beneficiary. A person or an institution named in a special needs trust to receive trust property that remains in the trust at the death of the disabled beneficiary.

Representative payee. Typically, a person authorized by a government agency, such as the Social Security Administration, to receive benefits such as SSI payments on behalf of a recipient who is not competent to handle his or her own money.

Resource. For purposes of determining SSI eligibility, any property that the SSI program considers available to the applicant. See Countable resource and Noncountable resource.

Revocable living trust. See Living trust. The term revocable refers to the fact that the person who sets up the trust can amend or revoke it.

Section 8 housing. A federal rent subsidy program under which landlords accept low-income tenants. Tenants pay a portion of their income, and the agency pays the rest.

Self-settled trust. A special needs trust funded with property belonging to the beneficiary, such as a direct inheritance, recovery in a personal injury lawsuit, or gift.

Settlor. Another term for grantor.

Shelter. For SSI purposes, any item commonly associated with housing such as rent, heat, utilities, and mortgage payments. Disbursements from special needs trusts for shelter are considered in-kind support and maintenance (ISM) and are deducted from the SSI grant up to a certain amount.

Sheltered workshop. A place of employment designed and managed to accommodate the needs of people with disabilities.

Social Security Act. A collection of federal statutes that govern a variety of federal programs, including Social Security retirement and disability benefits, Medicare, SSI, and Medicaid.

Social Security Administration (SSA). The agency charged with administering the programs created under the Social Security Act, including SSI and Medicaid.

Special needs. All needs of a disabled person for goods and services other than food and shelter, which SSI deems to be provided in the SSI grant itself.

Special needs trust. A trust designed to hold and disburse property for the benefit of an SSI recipient without the SSI and Medicaid programs considering the trust property or disbursements to be a resource or income. To accomplish this purpose, the trust typically gives the trustee sole discretion over trust disbursements and bars the trustee from making disbursements that would impair the beneficiary's eligibility for SSI and Medicaid. In addition, the trust must be for the beneficiary's sole benefit and bar creditors from going after trust assets. A special needs trust funded with the beneficiary's own property (a self-settled trust) is subject to additional restrictions.

Spend down. To spend resources on medical needs when an applicant for certain Medicaid benefits has resources over the resource limit. When the applicant's resources are sufficiently reduced, he or she will qualify for Medicaid.

Spendthrift provisions. Clauses in a trust aimed at protecting the trust property from the beneficiary's creditors, or allowing the beneficiary to use the trust property as collateral for a loan. All special needs trusts contain spendthrift provisions.

SSDI. Social Security Disability Insurance. This federal program provides monthly cash payments to disabled persons who qualify because they have paid enough Social Security taxes. There are no resource or income ceilings.

SSI. Supplemental Security Income, a federal program that provides cash payments to persons of limited income and resources who are disabled (according to federal standards), over age 65, or blind. SSI is the main form of government support for people who aren't eligible for Social Security retirement or disability benefits and who meet the program's income and resources requirements.

Successor trustee. A person named in a trust to take over as trustee when the first trustee dies or is otherwise unable to serve. In a revocable living trust, the first trustee is the person who sets up the trust (the grantor). The successor trustee is the person who carries out the provisions of the trust after the grantor's death.

Supplemental needs trust. Another name for a special needs trust.

Support trust. A type of trust that allows the trustee to make disbursements for the beneficiary's general support as well as other needs. A support trust does not qualify as a special needs trust for the purpose of sheltering trust property from consideration as a resource by SSI and Medicaid.

Term life insurance. A type of life insurance that pays out the face value of the policy at the policy owner's death but that does not have an investment or savings feature. Term life insurance is often used to fund a special needs trust.

Testamentary trust. A trust created as part of a will that goes into effect at the willmaker's death.

Testator. Someone who makes a will.

Third-party trust. A special needs trust funded exclusively with property given by people other than the beneficiary. The trust in this book is a third-party trust. Compare Self-settled trust, which contains property originally belonging to the beneficiary.

Transfer of assets. The act of getting rid of property for less than its fair market value in order to become eligible for SSI or long-term care benefits under Medicaid.

Trust. An arrangement under which a person called a trustee has a duty to manage certain property in a way that benefits a beneficiary. Trusts are created for many different purposes. See Special needs trust and Living trust.

Trust administration. A trustee's management of trust property according to the trust's terms and for the benefit of the beneficiaries.

Trust protector. A person given limited authority to review a trustee's actions. Depending on the terms of the trust, a trust protector may have the authority to remove and replace a trustee, review trust records, or make minor modifications to the trust document. A group of trust protectors appointed and working together is sometimes called a "trust advisory committee."

Trustee. A person named in a trust instrument, or chosen by an existing trustee, to manage the trust under the terms of the trust document. The trustee must be loyal to the trust and avoid conflicts of interest with the trust beneficiaries. In a special needs trust, the trustee owes a duty to manage the trust so that the beneficiary's special needs may be met without jeopardizing the beneficiary's eligibility for SSI and Medicaid.

Trustee powers. Specific grants of authority given to a trustee by the trust document in addition to, or in place of, authority granted by state law.

Unearned income. For SSI purposes, all income that does not result from employment.

Uniform Transfers to Minors Act. A law adopted by all but two states (Vermont and South Carolina) that provides a method for transferring property to minors and arranging for an adult, called a custodian, to manage the property until the child is older.

Whole life insurance. A type of life insurance that builds up equity in the policy owner's name and pays out a predetermined amount—when the insured person dies—to beneficiaries designated by the policy owner. Compare Term life insurance.

Will. A legal document in which someone leaves property and names a guardian to raise any surviving minor children after death. ●

Pooled Trusts

We've tried to make this list of pooled trusts as complete and up to date as possible, but you should always check with a local disability advocacy group, too. If a pooled trust exists in your locale or state, such a group will know about it. Also, the fact that a pooled trust program is listed here is not intended as an endorsement. Read Chapter 7 for tips on how to assess whether a particular pooled trust program is right for you.

Online Resources

These websites provide additional information about pooled trusts:

- Academy of Special Needs Planners: www.specialneedsanswers.com
- The Arc: www.thearc.org
- The National PLAN Alliance: www.nationalplanalliance.org

National and Regional Special Needs Trust Organizations

ARCare Trust Program
8417 Santa Fe, Suite 107
Overland Park, KS 66212
913-648-0233
arcare@crn.org

Charities Pooled Trust
1217 Ponce De Leon Boulevard
Clearwater, FL 33756
877-695-6444
www.charitiespooledtrust.org

The Center for Special Needs Trust
Administration, Inc.
4912 Creekside Drive
Clearwater, FL 33760
877-766-5331
www.sntcenter.org
contact@sntcenter.org

Disabled and Alone
Life Services for the Handicapped, Inc.
61 Broadway, Suite 510
New York, NY 10006
212-532-6740
800-995-0066
info@disabledandalone.org
www.disabledandalone.org

The Guardian Pooled Trust
901 Chestnut Street, Suite B
Clearwater, FL 33756
727-443-7898
800-669-2499
www.guardianpooledtrust.org

Midwest Special Needs Trust
P.O. Box 7629
Columbia, MO 65205
573-256-5055
877-239-8055
www.midwestspecialneedstrust.org
mftbt@midwestspecialneedstrust.org

National Planned Lifetime Assistance
Network
518-587-3372
npa@nycap.rr.com

National Pooled Trust
4912 Creekside Drive
Clearwater, FL 33760
877-766-5331
www.sntcenter.org
contact@sntcenter.org

Secured Futures Inc.
4747 E. Elliot Road, Suite 29-217
Phoenix, AZ 85044
877-734-8880
www.securedfutures-snt.org

World Institute on Disability: Info on
Special Needs Trusts
510 16th Street, Suite 100
Oakland, CA 94612
510-763-4100
510-208-9493
www.wid.org

State Special Needs Trust Organizations

Alabama

Alabama Family Trust
UCP Campus (Lincpoint)
100 Oslo Circle
Birmingham, AL 35211
contact@alabamafamilytrust.com
www.alabamafamilytrust.com
800-711-1303

Alaska

Foundation of The Arc of Anchorage
2211 Arca Drive
Anchorage, AK 99508
907-277-6677
www.thearcofanchorage.org

Arizona

PLAN of Arizona
5025 E. Washington Street
Suite 112
Phoenix, AZ 85034
602-759-8180
www.planofaz.org
planofarizona@yahoo.com

Arkansas

Midwest Special Needs Trust
P.O. Box 7629
Columbia, MO 65205
573-256-5055
877-239-8055
www.midwestspecialneedstrust.org
mftbt@midwestspecialneedstrust.org

California

Charities Pooled Trust
2911 Adams Ave.
San Diego, CA 92116
877-695-6444
www.charitiespooledtrust.org

Good Shepherd Fund
1641 N. First Street, Suite 155
San Jose, CA 95112
408-573-9606
888-422-4904
408-573-9609
www.goodshepherdfund.org

The Master Trust of California
Inland Regional Center
Mailing Address:
P.O. Box 6127
San Bernardino, CA 92412-6127
Street Address:
1365 South Waterman Avenue
San Bernardino, CA 92408
909-890-3000
www.mastertrustofcalifornia.com

Special Needs Trust Foundation
P.O. Box 1890
Lakeside, CA 92040
619-201-2672
www.sntf-sd.org

Proxy Parent Foundation
(DBA: PLAN of California)
17602 Seventeenth Street #102-240
Tustin, CA 92780
714-997-3310
888-574-1258
www.proxyparentfoundation.org
info@proxyparentfoundation.org

Colorado

The Colorado Fund for People
with Disabilities
1355 S. Colorado Boulevard
Denver, CO 80222
303-733-2867
www.cfpdtrust.org

Connecticut

PLAN of Connecticut, Inc.
P.O. Box 370312
West Hartford, CT 06137-0312
860-523-4951
www.planofct.org
director@planofct.org

Delaware

Delaware CarePlan, Inc.
2 South Augustine Street, Suite B
Wilmington, DE 19804
302-996-9400
decareplan@aol.com
www.arcde.org/decareplan

District of Columbia

PLAN of Maryland/DC
604 South Frederick Ave., Suite 411
Gaithersburg, MD 20877
301-740-8444
www.planofmd-dc.org

Shared Horizons, Inc.
5335 Wisconsin Avenue, NW
Suite 910
Washington, DC 20015
202-448-1460
www.sharedhorizons.org
info@sharedhorizons.org

Florida

Guardian Trust
901 Chestnut Street, Suite C
Clearwater, FL 33756
800-669-2499
Fax: 727-631-0970
www.guardianpooledtrust.org

PLAN of Florida
Jewish Family & Children's Services
5841 Corporate Way, Suite 200
West Palm Beach, FL 33400
561-684-1991
www.jfcsonline.com/pooled-trust

Georgia

PLAN of Georgia
A220 Century Parkway, Suite 510
Atlanta, GA 30345
404-634-0094
planofgeorgiainc@aol.com
www.planofgeorgia.org

Georgia Community Trust
3995 S. Cobb Drive
Smyrna, GA 30080
770-431-7070
www.georgiacommunitytrust.com

Illinois

Life's Plan, Inc
901 Warrenville Road
Suite 500
Lisle, IL 60532
630-628-7169
www.lifesplaninc.org

Midwest Special Needs Trust
P.O. Box 7629
Columbia, MO 65205
573-256-5055
877-239-8055
www.midwestspecialneedstrust.org
mftbt@midwestspecialneedstrust.org

ELCA Endowment Fund Pooled Trust
Evangelical Lutheran Church in America
8765 W. Higgins Road
Chicago, IL 60631
800-638-3522, ext. 2970
www.elca.org

Day One Reliance
1551 East Fabyan Parkway
Geneva, IL 60134
630-208-5555
www.dayonereliance.org
bmccrary@dayonereliance.org

Indiana

Life's Plan Inc.
901 Warrenville Road Suite 500
Lisle, IL 60532
630-628-7169
www.lifesplaninc.org

The Arc of Indiana Master Trust
107 N. Pennsylvania Street
Suite 800
Indianapolis, IN 46204
317-977-2375
www.arcind.org

Iowa

Midwest Special Needs Trust
P.O. Box 7629
Columbia, MO 65205
573-256-5055
877-239-8055
www.midwestspecialneedstrust.org
mftbt@midwestspecialneedstrust.org

Life's Plan Inc.
901 Warrenville Road, Suite 500
Lisle, IL 60532
630-628-7169
www.lifesplaninc.org

Kansas

ARCare—Master Trust I & II and
Guardianship
8417 Santa Fe, Suite 107
Overland Park, KS 66212
913-648-0233
www.arcare.org

Midwest Special Needs Trust
P.O. Box 7629
Columbia, MO 65205
573-256-5055
877-239-8055
www.midwestspecialneedstrust.org
mftbt@midwestspecialneedstrust.org

Kentucky

Kentucky Pooled Special Needs Trust
7984 New La Grange Road
Louisville, KY 40222
502-425-5323

Midwest Special Needs Trust
1500 Vandiver, Suite 100
P.O. Box 7629
Columbia, MO 65205
573-256-5055
887-239-8055
www.midwestspecialneedstrust.org
mftbt@midwestspecialneedstrust.org

Louisiana

The Louisiana Pooled Trust
www.sntcenter.org/TypesOfTrusts.htm

Evergreen Presbyterian Pooled Special
Needs Trust
2101 Highway 80
Haughton, LA 71037
318-949-5500
www.evergreenls.org

Maine

Maine Pooled Disability Trust
P.O. Box 495
Kennebunkport, ME 04046-0495
207-967-602
www.mainepooleddisabilitytrust.org

Maine Trust for People with Disabilities
P.O. Box 9729
Portland, ME 04101-5029
www.themainetrust.com
info@themainetrust.com

Maryland

PLAN of Maryland/DC
604 South Frederick Avenue, Suite 411
Gaithersburg, MD 20877
301-740-8444
www.planofmd-dc.org

Shared Horizons, Inc.
5335 Wisconsin Avenue, NW
Suite 910
Washington, DC 20015
202-448-1460
www.sharedhorizons.org
info@sharedhorizons.org

Massachusetts

Berkshire County Arc Pooled Trust
395 South Street
Pittsfield, MA 01201
413-499-4241
www.bcarc.org

Jewish Family & Children's Service
of Greater Boston
1430 Main Street
Waltham, MA 02451
617-244-5327
www.jfcsboston.org

PLAN of Massachusetts and Rhode Island
1301 Centre Street, Suite 102
Newton Centre, MA 02459
617-244-5552
www.planofma.org
director@planofma.org

The Massachusetts Pooled Trust
www.sntcenter.org/Types ofTrusts.htm

Michigan

Michigan Preservation Trust
Contact: Michele P. Fuller
12900 Hall Road, Suite 470
Sterling Heights, MI 48313
586-803-8500
michele@michiganlawcenter.com

The Arc of Midland
220 W. Main Street, Suite 101
Midland, MI 48640
989-631-4439
www.thearcofmidland.org

The Michigan Pooled Trust
www.sntcenter.org/TypesofTrusts.htm

Pooled Special Needs Trust from United
Cerebral Palsy of Michigan
4970 Northwind Drive, Suite 102
East Lansing, MI 48823
517-203-1200
800-828-2714
www.ucp.org
ucp@ucpmichigan.org

Elder Law of Michigan, Inc.
3815 West St. Joseph, Suite C200
Lansing, MI 48917
517-485-9164
www.elderslaw.org
info@elderslaw.org

Life's Plan Inc.
901 Warrenville Road
Suite 500
Lisle, IL 60532
630-628-7169
www.lifesplaninc.org

Springhill Housing Corporation, Inc.
4190 Telegraph Rd., Suite 3000
Bloomfield Hills, MI 48302-2082
248-731-3080

Minnesota

PLAN of Southeastern Minnesota
6301 Bandel Road NW, Suite 605
Rochester, MN 55901
507-287-2032
888-732-8520
www.arcse-mn.org/plan.html

The Pooled Trust of Minnesota
www.sntcenter.org/TypesofTrusts.htm

Minnesota Pooled Trust
325 South 7th Street, Suite 101
Fargo, ND 58103
701-297-8988
888-798-4277
www.gapsinc.org

Mississippi

The Mississippi Pooled Trust
www.sntcenter.org/TypesofTrusts.htm

Missouri

Midwest Special Needs Trust
1500 Vandiver, Suite 100
P.O. Box 7629
Columbia, MO 65205
573-256-5055
887-239-8055
www.midwestspecialneedstrust.org
mftbt@midwestspecialneedstrust.org

Life's Plan Inc.
2801 Finley Road
Downers Grove, IL 60515
630-628-7169
www.lifesplaninc.org

ARCare Trust Program
8417 Santa Fe, Suite 107
Overland Park, KS 66212
913-648-0233
arcare@crn.org
www.arcare.org

Nebraska

Midwest Special Needs Trust
P.O. Box 7629
Columbia, MO 65205
573-256-5055
877-239-8055
www.midwestspecialneedstrust.org
mftbt@midwestspecialneedstrust.org

ARCare Trust Program
8417 Santa Fe, Suite 107
Overland Park, KS 66212
913-648-0233
arcare@crn.org
www.arcare.org

Nevada

The Nevada Pooled Trust
www.sntcenter.org/TypesofTrusts.htm

New Hampshire

Enhanced Life Options Group
3 Executive Park Drive, Suite 269
Bedford, NH 03110
603-524-4189
603-472-2543
www.elonh.org

New Jersey

PLAN of New Jersey
P.O. Box 547
Somerville, NJ 08876-0547
908-575-8300

Sussex Arc
SCARC Guardianship Services, Inc.
11 U.S. Route 206, Suite 100
Augusta, NJ 07822
973-383-7442
www.scarc.org

New Mexico

The Arc of New Mexico
Master Trust One and Two Program
3655 Carlisle, NE
Albuquerque, NM 87110-5564
505-883-4630
www.arcnm.org

New York

NYSARC, Inc., New York State
Guardianship Services
393 Delaware Avenue
Delmar, NY 12054
518-439-8311
www.nysarc.org

FEGS Community Trust and PLAN
(in cooperation with UJA-Federation
of New York, Inc.)
315 Hudson Street
New York, NY 10013
212-366-8008
http://fegs.org

UJA-Federation of New York, Inc.
Community Trusts
(in cooperation with FEGS Community
Trust and PLAN)
130 E. 59th Street
New York, NY 10022
212-980-1000
www.ujafedny.org

Life Services Third-Party-Funded
Trust for People with Disabilities,
Disabled and Alone/Life Services for
the Handicapped, Inc.
352 Park Avenue South, 11th Floor
New York, NY 10010
212-532-6740
800-995-0066
www.disabledandalone.org

Westchester Arc Foundation
Community Trust
265 Saw Mill River Road
Hawthorne, NY 10532
919-949-9300
www.westchesterarc.org
info@westchesterarc.org

CLC Supplemental Needs Pooled Trust
600 Bedford Road
Mount Kisco, NY 10549
914-241-2076
www.clcpooledtrust.org
jjsignorelli@optonline.net

North Carolina

The Arc of North Carolina
343 Six Forks Rd. Suite 320
Raleigh, NC 27609
800-662-8706
919-782-4632

Life Plan Trust
122 Salem Towne Court
Apex, NC 27502
919-589-0017
888-301-0799
Lifeplan1@earthlink.net

The North Carolina Pooled Trust
www.sntcenter.org/TypesOfTrusts.htm

North Dakota

North Dakota Pooled Trust
316 N. 5th Street, Suite 112
Bismarck, ND 58501
701-222-8678
888-570-4277
www.gapsinc.org

Ohio

Community Fund Management
Foundation
14955 Sprague Road, Suite 290
Strongsville, OH 44136
216-736-4540
www.cfmf.org

The Disability Foundation, Inc.,
c/o The Dayton Foundation
The Ohio Community Pooled Trust
500 Kettering Tower
Dayton, OH 45423
937-222-0410
www.daytonfoundation.org

PLAN of Northeast Ohio
Cleveland Heights
5010 Mayfield Road, Suite 304
Lyndhurst, OH 44124
216-321-3611
www.planneohio.org

PLAN of Northwest Ohio
Cindy Brock, United Health Services
419-242-9587
Cindyb@uhs-toledo.org

PLAN of Southeast
NAMI Athens
100 Hospital Drive
Athens, OH 45701
740-593-7424
www.namiathensohio.org

PLAN of Southwest Ohio, Inc.
4300 Rossplain Road
Cincinnati, OH 45236
513-821-6111
www.planswohio.org

PLAN of Central Ohio
Anita Rigsby Szuch, Executive Director
2201 Riverside Drive
Columbus, OH 43221
614-586-4049
www.plancolumbus.org

The Ohio Pooled Trust
www.sntcenter.org/TypesOfTrusts.htm

McGivney Pooled Special Needs Trust
8101 N. High Street
Columbus, OH 43235-1406
www.mcgivneytrust.com

Oklahoma

Midwest Special Needs Trust
1500 Vandiver, Suite 100
P.O. Box 7629
Columbia, MO 65205
573-256-5055
887-239-8055
www.midwestspecialneedstrust.org
mftbt@midwestspecialneedstrust.org

ARCare Trust Program
8417 Santa Fe, Suite 107
Overland Park, KS 66212
913-648-0233
arcare@crn.org
www.arcare.org

Oregon

The Arc of Oregon
The Oregon Special Needs Trust
1745 State Street
Salem, OR 97301
503-581-2726
877-581-2726
www.arcoregon.org/osnt.htm

Pennsylvania

The Arc of Berks County
1829 New Holland Road, Suite 9
Reading, PA 19607-2228
610-603-0227
www.berksiu.org/arc/trust.htm

Achieva
The Family Trust
711 Bingham Street
Pittsburgh, PA 15203-1007
412-995-5000
888-272-7229
www.achieva.info/trustservices.php

PLAN of Pennsylvania
P.O. Box 154
Wayne, PA 19087
610-687-4036
mail@planofpa.org
www.planofpa.org

The Arc Community Trust of
Pennsylvania
1004 West 9th Avenue
King of Prussia, PA 19406
610-265-4788
www.arctrust.org
info@arctrust.org

Securet Pooled Trust
34 East Germantown Pike, #118
Norristown, PA 19401-1512
866-389-6339
www.securettrust.org

Rhode Island

NAMI of Rhode Island
154 Waterman, Suite 5B
Providence, RI 02906
401-331-3060
www.namirhodeisland.org

PLAN of Massachusetts and Rhode Island
1301 Centre Street, Suite 102
Newton Centre, MA 02459
617-244-5552
director@planofma.org
www.planofma.org

Tennessee

PLAN of Tennessee
Canoholland@comcast.net

The Tennessee Pooled Trust
www.sntcenter.org/TypesOfTrusts.htm

Midwest Special Needs Trust
P.O. Box 7629
Columbia, MO 65205
573-256-5055
877-239-8055
mftbt@midwestspecialneedstrust.org
www.midwestspecialneedstrust.org

Texas

The Arc of Texas Master Pooled Trust
8001 Centre Park Drive, Suite 100
Austin, TX 78754
512-454-6694
800-252-9729
www.thearcoftexas.org/programs/
masterpooledtrust

PLAN of North Texas
13151 Emily Road, Suite 240
Dallas, TX 75240
972-690-7526
www.plan-northtexas.org

PLAN of Central Texas, Inc.
Mailing address:
PLANCTX
P.O. Box 4755
Austin, TX 78765
Office address:
4110 Guadalupe Bldg 781, Suite 410
Austin, TX 78751
512-851-0901
www.planctx.org

The Texas Pooled Trust
www.sntcenter.org/TypesofTrusts.htm

Life's Plan Inc.
901 Warrenville Road, Suite 500
Lisle, Il 60532
630-628-7169
www.lifesplaninc.org

Utah

Utah Supplemental Needs Assistance
Pooled Fund
716 E. 4500 South, Suite N160
Salt Lake City, UT 84107
801-281-1100
www.utahspecialneeds.org
snap@utahspecialneeds.org

Virginia

Commonwealth Community Trust
P.O. Box 29408
Richmond, VA 23242
804-740-6930
888-241-6039
www.commonwealthcommunitytrust.org

Norfolk Community Services Board
Norfolk Community Trust
225 West Olney Road
Norfolk, VA 23510
757-441-5300
www.norfolkcsb.org

The Arc of Northern Virginia
The Personal Support Trusts
100 N. Washington Street, Suite 234
Falls Church, VA 22046
703-532-3214
www.thearcofnova.org

Arc of Virginia Future Planning
The Arc of Virginia
2025 East Main Street, Suite 107
Richmond, VA 23223
804-649-8481
www.tarcofva.org

Washington

Lifetime Advocacy Plus
444 NE Ravenna Boulevard, #208
Seattle, WA 98115
206-367-8055
www.laplus.org

The Arc of King County
233 6th Avenue North
Seattle, WA 98109
206-364-6337
877-964-0600
www.arcofkingcounty.org

Wisconsin

Wisconsin Pooled & Community Trusts
(WisPACT)
802 West Broadway, Suite 214
Madison, WI 53711
608-268-6006
www.wispact.org

Life's Plan Inc.
2801 Finley Road
Downers Grove, IL 60515
630-628-7169
www.lifesplaninc.org

Letter to Trustee

This appendix contains a wealth of information that you can put together for the people you choose as trustees. It explains the responsibilities the trustee will assume when he or she takes over the administration of the trust.

Read this appendix and think about any modifications you might want to make. For example, you will probably want to personalize the introductory letter and you may want to add notes about specific topics (such as investments or properties). Then, you can use the electronic version of this appendix to make your changes and print out copies for your trustees. For help accessing and using the downloadable eForms, see Appendix D.

Letter to Trustee

Dear _____:

Thank you for agreeing to be the trustee of a special needs trust for [*name of beneficiary*]. Here you will find some basic information about how that special needs trust works and what you will be expected to know and do as trustee.

You won't have to handle the trustee's job alone if the trust names a successor cotrustree to serve with you. In that event, the trust document will also tell you whether you can act independently or whether you and the other cotrustee(s) must agree to any actions taken on behalf of the trust. You should do your best to cooperate with other cotrustees to fulfill the purposes of the trust.

If you have questions that aren't answered here, the terms of the actual trust document are the final authority. The trust document was created using *Special Needs Trusts: Protect Your Child's Financial Future,* by Stephen Elias and Kevin Urbatsch (Nolo). You may want to look at that book for explanations of the various trust provisions. (If your trust document was drafted by an attorney, contact that attorney for specific instructions; don't rely on these instructions.)

You may also to want to review the book *Administering the California Special Needs Trust,* by Kevin Urbatsch (iUniverse). This book—written for trustees— covers nearly every situation that may arise during the administration of a special needs trust.

Again, sincere thanks for taking on this responsibility.

Managing a Special Needs Trust

This trust was created because the beneficiary is receiving—or will receive—benefits under the Supplemental Security Income (SSI) and Medicaid programs because of a disability. Both programs are available only to people with limited income and resources. The trust is designed to enhance the beneficiary's quality of life without interfering with SSI and Medicaid benefits.

As trustee, you have complete discretion over disbursements. The beneficiary has no legal control over trust property. As a result, the SSI and Medicaid programs don't consider trust assets to be a resource available to the beneficiary, and trust assets don't interfere with the beneficiary's eligibility for those programs.

An Overview

You are responsible for:

- communicating with the beneficiary
- investing trust assets prudently
- spending trust money to meet the beneficiary's special needs in a way that minimally interferes with his or her SSI and Medicaid benefits
- keeping good records
- preparing reports and notices required by SSI, Medicaid, and other interested parties identified in the trust document, and
- filing trust tax returns.

Each of these duties has a learning curve. You can get expert help with all of them, as discussed below.

Communicating With the Beneficiary

The core purpose of the special needs trust is to enhance the beneficiary's quality of life. This means you'll need to be sensitive to the beneficiary's special needs and have a basic understanding of how those needs can best be met. In some cases, there will be another person in the beneficiary's life—an advocate, a conservator, or a guardian—whose job it is to look out for the beneficiary. But in other situations, you will be the primary person the beneficiary depends on for help. If the beneficiary is unable to act independently, you may be called on to function as a surrogate parent.

If you are already well acquainted with the beneficiary—perhaps you are a sibling or other close relative—you will know what to do. But if you do not have much of a prior acquaintance with the beneficiary, you will need a lot of information. Ideally the person creating the special needs trust—the grantor—will have prepared a beneficiary information letter that informs you about such things as the beneficiary's family and medical history, education, employment, living situation, social life, routines, and religion. If not, you should try to find these things out by talking to others who are familiar with the beneficiary.

Your Fiduciary Duty

As trustee, you are a "fiduciary"—someone who occupies a special position of trust. And because you have been entrusted with someone else's money, you have a "fiduciary duty" to faithfully implement the trust's terms. This means you'll need to give the trust document a very close reading and make sure you understand what you can and cannot do. For example, no matter how much you want to make a particular disbursement, you can't if doing so would result in the beneficiary's losing SSI and Medicaid.

You must administer the trust for the beneficiary's benefit. If a conflict of interest arises, your first duty is to the beneficiary. For example, if you are also the remainder beneficiary—the person who will receive any money left in the trust when the beneficiary dies—there is a conflict of interest between your duty to spend money to benefit the beneficiary and a natural desire to conserve the trust money in case you inherit it. This conflict doesn't legally prevent you from being trustee, but it does require that you put your own interests aside and administer the trust in the interests of the beneficiary.

Others can benefit indirectly from your acts as trustee, as long as your primary purpose is to benefit the beneficiary. For example, you could use trust funds to buy the beneficiary a car even if a friend or relative might use it on occasion.

Spending Trust Money to Meet the Beneficiary's Needs

All spending decisions are completely up to you. When you use trust property to benefit the beneficiary, you must make sure your disbursements don't cause the beneficiary to exceed the SSI income and resource limits. The trust prohibits you from making disbursements that would cause the beneficiary to lose SSI and Medicaid benefits unless it is in the beneficiary's best interest to make such disbursements.

SSI and Medicaid Eligibility Rules

SSI and Medicaid are available only to people who have limited resources and income. In most states, someone who qualifies for SSI also qualifies for Medicaid.

To avoid running afoul of SSI resource and income limits, follow these guidelines:

- **Never give the beneficiary cash or items that could easily be converted into cash.** A beneficiary who receives too much income will lose SSI benefits—and so Medicaid—at least temporarily. Except for the first $20 a month, all unearned income that is reported to SSI is deducted dollar for dollar from the SSI grant. And if you give too much income to the beneficiary, the SSI grant will be terminated for that month, along with Medicaid benefits.

- **Make payments from the trust directly to the provider of the goods or services for the benefit of the beneficiary.** The reason? Payments directly to the beneficiary count as income (regardless of what it's spent for), but payments to a third party for the beneficiary's benefit do not.

- **Don't use trust funds to pay for food or shelter unless you know it won't cause the beneficiary to lose SSI benefits.** (See below.)

• **Don't buy the beneficiary items that would put him or her over the SSI resource limit of $2,000 in assets.** (Many items, however, aren't counted toward the limit. See below.)

Exceptions to rule that SSI eligibility equals Medicaid eligibility. In 11 states, Medicaid eligibility is determined independently of SSI eligibility. These states are Connecticut, Hawaii, Illinois, Indiana, Minnesota, Missouri, New Hampshire, North Dakota, Ohio, Oklahoma, and Virginia. If the beneficiary lives in one of these states, you'll need to contact the state Medicaid office to get an exact fix on the effect of resources and income on Medicaid eligibility. Medicaid eligibility standards in these states are roughly similar to those in the other states but, where there are variances, the rules tend to be a tad stricter. In these states, you will want to find a good contact person in the Medicaid department, or a private Medicaid specialist, to answer your questions.

Some Things Special Needs Trusts Can Pay For

There are an enormous number of things that a special needs trust can pay for because the primary intent behind such a trust is to enhance the quality of life of a person with a disability. However, some care needs to be taken so a disbursement will not interfere with the beneficiary's public benefits. Below is a list of some items and services (but by no means all) that can be purchased that will not interfere with public benefits.

Automobile (car, van)	Computer hardware, software, programs, and Internet service
Accounting services	Conferences
Acupuncture/acupressure	Cosmetics
Appliances (TV, VCR, DVD player, stereo, microwave, stove, refrigerator, washer/dryer)	Courses or classes (academic or recreational), including books and supplies
Bottled water or water service	Curtains, blinds, and drapes
Bus pass/public transportation costs	Dental work not covered by Medicaid, including anesthesia
Camera, film, recorder and tapes, development of film	Down payment on home or security deposit on apartment
Clothing	Dry cleaning and laundry services
Clubs and club dues (record clubs, book clubs, health clubs, service clubs, zoo, advocacy groups, museums)	

Some Things Special Needs Trusts Can Pay For (cont'd)

Education expenses including tuition and related costs

Elective surgery

Eyeglasses

Fitness equipment

Funeral expenses

Furniture, home furnishings

Gasoline and maintenance for automobile

Haircuts and salon services

Hobby supplies

Holiday decorations, parties, dinner dances, holiday cards

Home alarm, monitoring, and response systems

Home improvements, repairs, and maintenance (not covered by Medicaid), including tools to perform home improvements, repairs, and maintenance by homeowner

Home purchase (to the extent not covered by benefits)

House cleaning and maid services

Insurance (for automobile, home, or possessions)

Legal fees

Linens and towels

Magazine and newspaper subscriptions

Massage

Musical instruments (including lessons and music)

Nonfood grocery items (laundry soap, bleach, fabric softener, deodorant, dish soap, hand and body soap, personal hygiene products, paper towels, napkins, Kleenex, toilet paper, and household cleaning products)

Over-the-counter medications (including vitamins and herbs)

Personal assistance services not covered by Medicaid

Pets, pet supplies, and veterinary services

Physician specialists not covered by Medicaid

Pornography (as long as legal)

Private counseling if not covered by Medicaid

Repair services (for appliances, automobile, bicycle, household, or fitness equipment)

Snow removal, landscaping, and gardening (lawn) services

Sporting goods, equipment, uniforms, and team pictures

Stationery, stamps, and cards

Storage units

Taxicabs

Telephone service and equipment, including cell phone or pager

Therapy (physical, occupational, or speech) not covered by Medicaid

Tickets to concerts or sporting events (for beneficiary and an accompanying companion, if necessary)

Transportation (automobile, motorcycle, bicycle, moped, gas, bus passes, insurance, vehicle license fees, or car repairs)

Tuition and other educational expenses

Utility bills (satellite TV, cable TV, telephone —but not gas, water, or electricity)

Vacation (including paying for a personal assistant to accompany the beneficiary if necessary)

SSI and Medicaid Resource Rules: The $2,000 Limit

The beneficiary may own the following assets and still be eligible for SSI:

- a home, regardless of its value

- one vehicle of any value

- furniture and personal effects (such things as clothing, jewelry, recreation equipment, games and crafts, books, magazines, videotapes, telephone and answering machine, TV, radio, VCR, DVD, computers, musical instruments, and stereo)

- a total of $2,000 worth of any other kind of asset, including a bank account

- any property necessary for a plan (approved by the SSI program) of self-support (such as office equipment), and

- a life insurance policy and/or burial policy worth less than $1,500.

Trust funds are not, for purposes of SSI eligibility, counted as a resource available to the beneficiary. The beneficiary's special needs trust is called a third-party trust because the trust money in it never belonged to the beneficiary. It's important to keep it that way. So never put any of the beneficiary's own property into the trust. Doing so could jeopardize the beneficiary's eligibility for SSI and Medicaid.

Payments for Food and Shelter

If you never give the beneficiary cash, you probably won't have a problem with the SSI income limits. But you can also jeopardize SSI benefits by providing the beneficiary with food or shelter.

That's because trust money used to pay for food or shelter is counted as income to the beneficiary. It has a special name: "in-kind income" or "in-kind support and maintenance" (ISM).

SSI is intended to pay for food and shelter. If you use trust funds to give the beneficiary these items, the SSI grant will be reduced. The value of the food and shelter the trust pays for in a given month will be deducted, dollar for dollar, from the SSI grant—up to a maximum deduction of one-third of the federal portion of the grant, plus $20. In

2013, the maximum deduction is $256.67 per month. This cap will change every year, so you'll want to keep up to date.

If the SSI grant is wiped out completely by this deduction, Medicaid benefits will be lost as well. So to avoid even a temporary loss of Medicaid eligibility, make sure that ISM doesn't exceed the SSI grant. In most states, the beneficiary's SSI grant is more than the $256.67 cap, so you don't have to worry.

For example, depending on where the beneficiary lives and the amount of money in the trust, you might reasonably pay $1,000 a month for the beneficiary's rent, causing a reduction of only $256.67 in the SSI grant. Not a bad deal. But if the SSI grant were less than $256.67, paying that rent would disqualify the beneficiary for SSI and therefore for Medicaid.

If you are a tad nervous by now, here are two comforting thoughts to keep in mind:

- ISM payments count as income only in the month they're received. So if you blow it and give the beneficiary too much income of whatever type, SSI and Medicaid will be restored the next month, provided the resource limit isn't violated.

- Even if the beneficiary is kicked off SSI because of too much income, there may be a way of reestablishing Medicaid eligibility if the trust pays the Medicaid program a certain amount every month as a share of cost.

What is "shelter"? Expenses related to the beneficiary's residence count as shelter expenditures and can cause a reduction in the SSI grant under the ISM rule.

Items that count as shelter and trigger an ISM reduction	Items that don't count as shelter
• mortgage payments • rent • real estate taxes • gas • electricity • water • sewer • homeowners' insurance required by lender • condo charges that include the above items.	• telephone • cable or satellite TV • premiums for personal property insurance • laundry and cleaning supplies • staff salaries • capital improvements to the home • repairs to the home.

(416 C.F.R. § 1130(b); POMS SI 00835.465D)

Setting and Sticking to a Budget

Once you know the ground rules for keeping the beneficiary eligible for SSI and Medicaid, you'll want to decide how much the trust can reasonably spend every year on the beneficiary's special needs without bankrupting the trust. A ballpark budget would be based on four variables:

- value of the trust property
- the beneficiary's life expectancy
- the beneficiary's likely special needs, and
- how the trust property is invested.

You know, roughly, the value of the trust property. You can also obtain a rough life expectancy from actuarial tables and, if necessary, the beneficiary's doctors.

The information about the beneficiary's likely special needs will come from your personal knowledge or conversations with the beneficiary's family and friends. Also read any written information about the beneficiary that accompanies the trust document.

If you have financial skills, you may be able to sort this out yourself. But it would certainly be reasonable for you to hire a financial planner to help you arrive at a tentative initial budget.

One of the most difficult aspects of managing the trust may be sticking to your budget even if the beneficiary protests. For example, if the trust's budget is roughly $2,000 a year, and the beneficiary wants something that would cost the trust $10,000, should you honor the request or deny it? There is no easy answer. You'll have to use your best judgment. Whatever you decide, do your best to explain your decision to the beneficiary.

Investing Trust Assets

Your trust requires that you follow the investment guidelines set out in a law called the Prudent Investor Act. So when investing trust assets, you must:

- balance risk against return
- diversify investments
- consider the purpose of the trust, and
- evaluate the investment portfolio as a whole.

Because the purpose of the trust is to supplement an SSI grant, your investments will normally be conservative and favor liquidity over long-term growth. However, if you invest too conservatively, investment income will not keep up with inflation. It will be important to find a balance that will produce sufficient income at a low risk. A mix of money market funds, index funds, equity funds, and bond funds would be a typical investment portfolio for a special needs trust.

A closer look at these rules follows. A financial planner or another investment expert will be well-versed in these requirements.

Balance risk against return. The Prudent Investor Act allows high-risk investments only if there is the reasonable possibility of a high return.

For example, most investment advisers would tell you not to put trust money in a start-up business that you think will return about 13% on your investment. Given that you could expect close to 8% from much safer investments, the risk of the start-up failing is far greater than the extra return of 5%.

A high-risk investment can be justified, as part of a diversified portfolio, if, for example, the trust property has little value and the beneficiary has large projected special needs over a long period of time. In that case, you might want to invest as much as possible in a high-risk, high-return investment that will, if successful, have a much better chance of meeting the beneficiary's needs over time than conserving the small amount of trust property. On the other end of the spectrum, if you have a lot of money to work with, you might feel secure in investing part of it in a risky investment, given the potential return. The greater the value of the trust property, the more there is to spread around in different types of investments without serious risk that the trust will be depleted by a particularly bad investment.

Diversify investments. To reduce risk, the act requires you to diversify investments. For example, if all of the trust property were invested in high-risk volatile stocks or in a low-risk savings account, the investment would not be diversified. Similarly, putting all the property in equity stocks, rather than part in stocks and part in bonds or other government securities, would fail the diversification test.

Consider the purpose of the trust. The purpose of the trust is to pay for the beneficiary's special needs for as long as possible without jeopardizing eligibility for SSI and Medicaid. The purpose is definitely not to build the value of the trust assets beyond what the beneficiary will need. Although all special needs trusts have essentially the same purpose, that doesn't mean that one investment strategy is right for all special needs trusts. You must take into account:

- the type of assets in the trust
- their value
- the beneficiary's life expectancy, and
- the projected cost of the beneficiary's special needs.

For example, a typical investment strategy might be to keep some cash in the bank to meet immediate needs and invest the rest in diversified mutual funds, keep a house that the beneficiary lives in, and sell trust assets that the beneficiary isn't interested in and that don't generate income—jewelry or a car, for example.

Evaluate the portfolio as a whole. Every investment decision is looked at as it relates to how all the other trust assets are being invested. And to plan a coherent investment strategy for all trust assets, you are allowed to look at all kinds of circumstances, including the economic climate, taxes, and unique nature of some assets.

Discussed below are some of the factors the Prudent Investor Act allows you to consider.

General economic conditions. If economic conditions are good, it makes more sense to invest in a growth stock than if economic conditions are bad. Put differently, optimistic investing should be justified by marketplace conditions.

Possible inflation or deflation. In inflationary times, it makes more sense to invest in real estate than in bonds. Similarly, inflation renders the value of money in a bank account stagnant, but investing in securities gives the trust property a chance to grow with the rest of the economy.

Tax consequences. As tax laws change, so should the types of investment you make. For instance, if the tax laws someday removed the capital gains tax on appreciation in real estate, it might make a lot of sense to invest some trust funds in real estate, as opposed to an investment that is subject to capital gains tax.

The expected total return. When making investment decisions, you'll want to consider the income that the trust assets are likely to generate and the expected appreciation of the value of tangible assets such as real estate or art collections.

The beneficiary's other resources. If the beneficiary already owns a house (which is not considered a resource under SSI/Medicaid rules), investing trust funds in something other than real estate may make sense. But if the beneficiary needs adequate shelter, and the trust has enough cash for his or her special needs, it makes sense to buy a house.

Need for liquidity. A special needs trust always needs liquid assets that can be used to pay for expenses not covered by government benefits. So you must put a priority on investments that provide enough cash to pay for the beneficiary's special needs. It's not the trustee's goal to have trust property appreciate in value in a way that will benefit only the remainder beneficiary.

An asset's special value. If some of the trust property consists of family heirlooms, furnishings, or personal effects that are important to the disabled beneficiary, it may make sense to hold on to them, even if it would benefit the trust economically to sell them and invest the proceeds.

Handling Taxes

You'll need to file annual federal and state tax returns. The trust has a taxpayer ID that you will use for all your transactions with trust funds.

Trust income is taxed at a much higher rate than personal income. If the trust income is kept in the trust, this higher rate will apply. But if you spend the income on behalf of the beneficiary (but don't give it directly to the beneficiary), the income may be taxed at the beneficiary's lower personal rate and still not be considered income to the beneficiary for the purpose of SSI and Medicaid eligibility. To accomplish this result, the trust's records should match the trust income against the trust expenditures.

If you are also the beneficiary's guardian, don't mix the beneficiary's income with trust property. For instance, if, in addition to your role as trustee, you are authorized by the Social Security Administration to receive the beneficiary's grant on his or her behalf (termed a representative payee), you'll want to maintain one bank account for the beneficiary's income and another for the trust assets. This separation is necessary to keep the special needs trust from interfering with the beneficiary's SSI and Medicaid benefits.

Unless you are a tax expert, you'll be wise to work with one to set up your record-keeping system and to prepare and file the trust tax returns.

Making Reports

You'll need to keep careful records of all trust transactions so that you can make required reports.

Reports to SSI and Medicaid. SSI and Medicaid recipients are required to file monthly reports on any changes in their income, assets, or living arrangements and annual reports on trust activity. As long as you keep accurate books of trust activity, the beneficiary (or you, or the beneficiary's representative payee, guardian, or conservator) will have an easy time of meeting the beneficiary's reporting obligations.

Keep yourself informed about SSI and Medicaid. The SSI and Medicaid laws governing resources and income are subject to change. Because you must avoid trust disbursements that jeopardize the beneficiary's eligibility, you'll want to become and stay familiar with some key rules. You can probably find them online. There are two sets of rules for SSI:

- Regulations issued by the Social Security Administration and published in Volume 20 of the Code of Federal Regulations (C.F.R.), starting with Section 416.101 and ending with Section 2227. The income rules are found in Section 1100 and the resource rules in Section 1200. These regulations are available online at www.ssa.gov.

- Guidelines relied on by workers at the Social Security and local district offices are referred to as POMS (*Program Operations Manual System*). You can find information about POMS at http://policy.ssa.gov.

Each state issues its own Medicaid rules. Find them atwww.cms.hhs.gov.

Terminating the Trust

Someday, you'll need to wrap up the trust. The trust document gives you the authority to terminate the trust in the following cases:

- The beneficiary dies.
- The beneficiary is no longer disabled.

- The funds in the trust are exhausted.

- SSI or Medicaid regulations change to make the trust a liability.

If the beneficiary dies, you must distribute any remaining trust assets to the people named as "remainder beneficiaries" in the trust document (Article 13).

If the beneficiary is no longer disabled, then you will distribute the trust funds outright to the beneficiary. If the funds are about to run out, there is no reason to continue the trust. Simply close any existing accounts and file a tax return indicating that the trust has been terminated. Check with the IRS to see whether other forms are necessary.

If SSI or Medicaid regulations change so that maintaining the trust would knock the beneficiary off those programs, the trust requires you to give the beneficiary as much of the property as you can without making him or her ineligible for SSI and Medicaid. You would distribute the rest to the remainder beneficiaries.

If the regulations change so that there are no longer any resource limits for SSI or Medicaid, you would distribute the property to the beneficiary outright.

Before you terminate the trust, you are responsible for making sure that any debts and taxes owed by the trust are paid out of remaining trust assets. Specifically, you are required to:

- pay any legitimate debts that the trust still owes, such as legal or tax preparation fees

- file final federal and state income tax returns for the trust

- prepare what's known as a final account, showing a zero balance in the trust account

- pay any administrative expenses incurred in winding up the trust, such as attorneys fees, and

- pay the beneficiary's funeral costs if there are no other sources.

If there is not enough money in the trust to take care of all these expenses, get some legal advice on setting priorities.

Getting Help

Most trustees need expert help from time to time. You can pay a reasonable amount, from trust funds, to hire such help. Here are some examples.

Kind of Help You Need	Where to Get It
Bookkeeping and tax preparation	accountants, tax preparers
Investment advice	on the Internet brokers financial planners books
Help with SSI and Medicaid rules	on the Internet nonlawyer Medicaid experts elder law lawyers

Here are a few books that may help you:

• *Special Needs Trust: Planning, Drafting and Administration,* by numerous California lawyers and edited by Kevin Urbatsch (CEB). This book is written for lawyers but it is the most comprehensive book covering administration issues for third-party special needs trusts.

• *Administering the California Special Needs Trust,* by Kevin Urbatsch (iUniverse). This book is written for the administrator of a California special needs trust and goes into depth on all aspects of special needs trust administration. Much of it can be applied throughout the country.

• *The Trustee's Legal Companion,* by Liza Hanks and Carol Elias Zolla (Nolo), provides key information about trustee duties. It describes how to handle paperwork and keep beneficiaries informed and when to call in professionals when necessary.

Lawyers. You may find it necessary to get legal advice about your duties or the operation of the trust. Most lawyers who handle special needs trusts call themselves "special needs planning" or "elder law" attorneys. Because special needs trusts require knowledge of SSI and Medicaid rules, special needs trusts have become a specialty for these lawyers.

Two places to find special needs planning attorneys are:

- The Academy of Special Needs Planners website, www.specialneedsanswers.com, which lets you search for lawyers by state, and

- The National Academy of Elder Law Attorneys website, www.naela.org, which lets you search for lawyers by zip code or city.

Certified financial planners. Financial planners are people with accounting, investment, or insurance backgrounds who are adept with the numbers necessary to compute how much money you will need over time to accomplish a particular result. They are not licensed professionals, but a central board certifies them. They can provide a wealth of information on a feasible budget.

To find a certified financial planner in your area, enter "certified financial planner" and your city into your favorite search engine or visit these websites:

- www.fpanet.org

- www.paladinregistry.com

- www.wiseadvisor.com.

Documenting the Authority of Successor Trustees

The trustee must be able to show authority to invest or spend trust assets on the beneficiary's behalf. While the grantor serves as trustee, that person's signature on the trust document proves his or her authority to manage it. However, when a successor trustee—whose signature was not required on the face of the trust—takes over, it becomes more complicated to prove that authority. Successor trustees will need a paper trail that documents why each unavailable trustee cannot serve and who has taken his or her place. As trustee, you may also need to document your resignation or your appointment of a new successor trustee. The following sections show you how.

Assuming the Duties of Trustee

If the trust named you as a successor trustee, you will need to put together documents to show that all previous trustees are unavailable and that you have agreed to assume the position. For example, if the previous trustee died, you may need to produce that person's death certificate to show that he or she can no longer serve. If the previous trustee resigns or becomes incapacitated, you will need a letter of resignation or a doctor's letter attesting to the incapacity. If you are not the first successor, but the third or fourth successor trustee, you'll have to show that all trustees in line to serve ahead of you are unavailable.

In addition to showing that the trustee authorized to serve before you has become unavailable to serve, you must document that you have willingly assumed the trustee's role. An easy way to do this is to sign an affidavit to that effect and have it notarized. You can write the affidavit yourself and then sign it in front of a notary. An example affidavit is shown below—you can copy it, selecting and adding the appropriate terms and names to fit your situation.

After you've had the affidavit notarized, distribute copies to the beneficiary, the beneficiary's legal guardian or conservator, all successor trustees, all remainder beneficiaries, and all affected agencies, such as SSI and Medicaid.

AFFIDAVIT OF ASSUMPTION OF DUTIES BY SUCCESSOR TRUSTEE

State of _____ County of _____

[*Successor trustee's name*], of legal age, first being duly sworn, declares:

On [*date*] , [*name of grantor*] created The [*name of beneficiary*] Special Needs Trust.

The [*name of beneficiary*] Special Needs Trust names me, [*name of successor trustee*], as successor trustee to serve as [ ] trustee [ ] cotrustee if [*name(s) of trustee or trustees*] [*is/are*] unavailable to serve.

On [*date*] , [*name of unavailable trustee*] [*died / resigned/ was declared incapacitated by a licensed medical doctor*] and is therefore unavailable to serve as trustee.

Attached to this Affidavit is [*a death certificate for/a notice of resignation by/a doctor's letter attesting to the incapacity of*] [*name of unavailable trustee*].

[*Repeat these two clauses as necessary for each unavailable trustee named in the trust*].

I hereby accept the office of trustee of The [*name of beneficiary*] Special Needs Trust and now act as trustee of that trust.

Dated: _____

Signed: _____

            [*name of successor trustee*] , Successor Trustee

NOTARY ACKNOWLEDGMENT

Resigning as Trustee

If you need to resign your duties as trustee, you should do it in writing. Create a Notice of Resignation, have it notarized, and distribute it to the beneficiary, the beneficiary's legal guardian or conservator, all successor trustees, all remainder beneficiaries, and all affected agencies, such as SSI and Medicaid. Here's an example of a Notice of Resignation.

NOTICE OF RESIGNATION

I, [name of resigning trustee] , current trustee of The [name of beneficiary] Special Needs Trust, dated [date trust executed] , resign my position as trustee, effective immediately.

Dated: _____

Signed: _____

      [name of trustee] , Trustee

NOTARY ACKNOWLEDGMENT

Appointing a New Trustee

The trust document authorizes the trustee to appoint a successor trustee if there is no named successor trustee available to serve. If, as trustee, you find it necessary to appoint a successor trustee to replace yourself, you should create an Appointment of Trustee. Have it notarized and distribute it to the beneficiary, the beneficiary's legal guardian or conservator, all successor trustees, all remainder beneficiaries, and all affected agencies, such as SSI and Medicaid. Here is an example of that document.

APPOINTMENT OF TRUSTEE

I, [appointing trustee's name], trustee of The [beneficiary's name] Special Needs Trust, dated [date trust executed], appoint [name of person or entity being appointed] as trustee, effective immediately. This appointment is made under the authority granted to the trustee in Article 14 of the trust document.

Dated: _____

Signed: _____

      [name of current trustee] , Trustee

NOTARY ACKNOWLEDGMENT

Sample Beneficiary Information Letter

This appendix contains a sample beneficiary information letter that you can use as a model to provide your trustee with personal and intimate information about your loved one—information that will assist the trustee in making the best possible decisions about how the trust assets can best be managed and spent for your loved one's benefit. Of course every letter of this type will be different and tailored to each family's situation and experience. However, this example may stimulate your own thinking about the letter you will want to write about your own loved one. For your convenience, a copy of this letter is also available as a downloadable eForm. (See Appendix D.)

Sample Beneficiary Information Letter

May 6, 20xx

To the Trustee of the Special Needs Trust for Paul Sanchez:

We appreciate your future efforts on behalf of our beloved Paul and hope that you delight in him and his uniqueness as we have. We hope the following information will be helpful.

Family History

Paul has three older siblings who have always been affectionately involved in his life. We feel it is significant that each brother and his sister approached us individually years ago to ask to be his guardian if anything were to happen to us.

David Sanchez, 41 (wife Rebecca Chang, daughter Tiena Mei Sanchez, 2), 3211 Bayview Avenue, Alameda, CA 94501, 510-555-4567. Paul spends weekends with David and his family about once every six weeks and has phone contacts between visits. David often helps Paul find special DVDs he wants.

Mark Sanchez, 40 (wife Sonja Sanchez, sons Benjamin, 3, and Thomas, 1, and a child expected in a few months), 2445 Oak Avenue South, Minneapolis, MN 55405, 612-555-3219. Paul visits Mark and his family perhaps twice a year and has occasional phone conversations with Mark. Because Mark is a physician, we feel it is wise to consult him about any medical problems that Paul may have before making final treatment decisions.

Juliet Sanchez, 35 (partner Juliana Sorenstram, daughter Annika, 2, son Marcus, nine months), 815 Marcos Court, Santa Rosa, CA 95404, 707-555-9876. Juliet was a constant companion to Paul throughout his childhood, unbidden, a veritable "second mommy." Juliet and Paul share frequent phone calls. Paul spends the weekend with Juliet and her family about once per month. Among other helpful acts, Juliet is comfortable with Paul's personal needs, like helping him buy new shoes that accommodate his unusually small but wide feet, or even clipping toenails if she notices a need.

(Uncle) Steve Sanchez (wife Catherine Sanchez), P.O. Box 1750, Lakeport, CA 95453, 707-555-7895. Uncle Steve and Aunt Catherine have taken a warm and cheerful interest in Paul from his birth. One of Paul's first words was "Nunc" for "uncle." If Paul were ever to have any needs of a legal nature, we feel it would be wise to discuss them with Steve, who is an attorney.

(Cousin) Nicole Davis, 40, 1290 Eighth Street, San Francisco, CA 94122, 415-555-4369. Nicole spends time with Paul, usually at family celebrations, several times per year.

Other relatives with whom he has cordial but less frequent dealings are **Anne Davis and Richard Ross** and **Carol and Mickey Forlani** (aunts and their spouses), **Ken Sanchez and Sara Sanchez** (uncle and his wife), **Rubin Sanchez** (cousin), **Megan Sanchez** (cousin), **Dionne Davis** (cousin), and **Walter and Olivia Forlani** (cousin and wife).

General Medical History

Paul was born on July 31, 1975; he has Down syndrome. As a young child, he enjoyed good health but needed consistent medical attention for frequent ear infections, sore throats, and colds that regularly morphed into sinus infections. Fortunately he had no cardiac problems, an issue for half the children with Down syndrome. He had pneumonia two times as a child. We find that yearly flu shots and pneumonia immunization as directed by his physician are important preventive measures.

His dentition was irregular and late. His skin is very fair and he sunburns easily. He continues to need to use sunscreen daily and to wear dark glasses outdoors. He has dry skin; flaking on his face or hair is treated with Aquanil HC, an over-the-counter preparation.

When he was about 12 he had a difficult episode lasting many days of fearfully thinking he was changing into an animal. The episode faded, but as the years passed, occasionally other fears dominated his waking hours, basically unpleasant thoughts that he could not banish from his mind. When he was 17, his father (a psychiatrist) realized that Paul had a form of obsessive-compulsive disorder. Treated with Zoloft, the uncomfortable symptoms disappeared at once. He continues to take Zoloft.

As a teenager he underwent a hernia operation.

At 22, he became very ill when he was thrown abruptly from a supportive school program (work experience for a couple of hours a day and a few more hours spent learning to make his way in the community) into an eight-hour workday with a brand-new 1½-hour bus ride on either end of the already exhausting regimen. Whatever sort of illness he had resulted in a painful mouth and gum infection. He already was having some problems with his gums, and the illness greatly exacerbated them. Then began serious dental work: gum grafts that were unsuccessful, rigorous training in dental hygiene and oral rinses with Periogard, and extractions of a number of teeth. He does not wear a prosthesis because it would have to be attached to teeth that are already loosening and would hasten their loss. He now alternates appointments for cleaning and checkups between his dentist and periodontist every two months. (Contact information below.)

In his mid-20s he developed low thyroid, and now takes Levoxyl to normalize his thyroid levels. Nevertheless, he tires easily and needs significantly more rest than average. He uses Beconase inhalant to prevent sinus infections. Paul has had a lifelong tendency toward constipation. He takes mineral oil nightly to control the problem.

Paul has a high pain tolerance. If he says something is painful, it is advisable to obtain medical assistance. He may have difficulty in localizing or explaining what is happening to him physically. For example, he might say, "My throat hurts," when he is nauseated. His internist is Kent Yasuda, M.D.

None of these health issues is particularly alarming, but like most people with Down syndrome, Paul benefits greatly from regular, consistent medical and dental care.

Paul has a tendency to put on weight. We try to advise him and monitor his eating habits, but with limited success. We worry that this tendency may cause health problems eventually.

Paul has severe obstructive sleep apnea and must always sleep—naps included—with his CPAP (continuous positive air pressure) mask in place.

Some additional caveats: people with Down syndrome have a severe hypersensitivity to atropine, a substance that may be used in eye examinations and sometimes following a surgery. Doctors treating Paul should be reminded of this. People with Down syndrome have more problems with anesthesia because of "sloppy airways" due to their low muscle tone; surgery should not be lightly undertaken. Some people with Down syndrome develop weakness in their spinal cord due to atlanto-axial subluxation; Paul did not have the condition when he had spinal X-rays as a child, but it can develop later in life.

Paul handles the regimen of health measures and medicines described above on his own. He benefits from regular reminders, lists, and discussion. Often when asked, for example, if he is remembering to take his Beconase, he will say, "Oh, that's right, I forgot."

Paul had therapy and counseling for several years after some traumatic events. He enjoyed the support and benefited greatly from therapy. If he seems troubled, we would like him to have this opportunity again. It would be best to investigate which therapists are comfortable, experienced, and interested in working with Paul.

Current Medical/Dental Providers

We have always kept Paul on our medical insurance; at this time he uses Medicare and has a supplemental insurance plan from the County Health Plan. He has no dental insurance. We feel adequate medical and dental care are a priority and prefer to have Paul cared for by specialists who have treated other people with Down syndrome and are familiar with the medical needs that may accompany the syndrome.

Kent Yasuda, MD, internist, 4710 Yolanda Avenue, Santa Rosa, CA 95403; 555-8764

Robert Jeffords, DDS, dentist, 40 North Main Street, Santa Rosa, CA 95403; 555-4567

Richard Smithson, DDS, periodontist, 1416 Mountain View Lane, Santa Rosa, CA 95403; 555-6589

Education

Paul was "mainstreamed," as the practice of attending regular school classes was termed when he was a boy, until he was 17 years old. He was extremely well liked by other students, with many friendships extending to the present. He was usually supported academically by the Resource Room Specialist. He reads at about a fourth- or fifth-grade level, and writes perhaps like a third-grader. Paul can add a little and used to be able to subtract.

He developed a talent for writing unique poems. They are quite wonderful. If asked, he will write one for any occasion.

Paul's speech is often difficult to understand; his missing teeth compound the problem. Patience is sometimes required. His thought processes are much more advanced than one would expect listening to his articulation.

At 17, he began attending Special Education classes to prepare him for practical issues like work experience, bus riding, and money management. It was also an opportunity for him to have classmates who were true peers. He finished school at 22 years of age. During those years he enjoyed attending classes at Santa Rosa Junior College, and continues to talk of wishing for such an opportunity again. He lives in walking distance of SRJC, but the logistics of working during the day, doing chores with housemates when he returns home after a lengthy bus ride, and his fatigue have militated against taking more courses. He does delight in thinking of any meeting or class as a "graduate school class."

Employment

Paul has been in supported employment in the community since he was 22. He is with an enclave of several workers with a supervisor on site. We feel this situation is preferable to working alone since he takes a number of weeks of vacation, some without pay; this custom might be difficult if a business was depending only on Paul for certain services. During these approximately four weeks per year, spread out, he travels and celebrates family occasions, as when cousins visit from Sweden. We also feel it is beneficial for him to have peers who are work colleagues. It is possible that as he grows older, Paul may need a different work situation—less stressful perhaps, or perhaps with transportation provided. Time will tell.

Currently he is at Dynamat, a technology company in Rohnert Park. He does assembly work. He is accurate and quite slow compared to the average worker. His supervisor, Tom De Leon, is ideal for Paul. Paul has a tendency to become too easily offended by other people, especially authorities. Mr. De Leon is limitlessly pleasant and respectful with Paul.

The organization that currently supports Paul's employment is **North Coast Industries,** 555-9641. He takes part in the occasional social events such as The Human Race in May, and a dinner dance during the year. Generally speaking, Paul needs transportation to these and any social events. He is capable of riding the bus only on routes on which he has been trained. He rides the city and county buses to his workplace. North Coast Regional Center sends him his bus passes monthly.

At times, there have been recurrent issues of Paul's not going to work when he was not ill. We feel it is important for him to be out in the world working during the week, like everyone else. We find that giving him an allowance of spending money contingent on his going to work daily is effective. He receives $30 per week in spending money if he goes to work every day. If he does not go one day, he receives only $5 per day. So if he stayed home one day, he would receive only $20 allowance that week. Naturally if he is ill or has a conflicting engagement like a medical appointment, his allowance is not docked.

It is common for Paul to ventilate frequently about mild negatives in his life, and not comment on the positives. Therefore, it is best to pay attention, evaluate, and not react too quickly when he complains about work, his supervisor, or coworkers.

Lately he has been expressing a desire to work at Agilent Technologies, where his sister is employed, and which is near Arcangel House. Perhaps at some point he might try that, since there is a North Coast Industries work group located there that does assembly work.

In the past, Paul had jobs that involved too much heavy labor for him. For example, one job required him to lift many flats of soft drinks. He vastly prefers lighter work, more complex work, too.

Current Living Situation

Our opinion is that Paul currently needs an arrangement between an overly protective group home, where he probably would not have his own room, and living in an apartment by himself with little oversight and companionship. In our county, a continuum of alternatives was not available. Personally, we were very happy living with Paul, but for many years he had been saying, "I want to move out. I want to be independent."

When he was 25, Jane Ford, a lifelong friend and advocate for Paul, called to say, "You know that project we are always talking about for Paul? I'm ready to do it." What a surprise! Jane bought a house, 4567 Arcangel Avenue, in Santa Rosa, perfectly located near shops, markets, Santa Rosa Junior College, the Recreation Center, and buses. It is even across the street from a workshop for more involved people with special needs, so there are speed bumps in the street for safety. And wonderfully, the house is only two miles from our home and his sister Juliet's home. After living at Arcangel House for five weeks, Paul came home to celebrate Passover with all of us. He pointed to the place on the kitchen doorjamb where we have never painted over the dates and heights of our children. "Dad, you've got to measure me again. I'm tall now."

After a few years, Jane Ford wished to sell the house; we bought it so that the situation, which by then we knew worked so well for Paul and his housemates, could continue. The house has three bedrooms, two baths, and a modest garage apartment. Paul lives there with two other people his age who happen to have different special needs, but function roughly about like Paul. Paul has a voucher from HUD from the City of Santa Rosa, which means that he pays up to one third of his income (including Social Security) for rent. The housing authority pays the difference. Right now, his rent is $500, of which he pays around $200.

He and his housemates are supported by a person, currently Cheryl Frost, who lives rent-free in the garage apartment. She earns money by being the three housemates' IHSS (In-Home Supportive Services) worker. She helps organize housekeeping chores among the housemates, cooks their evening meal, and generally stays in tune with how their lives are going. **Oaks of Hebron** (555-5927) is an organization that supports the housemates too, by assigning a Community Support Facilitator (CSF) who is available to Paul, and who visits him weekly, helps him pay bills or straighten out problems with the buses—generally is available to help solve problems as they arise. The CSF also may take him to medical or dental appointments. It has been our practice to be at such appointments also, and we usually drive Paul home afterwards.

In Paul's situation, the caregivers can purchase food at the Food Bank, so Paul pays only $150 per month for food. We like to supplement this weekly by buying him melon (cut into chunks), cottage cheese, eight cans of tomato juice, and a bag of romaine lettuce. We do so because he needs low-calorie alternatives to help him control his weight, and because he needs fruit and vegetables in some quantity to help with his chronic constipation.

As is his wont, Paul often complains about aspects of his living situation. We find it best to listen and let him express his feelings, even though we usually judge that his living situation, or job situation, or relationship situation is probably optimal. Paul is not apt to tell us about the positive aspects of his life, for some idiosyncratic reason. He may say he "wants to live in the apartments in Rohnert Park." These are individual apartments for people with special needs with no one permanently on site if a need arises. We do not feel that this situation is safe for Paul over the long haul. We feel he needs more support, especially since he has always had and continues to have difficulty saying "no" to any suggestions by others, which could lead obviously to dangerous situations.

It is possible that Paul may need a more supportive environment, probably a group home, as he grows older. If he were to develop a condition such as diabetes, we would definitely want him to live in a group home where his increased medical needs could be met.

Day-to-Day Routines

Paul is quite self-sufficient. He rises and prepares himself for his workday independently. He fixes his own breakfast, packs a lunch, and walks to the bus stop by 7:30 a.m. He takes the bus to work and begins work at 8:30 or so. He wears a fanny pack with identification, bus passes, cell phone, and dark glasses. He has a backpack with his lunch and other necessaries like his treasured Walkman and favorite Beatles tapes.

Because Paul fatigues more readily than the average person, we have had his workday shortened. He walks to the bus stop to catch a bus home around 2 p.m. He arrives home, walking from the bus stop around 3 p.m. He then does assigned household chores, like sweeping and mopping the floors. Whoever is living in the garage apartment prepares dinner for the household and the four of them share the meal.

Paul is accustomed to calling us each evening at around 7 p.m. This is his own idea, though we admit we find it pleasant. He likes to recount a little about his day and his thoughts. It is perhaps a ten-minute chat. We feel happy that his living "on his own" has not lessened the affectionate connection that we have with him.

In the evening, he listens to his music collection or looks at a video or DVD. He and his fiancee Annie share a phone call.

He does his own laundry weekly. Paul likes to wear all clean clothes daily.

He is well groomed. He needs occasional reminders about what to do about, say, flaking scalp.

On weekends, he often visits a family member or his fiancee. He may attend a movie or a party, perhaps with housemates. He doesn't mind being in his home (Arcangel House) on weekends; actually he likes it. On Sundays, he likes to be there shortly after midday to make a transition to the upcoming workweek.

Paul has a longtime interest in and detailed knowledge of the Beatles, especially John Lennon. He likes to purchase tapes, books, videos, and DVDs, plus the occasional T-shirt about the Beatles or other topics. He likes to pore over books about the Beatles. He used to write poetry, and will do so now if encouraged.

He needs to exercise, but tires quickly on long walks or lap swimming. Something is better than nothing, we feel. He does better if the exercise is incorporated in his day—for example, walking to and from the bus stops.

Paul enjoys most foods. He always has, even as a small child.

Social Environment

Paul has always been a well-liked person. He dated frequently as a teenager. He and **Princess** (called **"Annie"**) **Priest** (Eddington Hall Apartments, Rohnert Park; 555-7693) began dating in about 2010, and became engaged in 2012. The relationship continues. We strongly feel that their relationship should be celebrated, but we do not believe that the couple should live together or marry. Paul and Annie seem to get along best when they spend most of a weekend together. Longer contact results in quarreling. Paul spends part of a weekend with Annie about two times per month. We regard Annie as a daughter-in-law; she attends most family celebrations.

As stated above, Paul has frequent and loving contacts with his brothers and sister and their families. He has developed skills in relating to his young nephews and nieces.

Lejf Jensen is a few years younger than Paul; they have been lifelong friends. They continue to see each other socially several times per year. Usually they do an activity together and share a meal somewhere. Lejf is currently a disc jockey at "Four More," a trendy radio station in San Francisco; he also works as a substitute special education teacher.

Matt Conrack is a friend since elementary school. Paul visited him in New York last year, where he was in graduate school. Again, they have cordial social contacts several times per year—usually an outing and a meal together.

Pat and Cassie Garcia, brother and sister, were neighborhood playmates when they were all toddlers together. They remain interested in Paul and sometimes contact and visit him.

Any of these friends would probably need help in setting up a social contact with Paul. If Paul received a phone message, he would not be able to call the person back on his own (although he can do so with family members who are in the speed dial of his phone).

Currently, it seems difficult for Paul to mix socializing and working. Activities that take place during the workweek are too much for him. He thinks of social activities as taking place on the weekend.

Paul usually says "no" if asked if he wants to do something, especially something social. This is a knee-jerk first reaction to most suggestions of any kind, and should not be taken too seriously. We try to help him keep his social life going by encouraging, sometimes almost insisting, that he take part in a social activity. Maybe one or two per weekend. He is often tired after two or three hours at a social event, and it is reasonable for him to return home then if he wishes to.

We believe it is important for him to interact with friends who also have special needs. He and Annie often double-date with Brent North and Julia South, who live in the same apartments as Annie. Her apartment is located near many restaurants and a cineplex, allowing them to choose independently.

In recent years, Paul (and usually Annie) have been delightedly participating in wonderful, low-cost travels arranged by Jane Ford, an old friend, and her organization. This year he is traveling to the Grand Canyon next month, and will cruise the Inside Passage of Alaska in the fall. Many of the same people are present on each trip. The group also went Christmas shopping in San Francisco this year. Paul considers it "his club." We hope this opportunity will continue.

There are others in the community who understand Paul and his needs from long years of contact and experience. They would be available to consult.

Sue Lake, MA, special education teacher (4672 Alejandro Drive, Santa Rosa, CA 95404; 555-4691), was his infant teacher and has remained in close contact with us. A great deal of problem-solving around issues that have arisen for Paul has included Sue's views.

Nancy Fernandez (9420 Glencannon Drive, Santa Rosa, CA 95405; 555-9321) is a longtime friend as well as the mother of Lejf Jensen. She is a special education teacher too. Again, problem-solving for Paul usually includes her suggestions.

Nancy Barlotti, RN, (679 Purrington Road, Petaluma, CA 94952; 555-0368), is a fellow parent of a person with special needs very different from Paul's and a former coworker in Early Intervention. Her perspective on Paul is wise.

Jane Ford, MSW, who originally bought Arcangel House where Paul lives so that he would have the opportunity, and who runs the trips for him and others, has known Paul all his life. Her views on any issues would be helpful.

Travel

Sometimes Paul flies to visit friends or relatives. He travels with a family member or on his own. When he flies alone, we buy what the airlines call their "unaccompanied minor program." This means that a staff person on board is assigned to be available to Paul if he needs help, or if the plane must change its itinerary due to weather or another exigency. Paul will be released only to the person whose name is given before Paul boards the plane. Under the program, whoever takes him to the airport or comes to pick him up is allowed through security to the gate. When he flies with a family member, we pay the family member the same amount of money for any supervision that may be helpful to Paul.

Religious Proclivities

As an interfaith family, we have always observed and celebrated both Jewish and Christian holidays. Very occasionally Paul attends First Methodist Church with me. He also participates with Oaks of Hebron personnel in occasional religious activities.

Preferences for Funeral Arrangements: We find it difficult to address this topic for one of our children, but here goes: We would like Paul to participate in organ donation, but are not sure if that is possible if a person has a different number of chromosomes from the average, as is the case with Paul's form of Down syndrome.

Arrangements should be whatever the surviving family deems appropriate. Perhaps a memorial service in a Methodist church or Jewish temple with spoken tributes from those of us who have loved him so, as well as thoughts from a clergyman. Certainly any service should include lots of Beatles music. We would very much like to have him laid to rest near us, his parents; we fervently hope he will never be far from us. Probably cremation is suitable. An informal family celebration of his life, with Beatles music and a buffet, might follow the service.

Other Relevant Information

Paul has a talent for choosing gifts for family and friends, as well as for planning parties.

Paul loves to have the opportunity to "be in charge" or be given a responsibility. For example, he was happy when he could volunteer at the Recreation Center, serving soft drinks. Sometimes when he travels with a small group, he is in charge of keeping track of the suitcases, or of calling everyone for dinner.

Paul is unfailingly punctual (far better than his mother); he organizes his belongings neatly; he remembers all appointments and engagements, and keeps an accurate calendar. He has an excellent memory for people, and for details about them like their birthdays (or even "half-birthdays").

He understands which amounts are more or less as far as money, but needs significant guidance in managing finances. Paul does not have a conservator, so it is necessary to obtain his cooperation through explanation and discussion regarding both medical treatment and financial management.

Paul cannot say something that is untrue, for example to manipulate a person or situation; he doesn't understand the concept. It may be important to know, however, that if he is asked a direct question, such as "Why did you do that?" he will probably interpret it as a demand for an answer. His response then will be his best guess, but he does not use niceties of expression like, "Well, it may have been because…. His answer will sound like a statement, because that is the syntax he understands how to use. This statement may not be accurate, but simply his effort at pleasing with a required response. Also, if he is worried about something, he may state it as a fact. He might say, "My supervisor said I have to get a new job," when what he really means is, "My supervisor reprimanded me today and I am worried that if he is mad at me maybe he won't want me to work here."

Paul is a lifelong client of **North Coast Regional Center**. A specific Client Program Coordinator, currently Dorothy Merriwhether, is assigned to him and available to discuss and help solve issues that arise.

If Paul disapproves of a comment or an opinion we express, he may hang up the phone or storm off angrily. After about ten minutes, he will return to discuss the matter calmly and without anger. He is reasonable and ultimately open to support in the form of suggestions presented in a friendly manner.

We hope you find this account helpful. Paul's welfare has been a priority for our family all his life. We are now entrusting his welfare to you.

Sincerely,

Lois and Bob Sanchez

Using the eForms

This book comes with electronic forms that you can access through it's Web page:
www.nolo.com/back-of-book/SPNT.html

TIP

Note to Macintosh users. These forms were designed for use with Windows. They should also work on Macintosh computers; however Nolo cannot provide technical support for non-Windows users.

Using the RTFs

The electronic version of the special needs trust is in rich text format (RTF). You can open, edit, save, and print the RTF files using most word processing programs such as Microsoft *Word*, Windows *WordPad*, and recent versions of *WordPerfect*.

Here are some general instructions about editing RTF forms in your word processing program. Chapter 8 provides detailed instructions about how to complete your special needs trust. Editing functions include:

- **Underlines.** Underlines indicate where to enter information. After filling in the needed text, delete the underline. In most word processing programs, you can do this by highlighting the underlined portion and typing CTRL-U.

- **Bracketed and italicized text.** Bracketed and italicized text indicates instructions. Be sure to remove all instructional text before you finalize your document.

- **Optional text.** Optional text gives you the choice to include or exclude it. Delete any optional text you don't want to use. Renumber numbered items, if necessary.

- **Alternative text.** Alternative text gives you the choice between two or more text options. Delete those options you don't want to use. Renumber numbered items, if necessary.

• **Signature lines.** Signature lines should appear on a page with at least some text from the document itself.

Every word processing program uses different commands to open, format, save, and print documents, so refer to your software's help documents for help using your program. Nolo cannot provide technical support for questions about how to use your computer or your software.

> **CAUTION**
> In accordance with U.S. copyright laws, the forms provided by this book are for your personal use only.

Using the PDF

At the Web address listed above, you can also download this book's Appendix A, which provides a list of pooled trusts. You cannot edit the list, but you can open and print it out at your convenience.

This document is in Adobe *Acrobat* PDF format. To open it, you need Adobe *Reader* installed on your computer. If you don't already have this software, you can download it for free at www.adobe.com.

List of Forms

Files in Rich Text Format (RTF)	
Form Name	File Name
Special Needs Trust	Trust.rtf
Sample Beneficiary Information Letter	SampleInfoLetter.rtf
Letter to Trustee	DutiesLetter.rtf
Florida Witness Statement	FLWitnessStatement.rtf

Files in Portable Document Format (PDF)	
Form Name	File Name
Pooled Trust List	PooledTrustList.pdf

Index

⚖ NOLO *Keep Up to Date*

 Go to Nolo.com/newsletters to sign up for free newsletters and discounts on Nolo products.

- **Nolo's Special Offer.** A monthly newsletter with the biggest Nolo discounts around.

- **Landlord's Quarterly.** Deals and free tips for landlords and property managers.

 Don't forget to check for updates. Find this book at **Nolo.com** and click "Legal Updates."

Let Us Hear From You

 Register your Nolo product and give us your feedback at Nolo.com/customer-support/productregistration.

- Once you've registered, you qualify for technical support if you have any trouble with a download (though most folks don't).

- We'll send you a coupon for 15% off your next Nolo.com order!

SPNT5

⚖ NOLO *Online Legal Forms*

Nolo offers a large library of legal solutions and forms, created by Nolo's in-house legal staff. These reliable documents can be prepared in minutes.

Create a Document

- **Incorporation.** Incorporate your business in any state.
- **LLC Formations.** Gain asset protection and pass-through tax status in any state.
- **Wills.** Nolo has helped people make over 2 million wills. Is it time to make or revise yours?
- **Living Trust (avoid probate).** Plan now to save your family the cost, delays, and hassle of probate.
- **Trademark.** Protect the name of your business or product.
- **Provisional Patent.** Preserve your rights under patent law and claim "patent pending" status.

Download a Legal Form

Nolo.com has hundreds of top quality legal forms available for download—bills of sale, promissory notes, nondisclosure agreements, LLC operating agreements, corporate minutes, commercial lease and sublease, motor vehicle bill of sale, consignment agreements and many more.

Review Your Documents

Many lawyers in Nolo's consumer-friendly lawyer directory will review Nolo documents for a very reasonable fee. Check their detailed profiles at **Nolo.com/lawyers**.